CHANGE THE WORLD

CHANGE THE WORLD

HOW ORDINARY PEOPLE
CAN ACHIEVE
EXTRAORDINARY RESULTS

ROBERT E. QUINN

JOSSEY-BASS
A Wiley Company
San Francisco

Credits appear on page 271.

Jossey-Bass books and products are available through most bookstores. To contact Jossey-Bass directly, call (888) 378–2537, fax to (800) 605–2665, or visit our website at www.josseybass.com.

Substantial discounts on bulk quantities of Jossey-Bass books are available to corporations, professional associations, and other organizations. For details and discount information, contact the special sales department at Jossey-Bass.

 Manufactured in the United States of America on Lyons Falls Turin Book. This paper is acid-free and 100 percent totally chlorine-free.

Library of Congress Cataloging-in-Publication Data

Quinn, Robert E.
  Change the world: how ordinary people can achieve
extraordinary results / Robert E. Quinn.
    p. cm. — (Jossey-Bass business & management series)
Includes bibliographical references and index.
  ISBN 0-7879-5193-5
  1. Organizational change. 2. Social change. 3. Change
(Psychology) I. Title. II. Series.
  HD58.8 .Q557 2000
  302.3'5—dc21   99–050826

FIRST EDITION
HB Printing 10 9 8 7 6 5 4 3 2 1

The Jossey-Bass
Business & Management Series

CONTENTS

*This book is dedicated to Kristin and Travis Quinn.
It is in contemplating their efforts to change the world
that I have found much of the inspiration for
writing this volume. I will be ever grateful
for their commitment and courage.*

Preface

Oliver Wendell Holmes once remarked that he placed little value on simplicity that lay on this side of complexity but a great deal of value on simplicity that lay on the other side. Put another way, there is a vast chasm between being simple and being simplistic. I would like to suggest something similar. I believe that in any activity there are many novices, a few experts, and very occasionally there is an extraordinary master. If you ask a novice about a topic, the novice will give you a very simple (simplistic) explanation that will be of little value. If you ask an expert the same question, the expert will give you a complex explanation that will also be of little value. If you ask a master the same question, the master's explanation may be simple, breathtakingly elegant, and remarkably effective. But the master's answer will only be valuable, breathtaking, and effective if you and I are ready to hear it and act on it.

The power of simplicity that comes from the other side of complexity can be most challenging. Indeed, the master's explanation of the answer that he or she offers is often paradoxical and therefore difficult to understand. Once we grasp it, it may become revolutionary.

It is clear to me that masters perform differently. In the heat of the moment, they wait calmly. They seem to have unconditional confidence that they will react in a way that is not only appropriate but highly effective. They have a minimum of performance anxiety. Masters know to trust their process. In the chaos of the moment masters see an underlying pattern and follow it. With minimum effort they shape the outcome. We watch the master's performance and we marvel at the understanding, skill, and influence of this person. We envy the creative power and the revolutionary impact they can make on the world.

Becoming a Master by Listening to Horses

Consider an example from the world of horse training. In his book *The Man Who Listens to Horses,* Monty Roberts tells about his own journey to mastery. He grew up with a father who trained horses through physical domination and fear, the very essence of simplistic (though certainly not "simple") thinking. Seeing how the animals under his father's tutelage suffered, the young Monty vowed to find a better way.

Monty's father based his approach to horse training on a common assumption, that he had to prove his superiority over the horse, that only if the animal was convinced that the man had total control of it would it be trustworthy. According to Monty, his father was usually abusive and often brutal in his methods, and approached horse training as though it were a war between man and beast. The object of the war was to subjugate the horse, to "break" it, and make it a slave to the rider's will.

When he was a boy Monty became a champion rider. Then, as a teenager, he visited Nevada and became fascinated with wild Mustangs. He spent long hours observing these horses in their herds. He did this in the heat of the day and the cold of the night. He watched how they used their bodies to communicate with each other, to establish relationships and shape behavior in the herd.

Monty began experimenting with ways to use his own body to communicate with the animals. He modeled their body language, learned to understand it, and thus was able to communicate with them. He used his eyes, his hands, and his own body to work with the animals, and soon they were as responsive to him as they were to other horses in their herd. Today Monty is training horses in a quarter of the time it ordinarily takes, and the animals he turns out not only do not fear their riders but clearly seem to trust and enjoy their relationships with humans.

Monty has since gone on to train thousands of other horse trainers and owners, proving that these animals do not need to be dominated or physically abused to be trustworthy. In fact, by training the animals this way, equestrians get much more cooperative steeds, horses who are trusting of people and trustworthy in their behavior. What he does now seems simple compared to the way his father worked.

Monty had discovered the simplicity on the other side of complexity. His methods are as profound as they are powerful. This was certainly not a simplistic approach, since it took Monty years of observation, experimentation, risking, listening, trusting, and remembering the suffering caused by his father's methods, to find his own "simple" way of working with animals. Like other masters, Monty has unconditional confidence. He can work with nearly any horse in any situation, transforming animals that other trainers have given up on. He has even trained wild Mustangs to be gentle mounts, a feat that many trainers consider nearly impossible. Monty experiences little performance anxiety. Watching him work one can see that his vision allows him to live in a state of unconditional confidence, thus winning him a place in his profession as an undisputed master.

The Content of This Book

What does the story of Monty Roberts have to do with this book? This book is about changing the world. It is about coming to a deep understanding of human beings and human relationships. Just as Monty came to master the process of changing horses, we can come to master the process of changing people.

The book focuses on vision, unconditional confidence, and profound impact. It is about the mastery of human influence, transformational power, and the capacity to accomplish extraordinary things. It argues that everyone of us is a change agent. There are times when we need to influence other people. The other people may be our teenage children, our spouse, our colleagues at work, our clients or customers, our students, our workforce, our congregation, or perhaps the team we coach. There are times when we need to create a new reality and a new world.

This book argues that every ordinary person can become like Monty Roberts. There is a language of transformation. Yet most of us are cut off from that language. All our lives we have been explicitly and implicitly taught to see human influence as an exercise in domination. Even the most sensitive among us is shaped by this paradigm or worldview. But this outlook prevents us from seeing more deeply into the actual working of human systems. This book demonstrates an alternative system. It offers a framework for having profound impact. The framework comes from the seed thoughts of people who, like Monty, have mastered the language of transformation. Here it is not a language for transforming horses but for transforming human beings.

By *seed thoughts* I mean some of the core notions that masters of transformation hold in common, the simplicity they send us from the other side of complexity. I focus on three people in particular. These are Jesus, Gandhi, and Martin Luther King, Jr. As historical change agents, these three exercised great discipline as they searched for and found an understanding of human systems. They were also connected by some common principles. They used these principles to operate in a very real world.

I select some seed thoughts, or core notions, and elaborate them into an enlarged set of insights about how to bring about change in our own real world. This enlarged body of principles I call Advanced Change Theory (ACT). *Advanced* does not mean complex. ACT seeks the simplicity from the other side of complexity. Yet ACT is advanced in that it is uncommon. In fact, it violates what you and I know to be true about our world. Herein is my problem as an author and herein is another parallel with the story of Monty Roberts.

Sharing the Simplicity on the Other Side of Complexity

Imagine Monty's excitement. As a teenager he had made a discovery that overturned thousands of years of human learning. He had developed a process that was faster, safer, simpler, and more effective. He had a story to tell. Yet telling the story proved to be surprisingly difficult.

The person he most wanted to tell was his father. Yet he had already been beaten for expressing some of his ideas. He knew he could not go directly to his father. So he went to his father's friend, who also broke horses. He begged the friend to come watch a demonstration. The man finally agreed. A horse was brought into the corral, and in thirty minutes Monty had a rider on the horse. With great anticipation, he waited for the man's excited approval. Instead the man seemed offended. He told Monty that his father was right, he was only going to get hurt and he should stop immediately. The rejection seemed incomprehensible. How could anyone reject this marvelous breakthrough? Monty was deeply hurt. He decided to make no more demonstrations.

As the years passed Monty accomplished miraculous things with horses, and he gained increased recognition. He was eventually invited by the Queen of England to work with her horses. Gradually he regained the courage to demonstrate his method. Yet the reception of his ideas was not much better. After a demonstration the experts in horse breaking would often claim his method was an illusion, some kind of trick. They would demand that he do it again with horses of their choice. Usually some demented animal would be brought into the corral. Before their eyes, Monty would successfully work with the animal they knew to be unbreakable. Certainly this evidence would gain their acceptance. It did not. Evidence did not seem to convince. In fact, it seemed to only increase the resistance. The experts simply shifted from arguments of illusion to some other rationalization that belittled the process.

Monty grew used to the rejection of the experts. He simply went on developing his techniques and generating impressive results. There was one expert, however, whom he did long to impress. Toward the end of his father's life, his mother arranged for the father to watch the performance of their son. At the conclusion of an impressive demonstration, the father once again refused to acknowledge the value of his son's breakthrough. The relationship remained strained.

Reaching the Experts

Monty suffered a great deal because of the rejection he experienced. Certainly we must attribute his suffering to the brutal and insufferable characteristics of the people who break horses in the more traditional way. Although this is the natural conclusion to draw, I submit that it is incorrect.

I would offer the perspective that the problem was not with the experts but with Monty. I think he suffered rejection because his deep love of horses caused him to reject men who broke them. He not only disapproved of these methods, he also denounced, perhaps in an unconscious way, the people. This denunciation led to an extraordinary man making an ordinary mistake. If he had put as much effort into the study of his father and his father's associates as he put into his communication with horses, Monty might have found more supporters in this community. He would have been able to "gentle" horse breakers as effectively as he gentled horses.

This may seem an unusual criticism. Certainly I am asking too much of Monty. Besides, was it not his father's responsibility to make loving sacrifices for his child, and not the other way around? In theory, we might like to believe that fathers do those things, but the fact is that Monty's father did not. Like us, Monty lived in the real world and the world rarely conforms to our expectations.

That being so, where are we left? Where Monty is concerned, it leaves a man with an impossible dream. Monty would love to share his achievements with his father and others who work with horses. But where this goal is concerned he fails. He therefore presses ahead, suffering the pain of rejection, and doing the best he can. Surely we all know and practice this strategy all too often in our own lives. Unfortunately, ordinary efforts bring ordinary results, and Monty is no exception.

I would suggest that Monty had the answer and never thought to use it. He knew how to study and learn the language of horses. He could have used those same tools to study and learn the language of horse breakers. If he loved his intended audience as much as he loved his horses (which was an extraordinary level of love) he would have not used an ordinary and failing means of influence.

Monty had developed a revolutionary method. It was a better method according to all criteria. So he assumed all he had to do was demonstrate his method to others who worked with horses. He reasoned that all he had to do to win their approval was to show them the evidence. What more should be necessary? However, instead of accepting the evidence, they attacked it. This is not unlike the experience of many inventors and innovators. Alas, many extraordinary people throughout history have been the victims of this same rejection.

The experts had spent their lives learning how to break horses. Their process was based on the common assumption of domination. Right or wrong, effective or not, it also required years of skill development. In some cases, those skills were acquired by risking their lives. Furthermore, the ability to break a horse was a symbol of one's manhood, one's core identity. Monty's methods, based on his love for the animal, of listening to the horse, was way beyond the paradigm of most horse breakers. The new method was based on finely honed understanding and skills in man–animal communication. This understanding and these capabilities were both outside normal experience. What Monty demonstrated was that their entire life investment, all that they stood for, was no longer of value. Monty also demonstrated their incompetence, their flaws. There was a better way and they were entirely incapable of using the better way. Monty was unwittingly negating them. Is it a surprise that they did not welcome his demonstrations? Through his demonstrations he brought their whole lives into question.

Ironically, Monty's demonstrations of gentling horses may have been his way of breaking men. It may have been an unconscious form of punishment, a way to get even with the men who caused both horses and him such grief. It was certainly an unconscious source of power for getting even with his father, of causing his father to experience the same kind of pain that he had inflicted on his son.

If Monty had been whole and free of the injuries he still carried from his childhood (few people are), he would have seen more deeply into what he was bringing to the situation. Instead of having a hidden desire to "break" the horse trainers he might have been able to apply the transformative skills he employed with the horses and "gentle" them toward opening their eyes to what he was doing. He might have learned to listen to their unexpressed message, that is, their fears that if his way really worked they would have to revise their approach. Instead, for all his efforts, the message he put across in his demonstrations was not his competence but their incompetence. He might have fulfilled his dream of winning their approval had he been able to entice them to empowerment. How?

Of course, we can only speculate. The real answer could have only emerged from experimentation, as did his method for working with the horses. However, here is a hypothetical answer. He might have started where the normal horse breaker was, perhaps with his macho outlook. He might have drawn on that macho outlook by challenging one of his naysayers to come down and stand in the corral with a crazed horse. He might then have taught the man a single technique for understanding what the horse was saying and then had the man practice a technique for getting the horse to respond.

Perhaps the trainer Monty had brought in to the corral would develop enough of the techniques so that at the end of an hour, that man would experience some of the exhilaration of "gentling" a horse. He would now experience the power of this technique in his own hands, as part of his bag of tricks for handling horses. That power would no longer be just Monty's, it would be his own.

Then, let's say that in the next hour or so that man, with all the excitement of his new skills, could teach some small part of the new method to another horse breaker. In other words, it may have been possible for the horse breakers to experience the potential that had always been embedded in them but had never before been tapped.

Maybe an experience like this would have opened their eyes and altered their being. Maybe it would not. If not, another experiment would be necessary. To be effective, Monty would have to give up control and further change himself. He would have to look at his own anger and pain, and how he might be using the horse-training demonstrations to punish those, like his father, whom he resented so much. So it is with each of us. And that brings us to the central message of this book: *We can all change the world, but we must first change ourselves.*

Who Should Read This Book

This is a book for ordinary people who have the ordinary need to have extraordinary impact. It is written for anyone who wants to make a difference. Yet let me issue a warning.

The principles in this book are much like Monty's principles. They have the potential for alienating the ordinary person. This even happens to me. I review this manuscript and I react like the horse breakers. I am truly impressed by the demonstrations and the seed thoughts of the three sacred servants. I am inspired by the principles of ACT. Yet the demonstrations of the three sacred servants tend to negate who I am. They make me feel that my assumptions and skills are inadequate. They call me to a higher standard.

They ask me to look within, to own my hypocrisy. They ask me to grow, to see more deeply and more realistically, to embrace great-ness and experience profound power, to risk being fully alive.

My first reaction is that I do not have the understanding, the skills, or the courage. So I search for a way out. First I argue that ACT is impractical. Theoretically, it is powerful, but it could never work in the real world. I also differentiate myself from the three sacred servants. I argue that the principles of ACT are not meant for normal people like me. They are meant for extraordinary peo-ple, people who are bigger than life. Like the horse breakers, I react by attacking. My attack is a cover for my fear. In fact, I am running from ACT.

Now please be warned. Because I expect the reader to run away like I run away, this book is filled with illustrations of normal peo-ple using the principles of ACT to change the world in which they live. Indeed, this is the message of the book. Ordinary people have the need to be profoundly effective change agents, and ordinary people can be extraordinary change agents.

As an author I cannot stand with you in the corral and help you practice a particular step in the method. So I have tried to reach out to you in another way. I have made clear the stories of ordinary people having extraordinary impact. In addition, I have tried to be as honest as I can about my own weaknesses and shortcomings, my own fears and failures, my own falsehoods and hypocrisy. I do this because I think this honesty serves as an invitation to transforma-tion. I think it serves as a system of support. That is my objective, to not only offer ACT as a body of principles but to try to support the reader in taking the risk of internalizing ACT. My hope is that you will come to see the simplicity on the other side of complex-ity, that you come to a deeper vision that gives the power to per-form in unique ways, to shape outcomes. It is my hope that you will have creative power and revolutionary impact. It is my hope that you will change the world.

Acknowledgments

This book relates many of my direct experiences, and it contains the stories of many associates. Most of the stories I have held con-fidential. I would nevertheless like to thank the many people who have shared parts of their lives. Their life decisions have shaped this manuscript.

In preparing to write I have read extensively. In the references are the books that were particularly useful. Within the list of references are the works of several authors who have had significant impact. I would like particularly to thank Debashis Chatterjee, Mihaly Csikszentmihalyi, Robert Fritz, and Parker Palmer. Each one has deep and useful insights into the notion of extraordinary impact. I have been most influenced and I am most grateful. I hope to some day come to know them personally.

I would like to thank the people who have taken the time to review parts of this manuscript. They include Doug Anderson, Corinne Coen, Jane Dutton, Mark Levine, Aniel Mishra, Ian Mitroff, Regina O'Neill, J. M. Sampath, Gretchen Spreitzer, Delsa Quinn, Ryan Quinn, and Shauri Quinn. Tricia Hackett has spent hours working on the manuscript. Carolyn Hansen has kept me organized during the process. Cedric Crocker and his many associates at Jossey-Bass have been, as always, invaluable. I am particularly grateful to Hal Zina Bennett, who has made marvelous input as a developmental editor.

Thank you to one and all.

Robert E. Quinn

Ann Arbor, Michigan
January 2000

The Author

Robert E. Quinn holds the Margaret Elliot Tracy Collegiate Professorship at the University of Michigan and is a member of the business school faculty. His research focuses on change. He has published a number of books. Among them are *Beyond Rational Management, Becoming a Master Manager, Deep Change, Diagnosing and Changing Organizational Culture, The Pressing Problems of Modern Organizations,* and the present volume. He is also senior partner in Wholonics Leadership Group, a firm dedicated to excellence in organizational performance.

CHANGE THE WORLD

CHAPTER ONE

AN INVITATION
TO TRANSFORMATION

My first real awareness of seeds came when I was ten years old. I had poison ivy so badly that I had to stay home from school. It was a beautiful spring day but there was nothing to do. As my boredom grew I had an idea. I would plant a garden! I picked a plot of ground by the side of the house and began to enact my silly fantasy. I spent much of the afternoon turning over the soil. That night, I pestered my parents to go out and buy seeds. They did, and the next day I planted.

During the entire process, I felt like a fake. I was a city boy who knew nothing about planting things. What were the chances that anything would come of my efforts? Nevertheless, in the face of self-doubt, I forged ahead. Weeks later bushy, green plants pushed toward the sun. I touched them with gentle wonder, filled with feelings of exhilaration. I was responsible! These were my carrots! I had put tiny seeds into the ground, and now they were magically transformed into growing plants.

Perhaps it was this experience that caused me to choose seeds as my metaphor for human action in this book. My dictionary tells me that a seed is "the part of a flowering plant that typically contains the embryo with its protective coat and stored food and that will develop into a new plant if sown and fertilized." An acorn is a seed. The acorn does not contain a small oak but contains the code for a process that may one day produce an oak. Place the acorn in the soil, with the right nutrients and moisture, and it begins to transform into something greater than itself. The external, protective coat splits and the internal contents mingle with the soil. It is a process full of creative tension. From the interactive process a new form may emerge. In one sense the outcome is determined. If the tree comes into being it must be an oak, not a maple. In another sense the process is free, emergent, or self-organizing. The number and placement of branches and other characteristics of the adult tree will depend on a variety of interactions with the environment, many of which will be impossible to predict.

This book is about the process of transformation in human systems. This can be an individual, two people in a relationship, or a group, unit, organization, or society. Human systems, whether of one person or a million, are always interacting with their environment. We know that over time, these interactions tend to become patterned or normalized. We develop individual scripts and collective cultures. Scripts structure the individual, whereas cultures structure the collective. These scripts and cultures resemble the shell of the seed. If they crack we can begin to interact with our environment in new ways, and these interactions can give rise to a new self or a new collective. We, like the carrot seed or the acorn, can transform into a more complex entity.

I like to use the word *seed* to speak about transformation because it can be used as either a noun or a verb. In a laboratory, for example, we might seed the process of crystallization by adding a small particle to a particular solution. In this way, a liquid is turned into a solid. The small particle becomes a catalyst for change. Similarly, a person can seed the culture of an organization with new ideas or a new vision that can transform it.

This book is about the process of seeding the transformation of human systems. It assumes that a small particle introduced into a human system at the right time may disrupt that system in a positive way. It can reduce the stasis or entropy and increase the energy, literally breathing new life into it. The seed or particle that is the catalyst for such changes usually comes in the form of some sort of behavior that itself emerged from a seed-like thought.

The Sacred Part of Change

Not long ago, I was working with a group of executives in a trust-building exercise. As the exercise progressed, the participants began to share more about themselves. At one point, a very senior member of the group told a story about a meaningful experience he has cherished over the years. He said that he had spent the first four years of his career as a ninth-grade teacher. He then left teaching to launch his managerial career. That was over twenty years ago. Recently, he was walking through a mall when someone called his name. He turned to see a lovely woman. She introduced herself as one of his former students. He remembered her, and they had a delightful few minutes of conversation. As she was about to walk away, she stopped, held his hand, and said, "I really need to thank you. You were the best teacher I ever had."

At this point in the story, the senior executive paused and started to weep. Finally, he said, "That event meant a great deal to me. It meant that I made a difference in her life."

As he said those words, I remembered how I had felt when I was a boy of ten caressing those carrot tops. These were feelings of joy that come only with a personal achievement in which we feel we have made an essential contribution. Oddly enough, those same feelings of achievement are often mixed with a sense of awe and humility. I believe the sense of awe stems from experiencing the magnificence of transformation. The humility stems from knowing we are necessary but, alone, are insufficient.

The process of transformation is always bigger than we are. It requires a supportive universe. As we take part in this process, experiencing the transformation of energy, becoming aware that the universe actually needs us and that we need the universe, we join in a dance of co-creation. We become aware of our own simultaneous potential and dependence. We awaken to the sacred potential that is in living systems. What I want to suggest is that all human systems, no matter how secular, are also sacred because the seeds of potential transformation exist there. Individually, we can contribute to the transformational process. We can each become transformational change agents. We do not need to be world leaders, leaders of an organization, or even the head of a family to do this. Each of us can make a significant contribution to positive change in ourselves, our relationships, and in any organization or culture in which we take part. If you have doubts about this, I urge you to read on.

On Being a Change Agent

Change agent is not a common term. As the individual words imply, it refers to any person who seeks to bring about some kind of change. Since we all sometimes seek to create change, we are all change agents. Children try to change their parents; parents seek to change their children and each other. Therapists attempt to alter individuals, dyads, and families. Executives seek to transform groups, departments, organizations, whole companies. Politicians attempt to alter entire societies. All of us, at some point, seek to play the role of change agent.

Being a change agent is not easy. Trying to change another person can lead to great frustration. Consider a story from the work of Terry Warner (1992, pp. 0–4).

In this case, an eight-year-old girl cares nothing about doing her schoolwork—she even cheats. The mother insists that the child complete her homework and spends hours working with her. The child complains. The mother tries to be cheerful but gets increasingly irritated. The mother states, "The trouble with Erin is especially frustrating because for years I have given her my best efforts." The mother then describes the self-discipline she has had to exercise not to compare Erin with her sister, who is a good student and highly motivated. The mother frequently gives Erin warm hugs, assuring the child that she is loved. The mother describes drilling Erin with flash cards and Erin's seemingly perverse efforts to frustrate the effort by knowingly giving wrong answers. The mother recounts the feeling of being "kicked in the teeth" and her feelings of helplessness.

I believe that this kind of frustration is universal. This mother is no different from the basketball coach who cannot get his players to excel, the executive who cannot get her sales force to accept a new technique, or the CEO who cannot achieve cohesion between conflicting groups in a merger. There are very few people who have not experienced themselves in the role of a change agent, frustrated in their efforts to effect changes that they are certain would improve a situation or a person's life. Transforming a human system usually requires that we transform ourselves, and this is a key to the process.

Reaching out for support, Erin's mother attended a self-help workshop run by Warner, and she was encouraged to look more deeply into herself. This process had considerable impact. She went through a personal change that also altered how she saw the world. In reflecting on her relationship with Erin, she noted considerable self-deception and implicit communication of her own negative feelings. She discovered something about herself: "I was outwardly encouraging, but inwardly I mistrusted her," the mother said. She then came to a critical insight: "She [Erin] felt that message from me."

With her new and more complex worldview, the mother took on a higher level of concern for her daughter: "I cried when I realized the price she had to pay for my inability to love her without reservation." With a new vision for the relationship, the mother stopped micromanaging the relationship and started modeling the importance of self-discipline by encouraging Erin to come to her for help when she was ready. The relationship dramatically changed. The little girl began to perform well in school. Her mother went on to report a particularly interesting moment:

> But this time I pulled her up on my lap and looked at her, and I had this overwhelming feeling of love for her that just seemed to flow between us. I hugged her tightly, and told her how much I loved her. I realized that, for the very first time in eight years, I was expressing true love for her. Previously, I had hugged her, but the love didn't flow. This time, the love just flowed. It was as if I was holding a new baby for the first time. Tears were streaming down, and she looked at me and said, "Are you crying because you love me, Mommy?" I nodded. She whispered, "Mommy, I want to stay with you forever."

The story of Erin and her mother provides an important model for this book, and you will find that I will refer back to it again and again. I see it as a key for transforming a marriage, a classroom, the Fortune 500, or an entire society. I have found that some people read it and say, "So the mother just withdrew and let her daughter make her own decisions. Is that the technique you are suggesting?" My answer is a resounding no! What occurred in the story is far more complex than that.

Read the story again: A change agent (mother) defines a problem—the unwillingness of an eight-year-old to study. She describes the purity of her own motives, the logic of her strategy, the resistance in the change target (Erin), and the frustration of the process. These are behaviors common to the normal change agent. What happens next is uncommon and transformational.

The mother finds herself in a situation where she is able to lower her defenses and examine her motives, thought processes, and behaviors. She makes the discovery that she has been self-deceptive. Her motives have not been pure and her analysis of the problem has not been accurate. Because of her own negativity, her strategies for changing Erin were far more punitive than she could originally see. With her new vision, her behaviors change. Her changed behaviors send a new message to her daughter, which causes the child to be more mindful. The child has to pay attention and has to make sense of the new patterns. The child interprets the new behaviors accurately. She is no longer being judged as a problem. Now the child feels loved. In the warmth and safety of that love, Erin finds increased confidence and feels safe to experiment with new behaviors of her own. The entire relationship between mother and child changes.

This is the story of a transformational change. The change agent was behaving according to a script she carried in her head. In changing, she had to transcend her old script. The shell of the acorn had to crack. The cracking of the acorn then led to a new pattern of interaction. The child was encountering a mother with a new self. She saw the doors opening to a more intimate kind of contact. The child responds to this new opportunity, and at this point mother and daughter become more richly connected than ever. In this interaction, there are new feedback loops. The child begins to change, and the mother continues to change. They reinforce each other. The relationship now consists of two more differentiated people who are making their own choices within this new, more integrated system.

Given this new system, Erin can now grow more effectively because her mother is now growing more effectively. Her mother is growing more effectively because she has encountered and altered her own self-deceptions. She has closed the gap between her script and the emergent reality in her life, that is, she can look beyond her own interpretations of Erin's behaviors and relate to her in the reality of the present moment. She can see this emergent reality more accurately.

The seemingly simple story is actually quite intricate. It is as intricate as the process that takes place when an acorn cracks. When we alter our scripts, we, like the acorn, initiate a new pattern of being, a pattern of high potential. This book is about developing as a person with increased potential for growth. It is about effectively transforming human systems by effectively transforming the self.

The Real World

The above story is played out within a family unit. In the family, we accept the notions of intimacy and love, particularly between mother and child, and it is here that we can see the potential for the sacred. But what about in the secular world? In the professional world, we make assumptions about expertise, competence, control, transaction, and exchange. People are valued if they perform and get along well with their coworkers. They are out the door if they don't. In the secular world, we see no space for the sacred, for honoring bonds such as we see between parents and their offspring.

I am reminded here of an executive who told me he understood the principles I was teaching. He and his wife used them in their family. He said that when he or his wife wanted to change the behavior of their teenager, they learned to look first at themselves. They practiced self-mastery and closed their own integrity gaps. The results were impressive. He had a deep grasp of what I was saying. Yet, he told me, "I cannot imagine how to bring these same principles into my professional setting." That is my challenge, for in this book, we will try to provide answers that would satisfy this man. Let's turn to a very real-world story.

Transformational and Incremental Change

In the early 1900s, Mohandas Mahatma Gandhi led India to independence from Great Britain. Most of us remember him for the model he provided through nonviolent protest, which won the Indian people greater freedom and self-determination. Trained as a lawyer, he was the architect of the constitution that established India's autonomy as a sovereign nation.

Gandhi's career began in South Africa, where he once bought a first-class ticket and boarded a train. Shortly thereafter, he was thrown off the train. Only whites were allowed to travel first class. After this incident, Gandhi made the momentous decision to confront the racist policies of the South African government. One of his first acts was to hold a public burning of the work passes required of all non-European people.

This event is beautifully captured in the movie *Gandhi*. The pass burning is held in the presence of South African police. After a short speech, one man burns a pass and is arrested. The senior police officer turns to threaten the crowd. As he does so, Gandhi, without comment, burns several more passes. For this, he receives a violent clubbing across his arm. As Gandhi lies writhing in pain on the ground, the police officer again warns the crowd. He then turns back to see the injured Gandhi lifting still another pass toward the fire. He strikes Gandhi in the stomach, and Gandhi again collapses. Yet Gandhi lifts himself and finds the strength to burn still another pass. The policeman becomes enraged and with all his might smashes Gandhi across the forehead. Gandhi falls. To his amazement, the policeman sees a set of trembling fingers struggle to grasp still another pass and move it slowly and painfully toward the fire.

At this point, there is a profoundly important change. The policeman's rage fades, and his lips make no more demands. As he raises his club, this authority figure, who just seconds before had seemed so much in control, suddenly appears desperate. His face is contorted with confusion, and his eyes beg for relief. At this extraordinary moment, control makes a paradoxical shift from the physically dominant man (the policeman) of external authority to the physically wounded man (Gandhi) of internal authority. It now appears that the policeman's greatest desire is to relent on the threats he has so forcefully uttered. The club hangs frozen in the air as the work pass moves haltingly, but certainly, to the fire.

What we have in this scene are examples of two types of change. Incremental changes are those that happen within normal expectations. For the crowd to lose its courage in the face of the policeman's brutality is an incremental change. It is a relatively small and predictable change. For the policeman to be suddenly frozen in his tracks by a wounded and seemingly powerless individual, however, is an instance of transformational change. It is outside our normal expectations. It is a profound change. *It is an example of Advanced Change Theory (ACT)—a body of principles based on seed thoughts of masters of transformation that reflect the simplicity from the other side of complexity—at its most advanced.* Before we examine ACT in more depth, we should first consider normal change theory.

Normal Change Theory

In this book, I use the words *norm, normal,* and *normalized* in a particular way. A *norm* is a pattern of behavior that has become routine in a given relationship or group. It is expected behavior, the accepted standard, model, or pattern. It is often considered average behavior in the given relationship or group. Similarly, behavior that has been *normalized* is behavior that has been brought into conformity with the standards and expectations of the relationship or group.

Normalized groups, and the participants in them, often become disconnected from emergent reality, that is, from the reality that is unfolding independently of that system. To be in touch with emergent reality is to be responsive to the present. Emergent reality requires new behaviors that the actors in a normalized system are not yet ready to embrace. Emergent reality tends to threaten deeply held values and to suggest the need for taking a risk by plunging into the unknown. It reveals how we all tend to be self-deceptive in interpreting the effectiveness of our own efforts. We become self-deceptive because we want to avoid the risk of losing what we presently have. A key assumption of normal life is self-interested survival. The change agent working in a normalized system will put self first. That's only natural. Such a change agent lives in a world of social exchange and economic transaction, and the central purpose of any person in such a system is to obtain status and resources while avoiding pain and punishment. These assumptions are accurate. They do reflect normal behavior.

Most of us are familiar with three general strategies for change in a normal situation. Here I will review a simplified version of a scheme originally offered by Chin and Benne (1969). The three strategies are *telling* (making logical arguments for change), *forcing* (using forms of leverage such as the threat of being fired or being ostracized), and *participating* (using open dialogue and pursuing win-win strategies).

The *telling strategy* assumes that people are guided by reason. If they decide it is in their best interest to change, they will gladly do so. Further, it is reasoned that any resistance to change could only be the product of ignorance and superstition. To counter that resistance, the change agent simply needs to persuade people or educate them to the truth. Their resistance should then dissolve. Unfortunately, this strategy often does not work.

Someone tells me my tire is going flat and that I need to get it changed. I can verify this by looking at the tire. I can make a clear cost-benefit assessment; I must have a good tire to drive my car. I am not emotionally tied to getting the work done, and I am quite certain that when it is done I can drive safely again. I know what to do; no learning is required. This is incremental change and it's relatively easy. But what if some expert were to tell me that I must change the way I drive because it is causing undue wear and tear on my car. It will be a good investment, I am told, and all I have to do is attend a weekend conference to learn the new technique. Now the equation changes. I have no way of assessing immediately whether that person is right or wrong. Besides, I would have to attend classes and learn a whole new way of driving. I see a large cost with an uncertain benefit. The proposed change seems logical to the change agent but not to me. Resisting the change seems logical to me.

When we are the change agent and this process unfolds, we often take a negative view of the ignorant change target. The change target takes a negative view of the ignorant change agent. The telling strategy has a narrow, cognitive view of human systems. It fails to incorporate values, attitudes, and feelings. Although people may understand why they should change, they are often not willing to make the painful changes inherent in many complex situations. Telling often leads to resistance.

The *forcing strategy* assumes that people are resistant and must be coerced into changing. Since they are not easily persuaded, the change agent must use leverage to manipulate the change target. Although the strategy is sometimes effective in the short-term, it engenders long-term difficulties. The forcing strategy usually evokes anger, resistance, and damage to the fundamental relationship. Therefore, it is not likely to result in the kind of voluntary commitment that is necessary to sustain the system.

A Two-Step Process

The normal way for the normal change agent to behave is to engage in the following two-step process:

First, tell the target why they need to change.
Second, if telling fails, figure out a way to force the target to change.

This two-step process is so normalized, that unless I stay very mindful, I may employ it and my life will fill with unproductive power struggles. The reader is likely to be guilty of this same pattern. We all tend to repeat this process. In doing so we refuse to recognize that in using force we damage the relationship and seldom obtain our desired long-term outcome. The fact that we seldom obtain our desired end seems to make no difference, however. We refuse to learn. If we have to choose between control or effectiveness, we tend to choose control.

The Participating Strategy

The *participating strategy* involves a more collaborative change process. It is much less normal than are the first two strategies. Here change targets are still guided by a rational calculus; however, this calculus extends beyond self-interest to incorporate the meanings, habits, norms, and institutional policies that contribute to the formation of human culture. The participative change agent welcomes the input of others as equals in the change process. Change does not come by simply providing information, as in the telling strategy. Rather, it requires the change agent to focus on clarifying and reconstructing values. In this model, the change agent attempts to bring to light all values, working through conflicts embedded in the larger collective. The emphasis is on communication and cooperation with the change target. The technique is to involve the change target in an honest dialogue, while mutually learning the way to win-win solutions.

I am a strong advocate of the participating strategy. I believe it to be extraordinarily powerful. I consider it an indispensable complement for ACT. Yet as normally practiced, it is often ineffective. The problem is not so much in the strategy as it is in the people who attempt to use it. Let's explore this point.

The Difficulties with the Participating Strategy

As an undergraduate, I took a rigorous course entirely devoted to learning a single skill. The skill was active listening. The notion was to listen in such a way that others were assisted in communicating feelings they are often not able to communicate. In so doing, two people together create an enriched relationship characterized by win-win commitments.

For the rest of my life, that course had provided me with a great source of power. I have been able to use the participating strategy to move through many seemingly impossible situations. Yet I know that not everyone left that course with the same abilities. During the last class a student raised his hand and asked, "Professor, what if I do all these listening things, and the person still will not do what I want?" The deeply disappointed professor seemed to shrink behind his podium. After all we had been through, this student could not comprehend the most basic point of the participating strategy; he could not comprehend the notion of reducing control enough to join with another human being in learning and mutual creation of a win-win solution. This notion remains a mystery to many people.

There is still another mystery associated with the participating strategy. Here I am reminded of a story told by Steven Covey. A disbelieving CEO told Covey, "Every time I try win-win, I lose." Covey replied, "Then you did not do win-win." The paradox is that this strategy calls for the reduction of control while remaining clear and strong about one's underlying values and intent. It is not a strategy of weakness, but of strength—the kind of strength that many people lack. Participatory strategies and active listening both require that people allow each other to express their truths while also making sure that one's own truth is heard.

Because participating strategies and active listening are so difficult to understand and implement, they are seldom used as they are intended but instead are used to manipulate. The change agent determines a solution, and then asks a group to join in a discussion. Any answer they come up with is acceptable, as long as it is the "right" one. Because so many people experience the participating strategy as a manipulative technique, they become deeply cynical. The participating strategy thus becomes a politically correct rhetoric but one that everyone is quite certain will not work. We thus get back only what we put out: distrust of the system and what passes for "proof" that the participating strategy doesn't work.

Advanced Change Theory

The telling strategy and the forcing strategy are at the heart of normal change theory. The participating strategy is not so normalized. It is more demanding and less used. The transforming strategy of ACT is even more demanding and even less used. A simple representation of the four orientations can be seen in Exhibit 1.1.

Exhibit 1.1 shows each of four strategies as being at different levels. I will explain the differences in level after discussion of Exhibit 1.2. Suffice to say that the lower the level, the more normal the strategy. The higher the level, the more difficult it is to observe and master the strategy. At level 1 is the telling strategy, which is about persuading others and emphasizing facts. Listed here are the types of questions we might ask ourselves when employing this strategy. At levels 2 and 3 are similar representations of the forcing strategy and the participating strategy. At level 4 is the transformational strategy of Advanced Change Theory (ACT). It is about engaging emergent reality and transcending self. Eight questions follow. A chapter of this book is devoted to explaining the meaning of each one of the eight questions. By the end of the book, the reader might find this list to be a helpful tool.

What is ACT?

ACT is a set of action principles for more effectively introducing change to human systems.

But do not look for a more comprehensive articulation and summary of the principles until the end of the book. (I summarize them

Exhibit 1.1. The Four Strategies.

Level 4. The Transforming Strategy (ACT)
Method: Transcend self; emphasis on emergent reality
     Am I envisioning productive community?
     Am I first looking within?
     Am I embracing the hypocritical self?
     Am I transcending fear?
     Am I embodying a vision of the common good?
     Am I disturbing the system?
     Am I surrendering to the emergent process?
     Am I enticing through moral power?

Level 3. The Participating Strategy
Method: Open Dialogue; emphasis on relationship
     Is there a focus on human process?
     Is everyone included in an open dialogue?
     Do I model supportive communication?
     Is everyone's position being clarified?
     Am I surfacing the conflicts?
     Are the decisions being made participatively?
     Is there commitment to a "win-win" strategy?
     Are the people cohesive?

Level 2. The Forcing Strategy
Method: Leveraging behavior; emphasis on authority
     Is my authority firmly established?
     Is the legitimacy of my directive clear?
     Do I understand their fears?
     Am I capable and willing to impose sanctions?
     Is there a clear performance-reward linkage?
     Am I controlling the context and flow of information?
     Am I using maximum leverage?
     Are the people complying?

Level 1. The Telling Strategy
Method: Rational persuasion; emphasis on facts
     Am I within my expertise?
     Have I gathered all the facts?
     Have I done a good analysis?
     Will my conclusions withstand criticism?
     Are my arguments logical?
     Are my arguments clear?
     Do I have a forum for instruction?
     Am I prepared to argue effectively?

in Appendix A.) In this book, ACT emerges from the teachings of Jesus, Gandhi, and Martin Luther King. Each chapter begins with a seed thought that is common to all three. Following each seed thought, I explore how it applies to transformational change in a modern setting. From chapter to chapter, the ideas and real-life examples grow and intertwine in a rich way. The book is written to take you on a personal journey of discovery. By the end you will have a deep feel for the notion of ACT and will then be ready for the abstract summary of ACT in Appendix A.

Action from Principle

One of the formative voices of the nineteenth century was that of Henry David Thoreau, a friend of Ralph Waldo Emerson. Both men were concerned about transcending the pressures for conformity in an industrialized society. Thoreau was born in 1817, and entered Harvard at sixteen years of age. After his graduation, he briefly taught school. He eventually gave up teaching and other professional pursuits. Subsequently, he built a simple cabin and lived alone on Walden Pond. His writing about this experiment in solitude would later become renowned. Perhaps the most noted statement in the account of his time at Walden is his description of men in the industrial age: "They become like machines whose sole purpose is to make a living. This mass of men lead lives of quiet desperation."

Whenever I read this line, I think of an incident that occurred in a company I visited. I was walking down a hallway lined with endless cubicles. People moved unenthusiastically from place to place. I must have signaled what I was thinking, because the woman who was escorting me read my mind. She said, "Yes, here we house the legions of the walking dead."

Thoreau was concerned with living a life of meaning. His purpose in going to Walden Pond was to find his own soul. It is important to understand that his intent was not to become a lifelong hermit. Quite the contrary: He pursued this quest so that he might return to society and more effectively cope with the pressures of conformity in that society. To do so, he felt he needed to fully know himself.

At one point, his taxes fell due. Although the amount was very small, Thoreau refused to pay. He did this in protest of slavery. He soon found himself in the local jail. He was in the jail for only one night because his concerned neighbors insisted on paying the tax. Nevertheless, the experience had great impact on Thoreau. Shortly thereafter, he wrote an essay that would be later studied by both Gandhi and Martin Luther King, Jr. The essay is entitled "Civil Disobedience." In the essay he makes the following statement:

> Action from principle, the perception and the performance of right, changes things and relations; it is essentially revolutionary, and does not consist wholly with any thing that was. It not only divides states and churches, it divides families; aye, it divides the individual, separating the diabolical in him from the divine. [Thoreau, (1849) 1946]

What does this statement mean? Altering our behavior to reflect what we really value is revolutionary because principle-driven actions tend to be outside the boundaries of exchange and transaction. In normalized relationships, we ask, "What does the group expect?" Around those group expectations we construct a set of rewards and punishments designed to bring conformity.

Engaging in a new behavior based on principle challenges the norms. The person with a moral purpose is usually willing to endure punishments in order to pursue the purpose. Such principled behavior sends the dreaded signal that perhaps "the emperor has no clothes." It questions whether the present system is moving toward stagnation and decay or toward new levels of life, complexity, and productivity. People in the system spilt into camps: one embracing the new behavior and the other condemning it; hence, the division of states, churches, and families.

Yet Thoreau's statement suggests that even the individual is split. In the face of principled behavior, the individual observer is constantly required to chose between preservation of the current self or the creation of the new self. When we discipline self in the pursuit of higher purpose, a new self emerges. This process is exhilarating because it makes us aware of the profound power we each hold. However, when we know that we should be walking a higher road and we do not, we bow to the diabolical that also lurks within.

We become divided. We loose psychic energy. We become flat, dull, and without enthusiasm, easy prey for those who would dominate or manipulate us.

ACT and Moral Reasoning

Thoreau's statement about principle suggests that moral power plays a major role in the transformational process. All change theories are rooted in assumptions of morality, but the assumptions differ greatly. Before we take any action, we ask ourselves, What is the right thing to do in this situation? The name for this process is *moral reasoning*. There are different levels of moral reasoning.

Kohlberg (1969) suggests that we can potentially move through six stages of moral reasoning (see Exhibit 1.2). The two earliest stages are based on anticipation of external rewards and the fear of external punishments. I decide what is right by what I think I will gain or lose by engaging in the behavior. External pressures determine who I am and how I will act. The next two stages are based on compliance with group norms and notions of what is fair and just. In this more developed realm, I decide what is right by asking what is expected and what is fair to everyone in the relationship. These questions reflect the normal assumptions of externally driven transaction and exchange, identifying the expectations and then transacting the process.

Only in the most evolved stages does moral reasoning become internally driven. In the final two stages, moral reasoning is based on principles. The fifth stage reflects the internalized principles of society, and the final stage reflects the internalization of universal principles. In stage six, internally driven people act according to conscience, even if the acts involve personal risk.

I believe that the change theories that most of us witness and enact are normalized, that is, they reflect and support the norms and expectations of the group. We are driven by the external conditions in which we find ourselves. Very few theories include the role of internalized principles; few theories suggest the need for a transformational change agent who is willing to sacrifice self in the pursuit of universal good.

The four strategies for change listed in Exhibit 1.1 are at different levels of moral reasoning. Strategies at levels 1 and 2 reflect

Exhibit 1.2. Kohlberg's Six Stages of Moral Reasoning.

Stage	Primary Behavior	Description
Pre-Conventional Morality (ages 1–10)	Decisions based on external rewards and punishments	Morality is almost entirely external
1. Punishment and obedience	Avoid punishment	Children obey because adults tell them to obey.
2. Individualism and purpose	Seek rewards	Children act in self interest; they obey when they think it is in their best interest to obey.
Conventional Reasoning (ages 10–20)	Decisions based on a combination of internal guidance and social rules	Morality is partly internalized, but still largely based on social norms.
3. Internpersonal norms	Gain approval/ avoid disapproval	Trust, caring, and loyalty to others shapes reasoning.
4. Social system morality	Conform to social rules	Social order, law, justice, and duty influence moral reasoning.
Post-Conventional Reasoning (ages over 20)	Decisions based on personal moral code	Morality is completely internalized and not based on other's standards.
5. Community vs. individual rights	Apply society's principles	Values and laws are understood to be relative and can be changed. Some values are understood to be more important than society's laws.
6. Universal ethical principles	Apply universal principles	Moral standards are based on universal human rights. People follow their conscience even though it may involve personal risk.

Source: From Mark Youngblood, in *Life at the Edge of Chaos: Creating the Quantum Organization,* edited by John Renesch, 1997, Perceval Publishing. Used by permission of Perceval Publishing, a division of Quay Alliance.

normal or conventional assumptions about what is right. Strategies at levels 3 and 4 reflect a more principled perspective on what is right. As we proceed through the book we will find other differentiations as well.

To observe transformational capability, we cannot observe normal people doing normal things. We must observe people who are living by principle. To develop transformational capability, we cannot be normal people doing normal things. We must stand outside the norm. To do that we need to go inside ourselves and ask who we are, what we stand for, and what impact we really want to have. Within ourselves we find principle, purpose, and courage. There we find the capacity not only to withstand the pressures of the external system but also actually to transform the external system. We change the world by changing ourselves.

ACT and the Quest for Freedom

Because ACT is found at the highest level of moral reasoning, I sometimes call it the theory that is too painful to be true. It assumes accountability and the exercising of choice. It says we are free and accountable. Although we usually claim to value freedom and accountability, we often behave in ways that produce the opposite. I have to admit that I sometimes behave in ways that are weak and that result in further weakness. When that happens, I am not very anxious to hear about high levels of moral reasoning. I get defensive and deny such notions. I argue that I have no choice. My life is determined by forces beyond my control. Any statement to the contrary is simply untrue.

The ideas I present here offer individuals and organizations a strategic advantage that is simple, differentiating, and difficult to copy. It suggests that the process of significant self-modification and change, of knowing and personifying our core values, leads to a sense of empowerment. Empowerment leads to increased experimentation, creativity, learning, and impact. These results, in turn, lead to the development of unique characteristics and the capacity to transform human contexts. Such a person, group, or organization brings positive energy to the larger community, while the larger community, in turn, experiences a decrease in entropy and an increase in energy. In doing the things I suggest here, we can seed the universe. We change the world by changing ourselves.

ACT Is About Action

It is not a coincidence that the acronym for Advanced Change Theory is ACT. ACT is about action, motion, and growth. To act is to do, behave, function, operate, or perform. There are, however, a number of other streams of meaning associated with the word *action*. For our purposes, two of these are particularly important. The first suggests that action often has an emergent element, and it is conveyed by words such as *materialize, develop, evolve, unfold, emerge, surface, arise, emanate,* and *originate*. Our actions, like seeds, can be seen as unfolding and evolving over time, causing other things to unfold or evolve. That is, each of our actions has the potential to create new outcomes.

Our actions stimulate others in that others must interpret and react to each new behavior we exhibit. We then respond to the reactions others are having to our actions. We are thus ever-involved in a process of co-creation with the world around us. We create the world that also creates us. This process can then be correctly interpreted in two opposite ways: The world creates us or we create the world. Both statements are true. Overemphasis on the first, however, can lead to resignation in which who we are increasingly becomes determined by external forces. An overemphasis on the second leads to self-deception in which we claim that all constraints are illusions. The focus here is on the reality of *constraints* and the reality of *potential;* both are real. In fact, potential requires constraints, and constraints make the transformation of potential a possibility.

The second important stream of thought has to do with how we create. It suggests that our actions can be symbolic representations. This stream of thought is captured through words such as *personify, embody, characterize, illustrate, symbolize, dramatize,* and *stage*. Here our actions are like seeds. They carry transformational potential. Each time we act, we represent our beliefs and values. We embody possibilities and illustrate constraints. With each action, we become a living symbol that others must interpret and to which they must respond. That is, our actions are signaling devices in the process of co-creation. What we represent matters deeply. What is more important, because we can control what we represent, we can change the world by changing ourselves.

In theory, this orientation can seem obvious. In practice, it is seldom considered. Our normal patterns of practice suggest that we can only expect small, incremental changes. The notion of bringing revolutionary and transformational changes is confined to the realm of mythological heroes. The notion that every one of us can change the world by changing ourselves seems most unrealistic. In this book, however, we will move from the seed thoughts of the sacred servants to the potential of the normal person, and demonstrate that perhaps it is quite within everyone's reach after all. As we do so we need to be clear about the nature of transformational power.

Transformational Power

A few pages back we considered the scene from a biographical movie in which Gandhi transformed the viewpoint of the violent policeman. By studying a later scene, we can gain some insight into this strange shift in control. We also gain an insight into Gandhi.

A Protestant minister named Charlie Andrews comes to join Gandhi. The two men are walking down a city street when three teenagers emerge from an alley, carrying rocks, calling names, and threatening violence. Charlie pauses and suggests that he and Gandhi take a different route. Instead, Gandhi moves forward and beckons Charlie to come along. As they walk, Gandhi notes that Jesus taught that if an enemy strikes a blow on one cheek, you are to turn the other. The danger grows with each forward step until the unnerved minister blurts out: "Surely that teaching was metaphorical."

Gandhi calmly replies:

> I am not so sure. I have thought about it a great deal, and I suspect he meant you must show courage. Be willing to take a blow, several blows, to show that you will not strike back, nor will you be turned aside. And when you do that, it calls on something in human nature, something that makes his hatred for you decrease and his respect increase. I think Christ grasped that, and I have seen it work.

In this scene, we find some important clues that might help us explain how, in the earlier scene, control moved from one man to the other. Here Gandhi explains how commitment and the courage to continue one's course in the face of externally imposed punishments tends to change the perception of others.

We might want to reflect more deeply on this process. In the scene where Gandhi is beaten by the policeman, formal authority and physical force are used with the intention of maintaining control. Instead of reacting as dictated by usual norms, Gandhi chooses to originate his own unique response. Such originating behavior is unconventional; it disturbs and distorts expectations. It disorients those who are expecting to get their way. It requires the policeman to stop his predetermined routine and search for understanding. The authority figure is no longer an actor but a reactor. As he searches for the appropriate reaction, he is momentarily open. During this moment of openness, he encounters the moral power Gandhi describes. It melts the policeman's hatred and commands his respect. Gandhi is no longer an object. He is now seen as a human being of noble purpose, someone worthy of respect. The policeman, like Erin's mother, no longer sees an object; instead he sees a human being of profound potential. The club cannot be brought to bear on such a person.

This scene is a microcosm of Gandhi's life. He eventually conquered the government of South Africa and then went on to India, where he overturned the British Empire. Over this period, as Gandhi searched ever deeper into his own soul, he continuously increased the extent of his external impact. As he did so, he not only transformed the external world, but also came to connect more fully to other historically great, transformational sages.

The Inaccessibility of ACT

Note an irony in the above scene. As Gandhi and his minister friend walk toward the threatening teenagers, Gandhi quotes the teachings of Jesus. The fearful Charlie suggests that the teaching is not literal but metaphorical. In making this claim, Charlie is representing the beliefs of many professed Christians. Surely Jesus did not expect such a standard, so there is no accountability to the standard. Since many professed Christians have never lived this or the other similarly demanding standards of Jesus, they cannot possibly understand the value of the standards or the wisdom of the original teacher. They are not at the same level of moral reasoning.

Note that Charlie is an ordained minister. He is a fine man. He is a graduate of a theological institution that certifies he is a student of the Bible. He has read the words, passed the tests, and learned the tactical skills of his profession. Gandhi, in contrast, is not a Christian. He is a Hindu, a heathen in the eyes of many Christians. He has never been baptized or ordained. Yet Gandhi seems to understand Jesus in an intimate way, a way that Charlie and other normal Christians cannot readily grasp.

This observation is most important. Understanding of the transformational process does not emanate from logical analysis of past documents; it does not come from external authority of the theological institution. It emanates from principled living and higher levels of moral reasoning. As we conquer ourselves, we come in contact with a source of internal power that is not experienced by normal people living normalized lives. As we become familiar with this power, we come to understand others who have possessed it. Yet most of the time we cannot access it because, like Charlie, we are operating at a lower level of moral reasoning. Our assumptions prevent us from accessing it. ACT is not about exchange and transaction. It is about transcending ourselves.

The Connectedness of the Sacred Servants

In my earliest attempts to articulate the principles of ACT, I focused on the lives of Gandhi and Dr. Martin Luther King, Jr. I was searching for the commonalities in philosophies and behaviors of these two men. It turns out that there are many such commonalities. Since King was a student of Gandhi, that shouldn't come as any great surprise. I was writing about the shared values of these two men when I began a sentence about Gandhi's understanding of Jesus. At that moment, I was struck by the obvious: Of course, Gandhi and King were both devoted students of Jesus as well! I then went to the New Testament and began a search for the philosophies and behaviors these three men shared. From that analysis came the seed thoughts at the beginning of each chapter. From the unfolding of each chapter came the principles of ACT.

The seed thoughts are conceptual statements intended to disturb our minds and send us into contemplation. They are arbitrary in selection, association, and interpretation. They are loosely connected. They are neither sequential nor mutually exclusive. The transformational realm tends to defy neatness. It is accessed through action and reflection. It emerges from the interaction of commitment and contemplation. The seed thoughts disturb our minds and attract us toward new actions and new thoughts. In such a state, we become new people. We also become seeds in the transformation of larger systems.

As I have already indicated, transformation tends to have sacred overtones because the experience of transformation teaches us that we are necessary but insufficient. Nevertheless, this not a religious book. It does not advocate the Judaism, Hinduism, or Protestant Christianity from which our three sages emerged. The book is not about religion, philosophy, or psychology. Here I would agree with Tracy Goss, who wrote insightfully about the question of how to make impossible things happen. As she points out, such questions require an ontological book. "Ontology is that branch of philosophy that deals with the nature of reality and different ways of being" (Goss, 1996, p. 10). This book, like hers, is about being and reality. It explores movement from the normalized state of being to the transformational. It argues that reality changes as we change from the one state of being to the other.

Featuring Jesus, Gandhi, and King as sacred sages will trouble some readers. Given the atrocities committed in the name of Jesus, the Jewish reader has a justified concern. People from other backgrounds may also worry about one or more of these three. Yet I believe that the eight seed thoughts featured here are consistent with the works of Moses and the prophets and kings of Israel. Likewise, I think they are consistent with the teachings of Mohammed and of Eastern sages of China and India. Transformational people are *connected*. Clearly, Abraham, Moses, Mohammed, Buddha, Lao-Tzu, and Confucius were transformational people. Their core experiences were inner driven and other focused. They lived by principle and changed the world.

Transformational people are unique, different from every other. Yet people who experience the transformational process are connected by shared values and shared experiences. I believe that nearly every transformational change agent, from the self-sacrificing teenager to the committed mother, from the visionary entrepreneur to self-authoring middle manager, is connected. When the ten-year-old caresses his emerging carrot tops, when the executive meets his former student, and when the mother connects with her resistant child, each of them is experiencing the transformational realm. They have a sense of the transformational power within themselves, and they are more likely to understand others who have accessed the same power. For them, the seed thoughts written here are not likely to be offensive.

Being Transformational Is a Choice

When I claim that anyone can be transformational, people get very uneasy. In fact, some get angry. When an idea makes someone angry, it leads me to suspect that it is a very important idea to explore. I therefore try to help people surface their arguments. Some people argue that ACT is very noble but unrealistic. It would fail in a real organization, in the real world. Others say that they can see the use of ACT by someone like Jesus, Gandhi, or King but that these men were bigger than life. They were heroes, superhuman, certainly not ordinary human beings. Others say the opposite. They point out that one or more of the three sages was flawed in objectionable ways and therefore ACT is not valid. I find that most of these statements are offered as rationalizations to escape the painful accountability that is embedded in ACT.

Precisely because of this tendency to rationalize, I have chosen to talk not about transformational leaders but about transformational change agents. As soon as we hear the term *leader,* we start to flee. It's natural to think that to be a leader we must hold some great position such as king, president, or CEO. Surely, ordinary people in positions like yours and mine cannot be transformational; surely this discussion does not apply to us. But it does.

We do not need to be in positions of high authority to be transformational. In fact, we need to have no authority except the authority of our own souls. We are all change agents. Holding a position of authority has little or nothing to do with our ability to access the transformational process. Being transformational is not about position but about values, thoughts, and behaviors. We become transformational change agents through choice—our own.

CHAPTER TWO

ENVISION THE PRODUCTIVE COMMUNITY

The First Seed Thought: Envision the Productive Community

JESUS *Jesus called them unto him, and said, Ye know that the princes of the Gentiles exercise dominion over them, and they that are great exercise authority upon them. But it shall not be so among you: but whosoever will be great among you, let him be your minister; And whosoever will be chief among you, let him be your servant. [Matthew 20:25–27]*

GANDHI *[I]n the orthodox army, there is a clear distinction between officer and private. . . . In a nonviolent army, the general is just the chief servant—first among equals. [Iyer, 1990, p. 257]*

KING *[N]onviolent resistance does not seek to defeat or humiliate the opponent but to win his friendship and understanding. . . . The aftermath of nonviolence is the creation of the beloved community, while the aftermath of violence is tragic bitterness. [King, (1968) 1986, pp. 7–8]*

Whether we recognize it or not, we each carry a mental picture or vision of how human relationships are supposed to work. This vision may reflect assumptions about relations between two people or a family, small group, or large organization. One of the most commonly held pictures is a vision of people in hierarchical relationships. In this picture it is normally assumed that parents are superior to children, teachers are superior to students, coaches are superior to players, bosses are superior to subordinates, and so on.

Within envisioned relationships of this kind, the key to being able to wield influence is to gain a position of authority. Once we have done this, we have presumably gained the right to tell other people to change. The problem is that telling people to change often does not work. Instead it results in power struggles. Normal families, groups, teams, and organizations are thus filled with conflicts. Because of the pictures or assumptions we carry, our communities are often less efficient and effective than they might be.

Productive Community

The three quotations cited above suggest a different picture of human community. These three change agents share an unusual vision. I consider their shared vision a seed thought, because the vision, if we come to understand it, can give rise to a major shift in our perception, thinking, and behavior. That is, we can envision and enact a new form of community, one in which ordinary people can generate extraordinary results.

The three change agents see a system of relationships in which the members share a common purpose and each works for the benefit of all. Throughout this book we will explore the creation of communities of this kind. These are what I call *productive communities*. When people become members of a productive community they tend to become more inner directed and other focused. They tend to be motivated by a calling that they feel deep within. They make contributions that exceed narrow self-interest. People in productive communities also have another unusual characteristic. They want to be connected to reality. They want to know what is real, even if the news is bad.

Given a choice between being effective or being in control, most of us choose being in control. I do this all the time. I deny emergent reality and in doing so I maintain at least a temporary illusion of control. When I am passionate about a purpose, I tend to become more inner directed. I am willing to sacrifice in order to make it happen. I also tend to be more willing to embrace emergent reality. I want to see clearly and accept what is true right now, because I want to be effective, even if it means giving up control. I am more willing to recognize the need to change and learn how to achieve the desired outcome. I have an unusual willingness because I am more clear about who I am. In productive community, many people feel and act this way.

A Surprising Characteristic of Productive Community

Normally this kind of discussion leads the optimistic, "right-brained" people of the world to condemn hierarchies and call for some kind of utopian commune. Such people will read the quotations at the beginning of the chapter and claim that all three of the change agents were for love, equality, and peace, and against hierarchy. This same line of reasoning leads the realistic, "left-brained" people of the world to shake their heads in disbelief. They argue that human nature being what it is, such idealistic nonsense will never work in the real world.

Which group is right?

First, note that none of our three change agents say anything in these quotations about abolishing hierarchy. Their message is much more demanding than that. In the community envisioned by Jesus, there are chiefs who achieve greatness relative to others. In Gandhi's nonviolent army there are still generals and privates. What we see in all three quotations is that the vision, in fact, does not reject hierarchy.

Jesus, Gandhi, and King were all dedicated to getting difficult things done in the real world. To do this they envisioned productive community. In these communities people have different roles, often distinctly different. Each person, being inner directed, is naturally going to be following a unique path, which in itself results in differences. When differences exist, there is, of necessity, a hierarchy. Yet this hierarchy is not like our normal picture of hierarchy. This hierarchy is paradoxical. People in higher positions see themselves as the servants of those in lower positions. Productive community is characterized by clarity of purpose, high standards of performance. Yet it is also characterized by highly trusting and supportive relationships. These kinds of purposes and relationships allow for learning and change.

We all have assumptions about the social world. These tend to become ideological and they tend to blind us to what is possible. Productive community is not easily envisioned by the right-brained optimist. The standards of achievement and discipline are much too excruciating. Neither is it readily envisioned by the left-brained realist. The necessary surrender of control in an emerging community of trust is much too idealistic. Since most of us fall into one of these two camps, all of us should have some difficulty envisioning productive community. Yet please bear with me. In this chapter we will more deeply explore each of the concepts associated with this concept. We begin with the notion of the inner-directed and other-focused person.

What It Means to Be an Other-Focused Person

Several years ago my wife Delsa and I were struggling to raise a family of six children. Demands on our time and finances were incredible. At the height of these pressures Delsa was asked to volunteer as a teacher for a religious class consisting of eleven-year-old girls. In spite of family demands, Delsa accepted the challenge enthusiastically.

Not long after her decision to take on this extra responsibility I came home to find the kitchen in extreme disarray. On the table was a beautiful cake. But it was no ordinary cake. It was quite large, sculptured in the shape of a doll, decorated like a work of art. Delsa had taken nearly the entire day to make it. She explained that it was for a girl in her class. It was the girl's birthday. Delsa was on her way to the class and was going to give it to the girl.

When Delsa returned, I was anxious to hear about the birthday celebration. She described the amazement and joy of the girl who got the cake. I asked Delsa how the other girls had reacted. She said they were very excited and wanted to know whether she was going to make a cake like this for everyone's birthday. Delsa replied that she intended to do exactly that, and she did! In the months that followed, she spent hours preparing thoughtful, highly focused, and creative lessons. She initiated service projects. She talked to the girls on the phone and spent time with them individually.

Over time, each of these girls' parents contacted Delsa and thanked her for all she had done. Virtually every girl had changed in ways that were quite heartening. Some thanked Delsa because their daughters had changed their attitudes toward church. Others told stories of how the girls were changing individually. Some were becoming more disciplined, some more sensitive, others more open to taking direction. The girls had had many teachers but Delsa was different. She was a transformational teacher and thus a transformational change agent. She had inspired the girls to change because she herself modeled the process of moving outside the normal system. Her unusual behaviors—the cakes, the creative lessons, the service projects, the phone conversations—and her very way of being, attracted the girls to change and to emulate her, to be more inner directed and other focused.

After they graduated from Delsa's class, most of the girls stayed in touch with her. Their relationships with her really mattered to them, and they mattered to Delsa. Even when the girls were in college, many of them would stop by our house to visit and tell Delsa what they were doing. I once commented to my wife about the richness of those relationships, and she shared an observation:

> When I first started teaching the girls, I was not naturally drawn to each one. But that did not last long. Since I saw it as my duty to serve them, I did, and as I started to make sacrifices to serve those girls, I started to see them differently. I started to see beyond their weaknesses. I started to see their potential. The more sacrifices I made in their behalf, the more I wanted them to grow. Pretty soon preparing the lessons, making the cakes, and designing the service projects were not a sacrifice. They were a joy. The more the girls felt my joy and concern, the more they were willing to try new things. The more new activities we tried, the more we could think of trying. One good thing seemed to produce another.

So what happened here? When asked to teach the girls, Delsa accepted the responsibility. As she executed that responsibility, she started to extend herself, doing much more than the normal teacher might do. The sacrifice of baking cakes, preparing creative lessons, designing unusual service projects, and spending time on the phone changed both the girls and Delsa. Those sacrifices led to increased commitment. The increased commitment resulted in new behavior, and the new behavior changed her vision. She could now see potential that no one else could see. She envisioned a productive community and behaved accordingly. Soon a productive community emerged. Note her comment, "One good thing seemed to produce another." Productive communities become synergistic. As one part of the community is enlarged, all parts are enlarged. What is good for the part is good for the whole. The individual good and the collective good are one. Productive communities usually emerge when one inner-directed and other-focused person begins to envision such a synergistic community.

Two Kinds of Heroes

How do we become inner directed and other focused? In his classic book *The Hero with a Thousand Faces,* Joseph Campbell described the journey of personal transformation. He pointed out that a core human experience is to descend into the dark valley where we have to face our core challenges and fears. As people emerge from this journey, they return "empowered and empowering to the community." Having undergone the transformation of self, they now see the world differently. They are more aligned with emergent reality. They have fewer illusions about themselves. The new worldview gives them new choices and new strategies that make them more effective. They are also more concerned. They are not self-focused but other focused. Such a person is excited about having others grow and experience the same kind of increased meaning.

In our culture we also carry another hero image. It is the image of the "ruthless hero" (Csikszentmihalyi, 1997). This hero is highly competitive and ego driven, aggressively pursuing the road to success. For the ruthless hero any means is justified by the "bottom line." Whereas Joseph Campbell's hero epitomizes the transformational process (empowered and empowering to the community), Csikszentmihalyi's ruthless hero epitomizes the transactional process (maintaining authority, control, and the illusion of power).

For the ruthless hero, most endeavors are self-focused and externally driven. This pattern is expressed by the obsessive pursuit of results. Here self-image is based on the accumulation of wealth and power. Driven by this image a person can become obsessive, destroying other people—and destroying his or her own health in the process. In our society, we often put this hero on a pedestal.

In spite of how we might glorify and reward the ruthless hero in our culture, the fact is that in the "real" world the ruthless hero is plagued by shortcomings. In fact, I am going to make this radical claim: The ruthless hero model does not work. Why? Because each of us lives in the world that we create. The ruthless hero usually reaps what he or she sows.

An Illustration of the Ruthless Hero

Csikszentmihalyi offers a wonderful anecdote that illustrates the frustration of the ruthless hero. It also illustrates how a small shift in perception can often alter the obsessive pattern and bring that which was initially unobtainable:

> Keith is one example of many managers I have met who have spent a decade or more desperately trying to impress their superiors in order to get promoted. He worked seventy hours and more a week even when he knew it was not necessary, neglecting his family and his own personal growth in the process. To increase his competitive advantage, Keith hoarded all the credit he could for his accomplishments, even if it meant making colleagues and subordinates look bad. But despite all his efforts, he kept being passed over for important promotions. Finally Keith resigned himself to having reached the ceiling of his career, and decided to find his rewards elsewhere. He spent more time with the family, took up a hobby, became involved in community activities. Because he was no longer struggling so hard, his behavior on the job became more relaxed, less selfish, more objective. In fact, he began to act more like a leader whose personal agenda takes second place to the well-being of the company. Now the general manager was finally impressed. This is the kind of person we need at the helm. Keith was promoted soon after he had let go of his ambition. His case is by no means rare: To be trusted in a position of leadership, it helps to advance other people's goals as well as one's own.
> [Csikszentmihalyi, 1997, pp. 113–114]

As long as Keith pursued the role of ruthless hero he was trapped in a power struggle. The world treated him as he treated the world. It was impossible to move up that ladder of power because this system, which he had helped to create, did not treat him fairly. From his perspective, he believed that he sacrificed all for the system and yet the system did not reward him. It was not until he gave up in frustration that there was hope. Once he let go, once he became other focused, the system began to respond to him differently. Keith was now co-creating a new world, where individual efforts, including his own, were appreciated. When he changed, the world changed.

The Strength of the Transformational Person

As change agents we are much more likely to be transformational—that is, truly making room for change—if we are inner directed and other focused. These two positive characteristics give rise to a positive tension. People who are inner directed and other focused are usually full of energy and tend to be enormously hard-driving. They feel a need to satisfy a deep personal calling that is linked to a positive and constructive change in the outside world. They can be tough and uncompromising about standards of performance and progress. Yet they are simultaneously concerned and caring. They want people to be at their best. This kind of person becomes "empowered and empowering to the community." They attract people to a higher level of experience.

Advanced Change Theory (ACT) is about being very disciplined. From what we know of him, Gandhi was one of the strongest, most demanding and courageous change agents in history. The same could be said for Jesus and Dr. King. These men were not weaklings. They operated at a level of courage and effort that far exceeds normal expectations.

Ordinary People

I see the same kind of behavior in Delsa. She is a person who is ferocious in the pursuit of the common good. Once she commits to serve a person or a purpose, she is not dissuaded from her path. Yet she is usually other focused. She is a dedicated servant to the common good. As the years pass, it is interesting to watch her take other assignments. A number of times, she has been asked to be preside over various organizations. She has accepted each assignment with the same dedication that she had when teaching the eleven-year-olds. Each time, there was a dramatic change in the organization. The process that worked with teaching the girls worked with leading adults.

I use Delsa as the first example in this chapter because she is a homemaker and volunteer, not a person holding a position of recognized authority in some large organization. She sees herself as a normal human being. Yet she is a reminder that each one of us is a potential agent of transformational change.

We find inner-directed and other-focused people in all walks of life. They are not more prevalent in one job than in another. They may emerge from the mail room but be absent in the executive suite. They may emerge from the executive suite but be absent in the mail room. When Erin's mother (whose story I shared in Chapter One) changed her relationship with Erin, when Delsa changed a class of young girls, and when Gandhi changed South Africa, these were all transformational acts. All of them brought about changes for the better, changes that empowered people around them. We all have this potential. But even though we are each quite capable of this kind of behavior, few of us choose this journey. Why? One reason is that we have to move outside our normal vision of community.

The Nature of Hierarchy

What is a hierarchy? It is a way of organizing elements or beings in order of rank, grade, or class. In the social world, a hierarchy will always emerge. It is as true in the animal kingdom as it is in the human realm. Interaction with other people over time gives rise to hierarchies. The process can be formal or informal. In the high school classroom, for example, the process is informal. One person becomes the class clown, another the academic nerd, another the bully, another the well-rounded leader, and so on. These roles are not assigned; they simply emerge as time passes. In formal hierarchies, such as corporations, jobs are designed and people are hired to fulfill highly defined roles within established hierarchies.

Hierarchies are often criticized. Two criticisms tend to dominate. First, hierarchies are often seen as epitomizing unresponsive bureaucracy. They are seen as not serving the needs of the intended customer, employee, or client. Second, they are often criticized as systems that dominate politically weaker people. This is said to waste human potential. These criticisms are often justified.

Nearly any hierarchy can evolve into a negative state that I call *frozen bureaucracy.*

The Ideological Flaw

I once sat with a woman at a professional conference who was on the cutting edge of feminist theory. She was convinced that one of the roots of evil in the world was hierarchy. She saw hierarchy as a form of domination practiced primarily by men to keep women down. She argued that hierarchy needed to be replaced with an alternative form of organization. She was practiced in this argument, and she was accustomed to having her viewpoint acknowledged and accepted. On this particular day, however, she got into a public debate with a man who was highly articulate about organizational issues. He proceeded to tear apart her best arguments. She was deeply upset and afterward I spent some time trying to help.

After some time passed, she asked for my opinion. Given her negative definition of hierarchy, I asked her to define the opposite of hierarchy. "It would be a responsive collective of people who cooperate in a system of openness and equality," she replied.

I indicated that she now had a negatively defined concept, hierarchy, joined with a positively defined concept. So I asked, What is the positive opposite of the responsive and open organization? She accused me of playing word games.

I was not playing word games. I was trying to bring to the surface a problem that existed in all of us. It is a flaw in our logic. Let me explain.

She defined hierarchy as a negative state. She was actually describing a frozen bureaucracy, that is, a dysfunctional hierarchy. Such hierarchies are inwardly focused and rigid. Human potential is wasted and people do not grow. My friend could envision a positive alternative in which there was equality, openness, and cooperation. Let us call it, for a lack of a better name, *adhocracy.* Adhocracies do exist. Basketball players on a fast break are operating in an adhocracy, as are any other group of people who are improvising as they go. Examples include crisis teams, therapy groups, movie crews, jazz bands, entrepreneurial business start-ups, and many high-tech firms. There are many more.

For people who are disenchanted with hierarchy, it is fairly normal to condemn hierarchy and call for some kind of responsive adhocracy. Many books have been written on this theme. They argue that because change is so prevalent, hierarchy must and will go away. The argument is distorted because it is not balanced. But let us not mistake a hierarchy for a frozen bureaucracy—they are simply not the same. Hierarchies become frozen bureaucracies due to the failure of human courage, but hierarchies themselves are not inherently dysfunctional. Here is a telling observation:

> The criticism often leveled at hierarchies has nothing to do with the essential structure and function of the pyramidal model. These problems all come from one source, conflict avoidance. Hierarchies become dysfunctional when decision makers don't want to confront redundancy and incompetence and instead bury the problems in another organizational layer. Or they find it too painful to confront difficult but key people who use legitimate roles and functions in illegitimate, destructive ways. Hierarchies don't do damage to businesses any more than alcohol creates problem drinking. Structures don't create problems; people do. [Shechman, 1994, p. 93]

Hierarchical organization is positive unless someone allows it to become negative. But the same can be said for the adhocracy. The positively defined adhocracy is assumed to be responsive, creative, and conducive to growth. From my perspective, adhocracy, like hierarchy, is inherently positive. Yet like a hierarchy, an adhocracy is difficult to maintain. Because humans lack courage and do not manage conflict well, adhocracies, like hierarchies, tend to become negative. In the real world they tend to move from being responsive adhocracies to chaotic anarchies. They become inefficient and unmanageable.

Now, why all the attention to these notions? Because we are all like the woman in the above story. We are biased in our observations and our arguments. Optimistic, right-brain people tend to condemn the frozen bureaucracy and see responsive adhocracy as the only alternative. Realistic, left-brain people scoff. They condemn chaotic anarchy and call for the predictable hierarchy. Both groups tend to be blind. They cannot see the positive opposites. Nor can they see the potential power in joining the positive opposites.

The Emergence of Hierarchy

For the moment, let's think of hierarchy as a form of organization that emerges over time. As we learn how to solve the problems that will confront us along the way, we become increasingly skillful at achieving the outcomes we seek. As this understanding emerges, based on the successes and failures we observe, we develop standards and expectations, routines, roles, and relationships that will allow us to function efficiently and achieve our stated purpose or mission.

Hierarchies can provide stability, control, predictability, and efficiency. These are all good things. But hierarchical methods are always based on past history, that is, on solutions to problems we have faced in the past. Inevitably, of course, the external world in which the organization operates changes. New realities emerge, demanding new responses. At this point, people and groups within the hierarchy may become threatened and self-serving, insisting that their way of operating in the organization works. After all, history has proved it to be so. When it doesn't, they become embroiled in political conflicts and lack the courage to assess and communicate the truth. They lose touch with emergent reality, choosing instead to live in the past, where their vision and knowledge worked.

Consider a hypothetical case. Joan comes to work for a team who is developing a new product. She is absorbed in very creative challenges. The team is making great progress and she feels gratified. Yet suddenly there is less support. The external competition is increasing. Senior management is pressured by the investment community to reduce costs. Resources that once came automatically to her project now require extensive justification. Her team leader promises to meet deadlines that everyone knows are impossible. Other teams, who were once cooperative, now see themselves in competition for the same scarce resources. They withhold essential information. Every day the conflicts increase. Everyone is wrapped up in preserving his or her own little territory, and no one is much concerned about the fate of the overall organization.

People tend to take the easy way out, the path of least resistance. We tend not to know how to live in a productive community or even recognize one when we see it. As more and more changes occur, with the original hierarchy still in place, the organization begins to stagnate. Gradually, it takes on more and more negative characteristics. Finally, it becomes a frozen bureaucracy where people subordinate the original purpose of the organization to their own self-interests. Every one strives to hold onto what they have. Collective purpose takes a back seat to self-interest.

The Emergence of Adhocracy

Under conditions of change and uncertainty, we do not know how to solve the problems that we face. In fact, that is the nature of change and uncertainty. We do not understand the cause-and-effect relationships that will bring the results we desire. For that matter, we may not even know what results we desire. It is at this point that most humans tend to form *adhocracies*. If hierarchies emerge from shared assumptions or known realities from the past, adhocracies are created by change. They emerge when there is a need to understand new trends and identify appropriate responses so that the organization can come into alignment with emergent realities. The key question here is not one of efficiency but of meaning and invention. Rather than maintaining the status quo, adhocracies arise when there is a need to discover new paths.

Driven by the challenge of discovering and meeting new needs, we group together in flexible networks and search for information. We try action experiments, compare observations, and attempt to make sense of things. In this search mode, we care little about the status that people might carry from past hierarchies. We are only concerned with the competencies they can bring to solving present problems, along with their ability to effectively relate to others in the problem-solving process. That dynamic is the essence of adhocracy, which is characterized by four key features: flexibility, learning, adaptation, and change.

In an adhocracy, predictability and control give way to the open mind of learning and adaptation. However, there's a potential downside: If we place too much emphasis on flexibility, learning, adaptation, and change, abandoning all consideration for predictability and control, the adhocracy is in danger of spinning entirely out of control. Such an organization evolves into chaotic anarchy.

The Integrated Picture

With these concepts in mind, and the language to talk about them, we can now discuss two kinds of opposites: the hierarchy is the positive opposite of the adhocracy. Both are useful. Hierarchy gives us predictability—but at the cost of flexibility. The other gives us flexibility—but at the cost of predictability. Furthermore, a frozen bureaucracy is the negative opposite of chaotic anarchy. Whereas frozen bureaucracy is on the verge of death by stagnation, chaotic anarchy is on the verge of death by disintegration.

But keep in mind that hierarchy and adhocracy are like the Chinese yin and yang. One opposite is always becoming the other. The more we strive for one, the more we stimulate the emergence of the other. Consider the woman in the above story who argued against hierarchy. She had differentiated two concepts, hierarchy and systems of equality. She devalued hierarchy and valued systems of equality. In so doing she was creating a hierarchy of organizational forms. Equality was good, hierarchy was bad. In trying to destroy hierarchy she was creating one. This paradox takes many forms. In working with people, if we push hierarchy to the extreme, it becomes a frozen bureaucracy, and people will cope with the disconnection from emergent reality by joining in emergent adhocracies. If we push adhocracy to the extreme, it becomes chaotic anarchy. People will cope with the uncertainty by creating mechanisms of control (hierarchies) and will cling to them tightly to avoid the pain of chaos. As time passes, the tight grip ironically but inevitably leads to the disintegration of control and the emergence of uncertainty. At this point the entire cycle begins again.

The Need for Certainty

Having said all this, let me point out that the woman who was arguing against hierarchy was mostly correct. Although she was advocating a fruitless end, the elimination of hierarchy, she was articulating a correct set of concerns. When given a problem, we humans tend to group together, just as our ancestors have done since the beginning of time. As people experience success, they bond and develop a set of common beliefs that are reinforced by more success. Through their successes they come to "know," or at least believe they know, that they are right. The beliefs and associated roles become the foundation for a culture with a set of related expectations. They create *norms,* that is, ways of behaving that mirror the decisions and actions that have allowed the group to enjoy success. To ensure continued success, the group requires conformity to those norms. Nonconformity typically brings some form of punishment, so most people conform.

For a while, the hierarchy holds us in orderly and even productive equilibrium. When the external reality changes, however, and the hierarchy ceases to be as effective as it once was, individual members exert increased pressure to maintain their established order. This can be positive when the external change is temporary—such as we might encounter with a natural disaster—but too often this resistance to change gives birth to organizational stagnation.

Change is not easy. Both organizationally and individually, we are continually faced with the choice between deep change and slow death (Quinn, 1996). We are all terrified by the prospect of deep change, since deep change means altering some of our most fundamental beliefs and commitments. In practical terms it can mean giving up an entire way of life—changing our job, our station in life, our salary, our daily activities, the people with whom we associate, and the place where we live.

When someone tells me they love change because it offers an opportunity to grow, it's a pretty good bet that they are talking about incremental change, that is, change over which they have some degree of control. Deep change is not incremental change; rather, it is radical or "out-of-the-box change." It usually requires letting go of control. It means facing the unknown, walking naked into the land of uncertainty. We spend most of our lives striving to avoid that very prospect. When faced with the choice between uncertainty and conformity, we will usually choose conformity. Oddly enough, we will cling to conformity even when we know the overall system in which we are operating, and which gives us our all-important illusion of certainty, is dying.

During the period when change in imminent, those in authority will often try to dominate. If the truth is threatening to those in power, it must not be stated. If the emperor has no clothes, nobody is allowed to say so. On the contrary, everyone is ordered to admire the clothes of their naked emperor. Organizations get disconnected from reality during such times. When this happens, fewer resources and less energy flows in or out of the system. This is the very essence of stagnation. At an individual level, people end up living lives of "quiet desperation." They now work for money, not meaning. They lose track of who they are. Gradually they discover that there is no longer any connection between what they need and what they want to get from their work.

Getting Stuck in Our Fears

The sense of disconnection occurs in virtually every kind of organization. I recently had lunch with a doctoral student from another school on the campus where I teach. He told me he was very discouraged and was considering leaving the university. When I asked why, he told me he was burned out. "Universities are supposed to be organizations of ultimate freedom," he said. "But I feel like I am in prison. Everywhere I turn someone is giving me advice on rules for being a good inmate."

For example, when he presented an idea to his peers, instead of getting help with developing the idea into something that might work, he was told why it would not work. The criticism he received often took the form of advice on political survival. For example, he was often advised about the preferences of the dominant faculty. His peers informed him that his ideas were not in the right "theoretical domain" for the faculty, or his idea would not yield to the "right" methodological treatment. He told me that he was proud of the fact that he had started a martial arts club on campus, yet he was advised against publicizing his part in it. A faculty member might conclude that if he was able to put energy into something like that, he was obviously not working hard enough.

The underlying message in all of this was quite clear to this student: The university is a dangerous place, a jungle. Be careful about your ideas and how you present yourself. If you create the wrong impression, the more powerful animals in the jungle will chew you up and spit you out. Since the message was coming from other disempowered, terrified observers—this young man's peers—it had great validity.

The litany of rules and rituals went on. Both of the metaphors that the student had used to describe his situation—prison and jungle—seemed appropriate. I could envision inmates in dark corners, talking over the implicit rules of survival. As for the jungle image, it was easy to imagine small animals furtively sniffing the air, checking to make certain they were a safe distance from bigger and faster animals that might prey upon them.

The student's dark descriptions were like the dark descriptions voiced by "insiders" of so many other organizations. I recently met with a talented and vibrant group of executives. Since we all knew each other well, the discussion soon turned to the inner workings of the organization with which they were associated. The conversation grew heavier as they told the stories of what had happened to people who had made political mistakes. Everyone agreed that this company was unfortunately a very dangerous place, indeed, where there was no choice but to leave or helplessly conform.

Here is a critical point. The stories those executives told were true; people had been punished for political mistakes. Even so, there were people at that very table who had taken enormous risks and flourished. *This fact was never introduced into the conversation.* Why? Because, when we are articulating the valid foundations of our fears, we are seldom interested in exploring contradicting facts that are also valid. That organization, like the university, was a place of both danger and opportunity. When people become fearful, they recognize and communicate the dangers. They do not recognize and communicate the opportunities.

Seeding the Universe

Before we parted company that day, I shared an insight with the doctoral student. I told him that if he were to learn every unwritten rule in the academic culture where he was presently studying, and if he followed every one of those rules to perfection, he would have a perfectly mediocre career. His life would become an experience of quiet desperation, filled with psychic entropy. This is the case in the life of many professionals. I told this young student that establishing a notable career requires that we break the rules. At some point, we have to know, accept, and express who we really are, not be content with being what others want us to be.

Our work in life takes on a distinctive voice only when we have something unique to offer. We do not become unique by learning and following all the rules. We must conform in order to master the professional technology, in the student's case the theories and methods of his particular field. Eventually, however, we must bring our deepest self to that technology. We must, like a musician, learn to rise above the technical rules and begin to create, to give what is uniquely ours.

To be truly creative, we must be willing to accept punishment. No one in the academic world, not even the most brilliant superstar, feels accepted. There is always someone around to criticize what we do. We are punished for failure. Surprisingly, we are punished for success. If we succeed, we come to stand for something, and that thing always gets criticized. Some of the criticism is justified and some is simply rooted in jealously.

The same is true in large corporations and even in families. We must know who we are and begin to create, not in hopes of approval, but because we are in love with an idea. We must create for the sake of creating. We cannot fall in love with our ideas if we live in constant fear of judgment. When we create, we experience deeper meaning. We begin to do the thing because we must. At that point, negative feedback takes on an entirely different value (Fritz, 1989). Because we are doing something we love, we can let go of the concerns that drive our egos. When we are doing what we love, negative feedback becomes part to the creation process. At the very least, it keeps us grounded.

Productive Community and the Flow of Energy

By the time my student friend and I finished lunch that day, he was beginning to brighten. He was beginning to see that the fear of punishment and a sense of inadequacy had caused him to get stuck. He had lost his sense of meaning. He was not growing.

The notion of growing is key to understanding a basic truth— that when we experience meaning, we are in the process of becoming. During this process, we get fully aligned with our emerging reality. The resources of the universe are attracted to us and us to them. As we unfold, we take on new levels of complexity. A most

unusual description of health, which mirrors the ideas I just articulated, is found in the writings of Carl Rogers:

> Life, at its best, is a flowing, changing process in which nothing is
> fixed. In my clients and in myself I find that when life is richest and
> most rewarding it is a flowing process. To experience this is both
> fascinating and a little frightening. I find I am at my best when I
> can let the flow of my experience carry me, in a direction which
> appears to be forward, toward goals of which I am but dimly aware.
> In this floating with the complex stream of my experiencing, and
> in trying to understand its ever-changing complexity, it should be
> evident that there are no fixed points. When I am thus able to be
> in process, it is clear that there can be no closed system of beliefs,
> no unchanging set of principles which I hold. Life is guided by a
> changing understanding of the interpretation of my experience.
> It is always in process of becoming. [Rogers, 1961, p. 27]

This statement suggests several things:

First, that the universe is never static. It is constantly changing.
There are no fixed states. A basic unit of the universe is energy. It
is ever-flowing from one form to another. We may see fixed points,
such as a planet, a mountain, a table, or a chair, but even these are
changing. They were once something else, and they will again
become something quite different. The illusion of permanence is
a function of our sense of time. Were it possible we might speed
up a video of these objects over a period of a century or two, and
we could watch them form and then transform in an unending
process.

Second, at some point I must surrender control and allow
myself to flow with the complex of forces all around me, letting
them carry me "toward goals of which I am but dimly aware." That
is, even my goals are not the permanent possessions I think they
are. They are co-created as I interact with the universe. I am change.

Third, in the flow-state that Rogers talks about, I am in the
process of becoming. That is, my "life is guided by a changing
understanding of the interpretation of my experience." I experience an increased awareness of how I interpret the world. I can
understand more effectively how I think. I am learning about how
I learn.

When I am in the transformational process, that is, when I allow myself to become the change that I am, I experience profound learning; I see emergent reality more accurately; I develop a new worldview. My altered understanding and interpretative systems allow me to see a world that was not previously observable. As I become the change that I am, I see that change is a natural state. I discover the world I am helping to create. When I myself am evolving with the evolving reality in which I am immersed, I know I am becoming more than I am. Because I am in a state of becoming, the universe is becoming more than it is.

In such a state, I can more clearly see how the old reality works. And I become increasingly aware that the hierarchy itself is not the problem. The problem has more to do with the human tendencies that are so quickly attached to the hierarchy—any hierarchy. These include (1) the tendency to put self-interest ahead of collective interest, (2) the tendency to rely on routines instead of thinking, and (3) the tendency to bury conflict and let fear drive out our desire to tell the truth.

In the altered state of flow, I can see the role that fear plays and why people get stuck. I become empowered because I no longer fear the sanctions within the old system. I feel whole and become filled with concern about relationships. With my new understanding and concern, I can imagine new and more effective patterns of behavior. I become "empowered and empowering to my community."

Flow at the Collective Level

One might accuse Carl Rogers of being more poetic than practical. What about the real world? Can this process really work in our families, groups, and organizations? I like the statement of Dee Hock, former CEO of Visa International:

> In the field of group endeavor, you will see incredible events in which the group performs far beyond the sum of its individual talents. It happens in the symphony, in the ballet, in the theater, in sports, and equally in business. It is easy to recognize and impossible to define. It is a mystique. It cannot be achieved

without immense effort, training, and cooperation, but effort, training, and cooperation alone rarely create it. Some groups reach it consistently. Few can sustain it. [Schlesinger, Eccles, and Gabarro, 1983, p. 486]

Hock describes human groups behaving as productive communities. Productive communities are synergistic. Getting to the state of productive community is not easy. It requires immense effort and cooperation. Getting there takes more than willing it to happen. In most cases, particularly in the ones he lists, people do bring training to the process. I disagree, however, that it requires training. Synergistic human experience can occur without any training. Even expertise, the knowledge of how to do the task, is not necessary. In fact, the absence of knowledge is often a key to getting there.

Let's go to Marine Corps basic training, which many people would describe as hyper-reality. Imagine the following scene as described by Smith (1995):

Eleven men are dropped into a hole that is eight feet in depth. The instructor drops in a "live" grenade and the men have ten seconds to escape. What happens next is a seemingly miraculous exercise in uncoordinated intelligence. With no training and with no boss making plans or giving orders, with no centralized control mechanism, eleven men escape. They are afterward exhilarated by their accomplishment. [Smith, 1995, p. 65]

Consider the same phenomenon in a large company. Florida Power and Light (FP & L) is a major utility. Traditionally utilities were slow-moving hierarchies. A number of years ago, Hurricane Andrew devastated Florida. For FP & L, being hit by Hurricane Andrew was like being in the hole with the live grenade. There was a crisis in every neighborhood. All semblance of order broke down. All the rules were suspended. Employees of FP & L worked for days without sleep and did so outside their normal job titles. Networks of employees joined together in responsive adhocracies and then dissolved as problems emerged and disappeared. In the end, their effort to solve the problems of emergent reality, brought on by Hurricane Andrew, was successful and heroic. Today, when I mention

Hurricane Andrew to a group of FP & L employees, their eyes light up. Many of them consider that event to be one of the high points of their professional lives.

If I talk to people at FP & L about adhocracy before I mention hurricane Andrew, their eyes glaze over. They cannot imagine what I am talking about. After I mention the hurricane, they connect. This is normal. Even when we experience adhocracy or the natural self-organizing processes that take place in that marine foxhole, we tend not to see the self-organizing process. Our experience tells us there cannot be order without centralized control.

There is another reason it is hard to see adhocracy. Adhocracies keep disappearing. Where do they go? The answer is surprising. They turn into hierarchies. At every moment in our journey outside the normal world, we are striving to learn. As the patterns come together, we start to see means-to-end relationships; we start to solve problems in new ways. We grow in expertise. We begin to normalize our behaviors. In the midst of adhocracy, we find hierarchy. Each is always giving birth to the other. Parker Palmer shares a profound insight about all this:

> The question assumes that community can happen only where there are no divisions of status and power—but such places do not exist. If community is to emerge, it will have to be in the midst of inequalities that appear whenever two or three are gathered. To argue that grades must be eliminated before community can emerge is to assume a utopian alternative nowhere to be found: It is to give up on community altogether. When authentic community emerges, false differences in power and status disappear, such as those based on gender or race. But real differences remain, and so they should, for they are created by functions that need to be performed if community is to thrive—such as the leadership task of maintaining the boundaries and upholding the standards that define community at its best. [Palmer, 1998, p. 138]

By *community,* I think Palmer means a collection of human beings who can effectively pursue a common purpose while also growing individually. Because they are all committed to the common purpose, each person is willing to sacrifice for the good of the whole, and the whole makes the pursuit of the individual good more likely. In such an organization, it is possible to discuss emergent reality. People are not defensive about their power and authority because they love the whole. They will change to preserve the whole. Here there is a kingdom in which the great are ministers to all (Jesus), an army where the generals are chief–servants–first among equals (Gandhi), and a beloved community of friends (King). In such communities there are differences, but we easily transcend them through our love for the common purpose and each other. The great sages understood that the objective is not to destroy hierarchy but to join it with its positive opposite so as to create a system of productive community.

Productive Community in the Real World

The cynic who works in the professional world reads about transcending the assumptions of hierarchy and responds, "What about the real world? In an entire career, I have never once seen such an organization!" This is a valid point. Even optimists ask me about the practicality or applicability of the principles I describe here. Many people claim they have never experienced a synergistic collectivity. My response to these people is that their claim is probably inaccurate. Whenever I have asked people to tell about their five most memorable career experiences, they usually share stories where examples of productive community abound. It is not that this seemingly ideal community does not exist; it is that such communities are difficult to see. In our heads, most of us are blocked by the assumptions, language, and concepts of hierarchy.

A Productive Community in the Corporate World

In fairness to the skeptics, it is likely that any examples of productive community that they experienced were probably transitory. In most organizations and relationships, productive community arises only during times of crisis or unusual challenge. Yet this is not always the case. As Dee Hock claims, "Some organizations reach it consistently."

When I encounter such organizations, I sense it immediately. Such was the case when I visited a highly recognized company that was part of a major pharmaceutical corporation. I was there only a few minutes when I knew I was in a high-performing organization. I could feel it.

As we started our session together, my colleague asked the top management team to make a list of the strengths of the company. They did. As the list grew, and despite my initial positive feeling, I began to suspect that they were posturing. The list was too good to be true. The characteristics were outside the normalized realm of organization. Consider their claims:

We are proactive: When a product is still climbing in the market, we move on.

We shape practices in the market.

We love responding to a challenge.

We think big and seek success at all costs.

We are the place you go in the larger corporation if you want to become a leader.

We cannot stand to be anything less than number 1.

We take strength from having done the impossible in past crises.

We are highly galvanized and rally in times of crisis.

We appear to have very few formal systems, but when a problem arises, a team spontaneously emerges, solves it, and then disappears.

We have quality people with a "can-do" spirit.

We have people-friendly policies; it is a place of high trust.

As this impressive list was being articulated, my attention was drawn to a particular conversation. The third to the last entry on the list came from the statement made during the conversation, "Whenever there is an important problem, a team of appropriate people spontaneously emerges, solves the problem, and then voluntarily disbands." I thought it the most extreme claim of all, but at that moment it was made, a woman on the management team responded, "That is right. I have been here three months, and it is driving me crazy. I have worked in a number of corporations, and I pride myself in being able to rapidly comprehend the culture of any organization. This place baffles me. I watch those teams form and disintegrate. It is like magic. I cannot understand or explain it."

To this statement, there was a rejoinder by another member of the organization: "I have been here more than a year. I am in charge of systems and processes. I cannot understand it either. It is an extraordinary phenomenon."

As the day unfolded, I became convinced that the list was for real. These were people with a powerful culture. The company was a productive community. It was a hard-driving organization making lots of money. There are, however, many hard-driving organizations that make money. This one was more. It was an organization in which people were as committed to each other's success as they were to their own. Because there was trust, people could communicate their problems and get help. Because there was trust, there was cooperation. The self-interest, which is the bedrock of most corporate cultures, was also operating here, but the collective interest and individual interests really were one. Here everyone was a servant to the system and to each other. This was a focused, money-making company that was also a productive community.

A productive community is a relationship or collectivity that is both structured and spontaneous. It is highly differentiated and integrated. Members are clear about their accountability and their freedom. This is true in formal organizations, small groups, and families. Consider the following statement:

> Much has been written about what makes families work. The consensus is that families that support the emotional well-being and growth of their members combine two almost opposite traits. They combine discipline with spontaneity, rules with freedom, high expectations with unstinting love. An optimal family system is complex in that it encourages the unique individual development of its members while uniting them in a web of affective ties. Rules and discipline are needed to avoid excessive waste of psychic energy in the negotiation of what can or cannot be done—when the children should come home, when to do homework, who is to wash the dishes. Then the psychic energy released from bickering and arguing can be invested in the pursuit of each member's goals. At

the same time, each person knows that he or she can draw on the collective psychic energy of the family if needed. Growing up in a complex family, children have a chance to develop skills and recognize challenges, and thus are more prepared to experience life as flow. [Csikszentmihalyi, 1997, p. 88–89]

You might want to try an experiment. In the above paragraph, substitute the word *organization* wherever the word *family* appears, and substitute *the employees* for *children*. Then reread the paragraph.

Creating Productive Community

As Palmer suggested in the earlier quotation, "If community is to emerge, it will have to be in the midst of inequalities that appear whenever two or three are gathered." We start in a context of hierarchy but the key is to not start by focusing on hierarchy. Our job is to transcend the assumptions of hierarchy. But what exactly does this mean?

Katzenbach (1995) and his colleagues published a book entitled *Real Change Leaders*. It was a study of people who are not in top positions yet brought significant changes to their companies. They were transformational change agents. In the book, the authors identify a number of characteristics that differentiate these real change leaders from normal managers.

First, real change leaders get outside the hierarchical box. They may even lack authority for the task at hand. They are not defined by their positions. Although they avoid unnecessary violations of expectations, they do violate them. They seldom focus on what the hierarchical culture suggests is possible: "Instead, they think first of what is the right thing to do and who they need to involve to get it done."

Second, real change leaders do not start with structure because they realize that changing the structure seldom leads to increased performance and that such changes are highly resisted. "Instead, they use informal, ad hoc networks and find ways to cross functional boundaries and hierarchical levels by focusing on action flows and objectives, not on functions and positions." They find key actors and build committed teams; these teams are examples of what we are calling productive communities.

These two claims suggest that transformational change agents practice a higher level of moral reasoning. In asking, "What is the right thing to do?" they are not asking what is fair, expected, rewarded, or punished within the system. They are asking about the state of the system. This is a perspective that is higher than self. This perspective takes them from the realm of transaction to the realm of principle. In asking what is the right thing to do, they are no longer servants of the system. Instead, they align themselves with the potential of the system. Then they become servants to that system.

Most of us see ourselves as servants of the system. Seeing ourselves as servants *to* the systems in which we are embedded is quite different. I may have a little girl who will not do her homework or a workforce that will not embrace the new culture. If instead of seeing them as the problem, I see us as a system and see myself as both an actor within the system and also an external servant to the system, I am beginning to take a transformational perspective.

In asking, "What is the right thing to do?" the transformational change agent is asking a second critical question: What result do I want? Such change agents are not asking, How do I get what I want? They are asking, What result do I want? Robert Fritz (1989) tells us that the difference between these two questions is profound. One keeps us on our present unexamined course. The other aligns us with the potential to be empowered and the potential to be empowering to our community. The transformational change agent is willing to go outside his or her defined position and violate expectations in order to originate productive community. Rather than starting with structure they go out and attract other actors to the experience of productive community. In doing so, they initiate a social movement.

Creating Social Movement

In over twenty-five years of working on issues of organizational change, I have come to the conclusion that most important changes require the creation of a social movement. It is, in fact, more accurate to say that change is social movement. The first step in creating a social movement is having a single actor who asks questions:

- What is the right thing to do?
- What result do I want?
- How do I behave in a more authentic way?

In Palmer's (1998) words, the person chooses to "live divided no more." This is what Peter Block means when he describes the effective change agent.

> Our ability to facilitate the learning of others is absolutely dependent on our own consciousness and on our willingness to make our own actions a legitimate subject of inquiry. Allowing the personal to become public is the act of responsibility that initiates cultural change and reforms organizations. Our need for privacy and our fear of the personal are primary reasons why organizational change is more rhetoric than reality. Real change comes from our willingness to own our vulnerability, confess our failures, and acknowledge that many of our stories do not have a happy ending. [Block, 1995, p. xii]

Notice that Block sees organizational change as "facilitating the learning of others." This is very different from seeing change as telling and forcing. Block understands that the most effective form of organizing is productive community and that it emerges as a social movement. The social movement begins when someone, allows the "personal to become public." When the change agent chooses to live undivided, focuses on the good of the system, and becomes a servant to the system, other people are attracted to empower themselves and the system changes.

The central claim in all of this is that when a change requires people to alter ingrained behavior patterns, a social movement is needed. An actor in the system must become a social insurgent, the leader of the movement. For people in formal positions and for people operating at conventional levels of moral reasoning, this is a radical thought. The notion of change driven by authority, and change driven by social insurgency, are assumed to be mutually exclusive, even at war with one another. Authority exists and justifies its existence by resisting insurgency in organizations. Contrariwise, insurgency exists to overthrow authority.

The notion that a CEO, supervisor, coach, or parent needs to model moral power and become the leader of a social movement is both intellectually and behaviorally difficult to accept. It means we must become servants who are inner directed and other focused. We must put into action the first seed thought: We must envision the productive community. Doing so is the first step in enacting such a community into being.

CHAPTER THREE

FIRST LOOK WITHIN

The Second Seed Thought:
First Look Within

JESUS   *And why beholdest thou the mote that is in thy brother's eye,*
but perceivest not the beam that is in thine own eye? Either
how canst thou say to thy brother, Brother, let me pull out the
mote that is in thine eye, when thou thyself beholdest not the
beam that is in thine own eye? Thou hypocrite, cast out first
the beam out of thine own eye, and then shalt thou see clearly
to pull out the mote that is in thy brother's eye. [Luke 6:41–42]

GANDHI   *The function of violence is to obtain reform by external*
means; the function of passive resistance, that is "soul-force,"
is to obtain [reform] by growth from within; which in turn is
obtained by self-suffering, and self-purification. [Iyer, 1990, p. 90]

KING   *The words I spoke to God that midnight are still vivid in my*
memory. "I am here taking a stand for what I believe is right.
But now I am afraid. The people are looking to me for leader-
ship, and if I stand before them without strength and courage,
they too will falter. . . ." Almost at once my fears began to pass
from me. My uncertainty disappeared. I was ready to face
anything. The outer situation remained the same, but God had
given me inner calm. . . . I knew now that God is able to give
us the interior resources to face the storms and problems of life.
[King, (1968) 1986, p. 509]

Reform from Within

In the normalized world, the dominant approach to change is the two-step process we explored in Chapter One. Step One: Tell the person to change. Step Two: If the person fails to respond, find some way to coerce them into changing. Watching others do this over time, we may notice the futility of their efforts. It is at such times that the above quotation from the teachings of Jesus might come to mind, suggesting that we might better understand and influence others if we first gained a deeper understanding of ourselves.

When we watch others tell and coerce, we can sense that they are suffering from two problems. First, their efforts are far less effective than they would like. Second, they are probably imposing some form of injury on the larger relationship in which both persons are involved. Gandhi tells us that such a change agent is trying to bring change by only external means and in so doing brings violence or injury to the relationship. He suggests that the transformational alternative is to "obtain reform by growth from within, which in turn is obtained by self-suffering, and self-purification." We may greatly increase the likelihood of changing the world if we look within, clarifying our own values as we go, and then disciplining ourselves to more fully live those values.

Dr. King advocates the same principle. His quotation at the beginning of this chapter refers to an evening before an important civil rights demonstration. As thousands waited to march, King received a racist phone call, threatening his life. As he hung up the phone, he was filled with fear and panic. He knew that as long as he was driven by this fear, he could not lead. People would sense what he was feeling and they would falter. They needed to feel his courage, determination, enthusiasm, and trust. His awareness that his supporters needed this from him drove him to prayer and to an internal transformation. His final sentence is instructive: While the outer situation remained exactly as it was, with a potential assassin still out there, the presence of the assassin did not matter. King now had the interior resources to lead with confidence. By changing what was happening within him, he gained the power to more effectively change the world.

An Extraordinary Woman

Occasionally, I have the opportunity to work with people who embody many of the principles of ACT. When I think of the seed thought at the beginning of this chapter—first look within—I am reminded of an extraordinary woman I'll call Eleanor. My first encounter with her was through an e-mail request. In it, she asked me to help her transform a major medical facility. My initial reaction was to express my appreciation for her efforts and tell her that my schedule was too tight. I could not accept her kind invitation. A short time later, I received the following letter:

Dear Dr. Quinn:

Having worked in large health care organizations for a number of years, I am intrigued with the concepts in your book, *Deep Change*. In particular, the "power of one" parallels my personal philosophy and it is a message I try to pass along to others. As you have so aptly stated in this book, "Organizational change cannot occur unless we accept the pain of personal change." I fully concur with you that the commitment to make the personal changes necessary to impact a complex organization comes only through the courage to take a major risk—a risk of one's job as well as the risk of relationships with others. Your scenarios point out that where these risks have been taken, the outcome is often one of significant value—to the individual, the team, the organization, and ultimately, to the consumer. Significant change has been imposed upon health care institutions through decisions made externally (for example, third party reimbursement decisions, etc.), and the public has demanded a higher level of quality and customer service. As a result, we have downsized, restructured, and redesigned the work. We have examples of successful change that could be added to the examples in your book. On the other hand, we have scenarios where the impact of the downsizing and redesign has been significantly less than what we planned.

   To be very frank, the data from our customer service surveys have indicated that in spite of what we perceive to be tremendous change, we have not made the type of "deep change" that is necessary to meet the expectations of patients and families. And Dr. Quinn, the patients and families are not the anonymous "they." "They" are our friends, our neighbors, our colleagues. "They" are our families. "They" are you and me. Unfortunately, I have had the personal experience of being a consumer when I lost my spouse to cancer just a few short years ago. During his valiant battle over the course of several years and in multiple health care settings, my family and I had first-hand knowledge of the good and the bad of the health care system. When it was good, it was wonderful but when it was bad, it was absolutely devastating. One is never so vulnerable nor so powerless than when confronting a complex, unresponsive system in the midst of significant personal crisis.

This is my passion, my life's mission is to use my influence as a health care executive to impact the [names her organization] so that we can make a difference to the customer we serve. We have the resources to provide excellent patient care, to educate the community as well as health care students and residents, and to conduct research that can impact the world. We have an institutional goal of patients and families first and values that include respect and compassion for our customers and one another. Yet we hear from patients and families and employees that we consistently fall short of the mark. Based upon your beliefs and values as stated in *Deep Change*, I am convinced that you are the one person who can partner with me to inspire the fundamental personal change necessary to make a significant difference in the world of health care.

I am planning to hold a leadership retreat this fall and I am inviting you to provide the keystone presentation and hold some discussion with the group. (In anticipation of the retreat, I purchased and distributed *Deep Change* to the group for their "summer reading pleasure.") I also have an interest in your ongoing work with us on a consultant basis to challenge and guide us on this journey. While I know that you have multiple commitments and that your time is limited, I am more than willing to work around your schedule.

Thank you for your time in reading this letter and your consideration of this request. I would be pleased to speak further with you about this and invite you to contact me. . . .

I read Eleanor's letter and immediately knew this was no ordinary executive. This was a person living the principles of ACT. I knew I had to meet with her. I turned to my computer and wrote the following message: "Given the intensity of my schedule, I have been trying to turn down all invitations and commitments, but your letter penetrates my heart. You are a dangerous character! When can we meet?"

A few days later, I met with Eleanor for the first time. When she shook my hand, she looked me in the eye and expressed her deep appreciation for my agreeing to meet with her. It was clear that what she said was what she felt. Her expression of gratitude made me feel that I mattered to her, that her enthusiasm was more than the usual professional courtesy. I found myself immediately opening up to the influence of this woman.

After a few moments, she began to describe her organization. I have been through this process many hundreds of times, but never before did it bring tears to my eyes. It was not what she was saying about her organization that moved me: Her words were like the words of many other executives. It was how she spoke the words that had impact. This was a woman who knew what she was about.

An Unusual Story

Eleanor told an unusual story. Her boss had written a memo indicating that every division in the organization would have to take a large cut in personnel. She wrote back a memo saying that this would simply not be possible for her division. The boss called her in and challenged her. She explained to him why she could not take the cut. Finally, he started to back down and said, "I would like you to rewrite this message, saying that you cannot take the cut at this time."

She paused as she told me this and I assumed she was going to tell me that she had agreed to rewrite the message. Even so, I was thinking that this was an impressive victory. However, Eleanor's story took a radical turn. Instead of accepting the compromise, she told her boss, firmly and clearly, "We cannot take a cut in staff." He pushed back several times, but each time she repeated the same sentence. Finally, the boss relented and withdrew his demand completely.

Eleanor told her story without pride or self-aggrandizement. Nor was she judgmental about her boss. In fact, she conveyed a sense of respect for him. She was simply telling the story to make a point about the dynamics in her organization. I asked her, "Why weren't you fired?" She looked at me in surprise. She thought about the question. Again, without any sense of self-aggrandizement, she said: "Because he knows I am not doing any of these things for myself. My central concern is the good of the customer. I will do anything he tells me that is good for the system and its capacity to serve the customer. I will not do anything that is not for the good of the system. If he can show me that there is something I do not understand, then I will gladly comply. I try to stay very clear about who I am. I am willing to risk my job but I do not feel like I am taking any risk at all."

Clearly, Eleanor was a woman of commitment and purpose, a heroine on the transformational path. Her power came not from stubbornness or pride but from an inner truth that she knew she could not compromise.

Looking Within: Making a Fundamental Choice

A change agent needs to look within for at least two reasons. The first has to do with purpose. In the above story, Eleanor did not define herself according to the signals she received from the outside world. She wasn't competing in a popularity contest, nor was she motivated by holding her position in the hierarchy. Her direction was determined from within.

Many people will read this and agree that clarity of purpose is important, but they will be left with a helpless feeling. "I do not have clarity of purpose and would love to be like Eleanor, but how do I find purpose?" I would suggest that we do not find a purpose: A purpose finds us. The process does not begin with some kind of goal-setting process. It begins by making fundamental choices about our own life and what we stand for. Robert Fritz (1989) spells out three kinds of choices:

1. Fundamental choice. This has to do with our state of being or basic life orientation.
2. Primary choice. These are choices that involve specific results.
3. Secondary choice. This kind of choice supports specific results of the above.

There are many people who have chosen the religious path (primary choice), without making the fundamental choice to live in accordance with their highest spiritual truths. There are many people who have chosen to be married (primary choice), without making the fundamental choice to live from within a committed relationship. . . . Fundamental choices are not subject to changes in internal or external circumstances. If you make the fundamental choice to be true to yourself, then you will act in ways that are true to yourself whether you feel inspired or depressed, whether you feel fulfilled or frustrated, whether you are at home, at work, with your friends, or with your enemies. . . . When you make a fundamental choice, convenience and comfort are not ever at issue, for you always take action based on what is consistent with your fundamental choice. [Fritz, 1989, p. 193]

When we make a fundamental choice, it changes our outlook and our behavior. As Fritz argues, "When people make a fundamental choice to be true to what is highest in them, or when they make a choice to fulfill a purpose in their life, they can easily accomplish many changes that seemed impossible or improbable in the past." I would suggest that when we do the first—make a fundamental choice to be true to the highest in ourselves—that we are then far more likely to "make a choice to fulfill a purpose." When we align ourselves with our values, we know where we need to go. The purpose we need to fulfill becomes clear. Whatever suppressed or hidden purpose we may have had rises into our consciousness.

A Fundamental Choice Can Alter What You See

When we finally do make a fundamental choice, that commitment itself is transformational. It immediately alters how we see the world and how we behave. I remember a man—I'll call him Garret—who attended my Leading Change course in the Executive Education Program at the Michigan Business School. He was a company president. During the first three days of the course, he said very little. On Thursday morning, he asked whether we might have lunch together and I agreed. Over lunch he told me that if he had attended my course any time in the last five years, he would have been wasting his time. He had successfully turned around two companies and felt he knew everything there was to know about leading change.

He told me that he was now a lot more humble. There were five companies in his corporation. He had turned two of them around and was seen as the shining star among the presidents. He

had earned the right to lead the largest company in the corporation. The current president of that largest company still had, however, eighteen months left until his retirement. In the meantime
Garret had been asked to try his hand at one more turnaround.
There was a company in the corporation that was considered hopeless. It had once commanded a large market share for its product.
Today, it had only a small percentage of the market and was still
shrinking. Nobody believed this company could be turned around,
so if Garret failed in his efforts, no one would hold it against him.

It had now been twelve months since he took on the challenge.
He felt defeated. Everything that had worked for him before, everything his past had taught him failed in the present situation.
Morale was dismal. The numbers were dismal. The outlook for the
future was dismal.

I asked Garret what he thought he would do next. On a paper
napkin he listed his short-term objectives. He began to draw an
organizational chart. He described the people in each of the senior
positions and described the assignments and changes he was going
to make in regard to each person on the chart. I found his answer
unexciting. There was no commitment or passion in what he was
telling me. Yet it was clear that Garret was a man of character with
a sincere desire to succeed. I took a deep breath and asked a hard
question.

"What would happen if you went back and told those people
the truth? Suppose you told them that you have been assigned as
a caretaker for a year and a half. No one believes the company can
succeed and no one really expects you to succeed. You have been
promised the presidency of the largest company, and the plan is to
put you into the plum job. Tell them that you have, however, made
a fundamental choice. You have decided to give up that plum job.
Instead, you are going to stay with them. You are going to bet your
career on them, and you invite them to commit all the energy and
goodwill they can muster into making the company succeed."

I was worried that I might have offended Garret. I half expected
an angry response. He looked at me for a moment, then it was his
turn to take a deep breath. To my surprise and relief, he said, "That
is pretty much what I have been thinking." He paused, and in that
moment I watched him make the fundamental decision. Almost

immediately, he picked up the napkin and started doing a reanaly-
sis. He said, "If I am going to stay, then this person will have to go;
this person will have to be moved over here; and this person. . . . "

As he talked, there was now an air of excitement in Garret's
words. Once he had made the fundamental decision to stay, everything changed. His earlier plans to move on to the larger company
were suddenly scrapped. Garret had made a fundamental choice,
and now he had a new life stance, a new outlook, and a new way to
behave. The organization chart that made sense a few moments
before now made no sense at all. None of the original problems
had changed but Garret had changed, and this made all the difference.

Becoming a Creative Force

Clarifying our purpose and committing to pursue the highest in
us is transformational. Although Garret would not have admitted
it at the time, prior to making his fundamental choice he had been
reacting to circumstances, not acting from a core of commitment
and personal beliefs. He had been offered an attractive external
reward: the presidency of the largest company. The natural reaction had been for him to do whatever he was asked in order to
secure that reward. Until he was faced with making his fundamental choice, it had not occurred to him that in taking the short-
term assignment and making no commitment to the sick company,
he was choosing to live divided.

Lacking that fundamental choice, Garret had actually been
selling short all the people who worked for him in the turnaround
company, to say nothing of their families and the community that
depended on the company to succeed. Without Garret's commitment everyone in that organization was marching to a slow death.
Garret's lack of commitment was only continuing that process and
inviting that experience of failure into his own life. Making his fundamental choice about staying, and telling his employees the truth,
placed him in a very different position. No longer a mere reactor,
he had chosen to live undivided, and in the process he became a
primary, creative force that would drive the whole organization
toward success.

It's important to recognize, however, that making a fundamental choice of this kind is not a gimmick or a technique: The choice to be the predominant creative force in your own life does not mean forcing yourself into a different view of reality, nor is it a form of self-manipulation through willpower, a change of "attitude," a motto to recite, an affirmation to make, or a posture to assume. It is a choice. It comes from a desire to be the predominant creative force in your own life; not out of need, or out of conflict, or even out of the circumstances; but because that is what you want. [Fritz, 1989, p. 194]

We all want to experience ourselves as a creative force. That's when we are most influential and happy. The problem is that the normalized world will always entice or threaten us into mindless choices. The normalized world will take us to the routine, unexamined response. When this happens, we focus on the external and forget to examine the internal. We become driven by circumstance and begin to live as a divided self.

Fundamental choices do not shift with circumstance. Once we make such a choice, we stick to it even if we are angry, frustrated, or depressed. Whether we are winning or losing, whether we are surrounded by supporters or detractors, does not matter—our choice remains the same. We pursue it even when it is inconvenient or uncomfortable to do so. This kind of choice and this kind of action reflects who we are. And the choice we have made becomes an internal compass, showing us the way. It allows us to behave creatively when others would simply conform, falling into habitual patterns that have no creative challenge. Think about the letter written by the health care administrator. She had made a fundamental choice. It was her passion and life mission to influence her organization to make a difference to the customers they served. No one, including her boss, could dissuade her from her purpose.

The Loss of Purpose in the Normalized World

Some readers might ask, If experiencing ourselves as a creative force is such an essential drive, how is it that we get so far off course? One reason is that the normalized world tends to destroy purpose and reward compromise, transaction, and exchange. In the last chapter, I suggested that as soon as a group of people learns to solve a puzzle, they swiftly become an efficient hierarchy. When new people enter the culture, the old group socializes the newcomers, teaching them what to believe and how to behave.

The values that the hierarchy imposes on newcomers, as well as on its members, insulate the group from emergent reality. The following case of socialization in a medical school, which I summarize from an account by Parker Palmer (Palmer, 1998, p. 124), can help illustrate this point:

The dean of this particular medical school was concerned with educating doctors. Although the process in his school was much like most others, he was concerned about final outcomes. Most medical students enter school with some degree of compassion for serving human needs, but by the time they graduate they are beginning to see patients as "cases" rather than human beings. Patients become diseases to be treated, mere objects to be acted upon. In addition, many medical students never learn how to learn. Part of the reason for this is that their educational experience consists mainly of memorizing concepts and facts that they feed back on tests. They tend not to develop skills for staying current in their own field of knowledge, which is constantly changing. Not only is there new research to keep up with but older treatments are constantly being updated and revised, sometimes quite dramatically.

During the first two years of most medical schools, students meet in large groups and listen to professors who identify the bones of a "skeleton hanging on a rack." They memorize the information and feed it back on demand. It is generally a passive process. Given the pressures of their training, few have time or energy to discover things on their own initiative. The process teaches the student to be a reactor; it does not teach exploration nor does it call for generative action. During their third year, students meet the first live patient, and their tendency is to treat the patient like a skeleton on a rack.

The educational process for doctors is also highly competitive, and this sometimes leads to discouraging outcomes. For example, when an assignment is made to read a journal article in the library, that article sometimes disappears. Trying to gain a competitive advantage, a selfish student may cut it from the journal. Notice that the objective here is to beat the other students rather than focus on doing one's best. There is virtually no concern for the patients they will one day, presumably, serve. The process unintentionally, but most definitely, teaches students to be self-focused and to engage in behaviors that divide the self.

This particular dean, however, introduced a new approach. From the very first day in the medical school, the students now meet in groups with a live patient, and they are asked to produce a diagnosis and treatment plan. Each group has a teaching physician who facilitates the process. Instead of providing only traditional answers, this facilitator asks questions that prod students to use their own inner resources for seeking explanations and solutions. Each student is thus encouraged to engage emergent reality, and is expected to establish a caring, interactive, and impactive relationship with the patient as a real person with an illness rather than a "case number" or disease to be treated.

From the very beginning, students encounter the real world and experience the complex needs of real human beings. The results are encouraging. According to the dean, students learn to relate more effectively with each other as well as with the people who come for treatment. Moreover, under this new system, medical students learn to learn. They stop cutting articles out of journals in order to beat down their competition. They develop increased integrity through having a greater sense of purpose. Because they are in direct contact with real people and emergent reality, they are more likely to make fundamental choices about their own state of being.

Socialization and Emergent Reality

Although the above story describes socialization in medical school, I suspect that it approximates socialization for all human organizations. We are continually taught to engage secondary reality, that is, reality already interpreted and defined by others before us. For example, doctors are encouraged to go by the book, never to deviate from the accepted treatment modes, which are recorded in books and memorized by every physician. Similarly, most organizations have standards of operation that employees are expected to learn, either by being formally taught or by observing which of their actions are rewarded and which punished.

This socialization and standardization process happens because it is necessary. It provides order, equilibrium, predictability, and efficiency. There is, however, a trade-off. The process keeps us from examining emergent reality. The young physician, for example, compares the symptoms she observes in her patient and matches them to the official treatment plan recommended in current diagnosis and treatment literature. She goes by the book rather than doing any research on her own. Similarly, the sales department in a large business organization may continue to pitch their products to customers in their thirties even after demographic studies have shown that their customer base is fifty and older. They do this because it always worked in the past, not because their immediate experience demonstrated it was the best way to go. We see from this that the more the world changes, the more the gap between old interpretations and current reality widens.

Looking Within: Changing Self First

As I have indicated, we need to look within for at least two reasons. The first has to do with purpose: making fundamental choices about who we are. The second involves revisiting our fundamental choices and continuously realigning our behavior accordingly. By honoring and acting in alignment with our ideals, we grow within and increase what Gandhi called "soul force." We gather the "interior resources" that Dr. King said were necessary to face the problems of life.

The clearer we are about ourselves, the greater is our capacity for change. Instead of responding in expected ways, we can step outside our routines. Instead of reacting as expected, we choose our response to meet the present circumstances. Consider another illustration concerning the health administrator I discussed at the beginning of this chapter. This second incident occurred shortly after our first meeting. We were in a workshop, and she was addressing the professionals in her organization. A discussion transpired about why it was so difficult to effect change. The name of a senior administrator entered the conversation. We'll call him Dr.

Jones. Though I did not know this man, it was clear from the reactions from the group that he was a difficult authority figure. He was the reason that it would be impossible to do the proposed change. He was the excuse.

Eleanor's reaction was not to argue but to tell a story. She told her people about a time when she and her husband were driving across town. He was doing something that irritated her immensely. It was something he always did, and she was getting angry at him—again!—as she always did. She said to the group, "I told myself, 'This man is driving me crazy!' I was about to tell him a thing or two when another thought crossed my mind. 'He is not driving you crazy, you are driving yourself crazy. The issue is not what he is doing; rather, the issue is how you are reacting to him.' I thought about this and decided to change my reaction. Pretty soon he started to change his behavior.

"Now you all know what Dr. Jones is like," she continued. "Well, two months ago he was behaving as he always does and I said to myself: 'This man is making me crazy.' The phrase led me to recall the episode with my husband. It dawned on me that the two contexts were the same. I decided that I would change how I reacted to him. That was two months ago. Let me tell you how he is treating me now."

She went on to describe a series of incidents with the good doctor. People sat in disbelief. They could not imagine the man behaving as this woman was now describing. But here was evidence that the internal changes that we make can indeed have an impact on the external world, on our relationships with others, and on the operation of the organizations in which we are participants.

Boxed In

In my meetings with executives over the years, I frequently hear stories about the impossible boss. It seems to be a universal dilemma. People will often tell me, "The ideas I am learning in your seminar are great but you just don't know my boss. I could never implement these ideas as long as he is at the helm."

There are legions of people who completely give up because of a difficult boss. They feel totally boxed in. There seem to be no alternatives. At the opposite end of the spectrum, there are people like Eleanor who do see alternatives. In fact, they create alternatives. They refuse to be disempowered.

People like Eleanor understand that the world creates us and we create the world. Because they understand this reciprocal interaction, they have the power to change the world. They know they are free to choose their own responses, and they do. By changing their response, they cause the world to change. In addition, they have an impact on others. In telling the above story, for example, the health administrator was teaching her people how to deal with the mote in the eye of another. She taught them how they are responsible for the world they live in. If there is a bad relationship, it is a relationship they were helping to create. They could change it, if they first would change themselves. The key is to first look within. Eleanor taught her people about "soul force" and how to gather the inner resources that allow us to change the world by changing ourselves.

CHAPTER FOUR

EMBRACE THE HYPOCRITICAL SELF

The Third Seed Thought:
Embrace the Hypocritical Self

JESUS   *So when they continued asking him, he lifted himself up, and said unto them, He that is without sin among you, let him first cast a stone at her. And again he stooped down, and wrote on the ground. And they which heard it, being convicted by their own conscience, went out one by one, beginning at the eldest, even unto the last: and Jesus was left alone, and the woman standing in the midst. [John 8:7–9]*

GANDHI   *[M]odern organized artificiality . . . cannot have any accord with true simplicity of heart. Where the two do not correspond, there is always either gross self-deception or hypocrisy. [Iyer, 1990, p. 108]*

KING   *It is the method which seeks to implement the just law by appealing to conscience of the great, decent majority who through blindness, fear, pride, or irrationality have allowed their consciences to sleep. [King, (1968) 1986, pp. 148–149]*

The three sacred servants all express a profound awareness of how hypocrisy operates in the change process. Gandhi tells us that in the organizing process there is a tendency for the self to split. We embrace what he calls "modern artificiality," that is, the truth as defined by the external world at any given moment, and ignore the truth of our conscience. Dr. King tells us that there is a tendency, even for the "great, decent majority," to be externally driven, that is, failing to live in accord with their conscience.

With most change, it is a challenge to awaken the conscience. In the most classic of transformational stories, the stoning of the adulterous woman, Jesus illuminates the hypocrisy of collective action when he asks that the first stone be cast by a sinless person. This story illustrates the powerful impact that moral leadership can have in the transformational process. Jesus' single request—to let the person without sin to step forward—brings to light the unexamined truth in each individual conscience. In the process, the behavior of the entire collective is changed.

The Hypocritical Change Agent

David Whyte (1994, p. 43) tells the story of a frustrated change agent named Joel. The young management consultant was pleased with the work he was doing with an important client organization. One day he received a surprise phone call from the CEO. Joel was invited to meet with the CEO in a couple of hours. Attending the meeting meant dropping what he was doing, which included the session he was chairing when the call came. Joel rushed to the company headquarters, thinking that he was at last going to get an opportunity to influence the company in a significant way. It would be his first meeting with a figure of such prominence.

When Joel entered the office, the CEO greeted him warmly and thanked him for everything he was doing for the organization. Joel was warmed by the praise, even if the CEO continued to call him Jack. Joel did not bother to correct the inaccuracy. The CEO got down to business, pointing out that it was his understanding that Joel had become close to Robert, one of the vice presidents. The CEO wanted Robert to take a position in an overseas division of the company and Robert did not want to go. The CEO asked Joel to take Robert aside and explain why this was an assignment he should take.

Joel was taken aback. To increase the level of trust in the organization he had invested a good deal of time encouraging others to risk telling the truth. He paused and timidly suggested to the boss that it might be better if the CEO himself had an open conversation with Robert. The CEO flushed with anger and said, "Jack, I don't find that remark helpful for my purposes, or for your future with this company!"

Joel became fearful. He could see himself losing the contract, the story of his incompetence then spreading across the world. If he failed to please the CEO, he was sure he would spend the rest of his life as a pauper. He quickly backed off his position and agreed to talk to Robert.

Joel still feels badly about that moment. In training young consultants, he is careful to tell this dark story. Why? First, because he wants to acknowledge that the world is a dangerous place. Second, he wants to illustrate that the young consultants are not the only ones experiencing fear. He wants them to know that the transactional world tends to drive us all toward hypocrisy.

I believe that his ability to see his own hypocrisy is a source of transformational power. By sharing the story of his hypocrisy, he is opening the way for the young people to see and confront their own hypocrisy. If they do this they are much more likely to become transformational.

Hypocrisy and the Choice of Slow Death

In the world of professional change agents, few people are better analysts than Chris Argyris. He makes two points that have relevance to our present topic. First, he claims that hypocrisy is ubiquitous in collective settings (Argyris, 1988). He claims that we all have an espoused theory (how we claim to behave) and a theory in action (how we actually behave). He argues that there is a recurrent discrepancy between what we espouse and how we behave. His claim, if it is true, suggests that, like Joel, we are all hypocrites. Furthermore, he points out that we are mostly unaware of this discrepancy. We simply do not see our own hypocrisy. In fact, we are sure it does not exist. This personal condition has a collective outcome that complicates matters. It results in "miscommunication, self-fulfilling prophecies, and escalating errors." Fueled by our individual hypocrisy, we fizzle out before we achieve our personal or collective potential. We do not establish or maintain productive community. Instead, we create relationships of distrust and succumb to living in a community that prevents virtually every member from achieving their potential.

Argyris (1991, pp. 99–109) believes there is a universal pattern in professional life. He says that we tend to organize our lives around four basic values. We strive to (1) remain in control, (2) win,

(3) suppress negative feelings, and (4) pursue rational objectives. In light of these values, any suggestion of failure is going to feel like a threat. We avoid negative feelings through "dissociation," that is, by separating ourselves from anything that might cast us in a less than favorable light. Ironically, we shut down at the exact moment that we most need to be open to learning. In doing so, we begin the process of stagnation, or slow death.

An Illustration of Dissociation

When I think about the process of dissociation, I often think of an incident that happened to me in the ninth grade. One of the best men I ever met was Ray "Chesty" Carr. He was a schoolteacher and a ninth-grade basketball coach. He was excellent in both roles. He was positive, energetic, competent, and caring. I always enjoyed being around him. I look back at the year I played for him with warm memories. Whenever I think of the notion of dissociation, however, I think of him and one sixty-second incident that was entirely out of character.

The year I played for Ray, he was coming off two consecutive undefeated seasons and two junior high school state championships. Our team had reasonable talent and our expectations were high. In the first two games of the season, we lost. At the conclusion of the second game, the team boarded the bus for the trip home. As the coach joined us, he heard several people in the back talking and laughing. He yelled at this group and told them to keep quiet. As he turned in disgust, he said, "You guys have lost more games in two weeks than I have in two years!"

I could not believe my ears. I felt rejected and hurt. For decades those words have continued to echo in my mind. Suddenly, he was separate from us. He was a winner, and we were losers. Logically it made no sense. He and his teams had won together, and now he and his present team had lost together.

Avoiding Negative Feelings

From a strictly emotional point of view, it's not difficult to see what was happening. Remember what Argyris tells us about how professionals organize their lives around four basic values of staying in control, winning, suppressing negative feelings, and pursuing rational objectives. Ray was used to believing he was in control. And he certainly saw himself as a winner. Losing two games suggested that he was not a winner anymore. Any testament to the contrary was bound to trigger negative feelings. In an effort to escape the evidence that triggered these negative feelings, he came up with a defense mechanism, a rationalization, to escape the pain he felt about losing. He did not lose; we lost. We, therefore, were not a part of him.

What Ray Carr did was natural enough. And here is the key point: like Joel, the intimidated consultant who caved in to the CEO, we all make mistakes or have bad experiences. Like Ray Carr, the frustrated coach, we all practice dissociation. We all want to be in control, win, suppress negative feelings, and pursue rational objectives. We all use defense mechanisms to avoid the emotions we experience with the dark feelings of life.

What's the bottom line? As painful as it might be for us to accept, the truth is that we are all hypocrites. And this is information that we either do not know or do not want to know. Why? Because we value control, winning, suppression of negative feelings, and the pursuit of rational objectives, we find ways to neutralize the slightest signal that we might be making a mistake or failing. We resist any evidence that would suggest that we are less than perfect.

Our hypocrisy leads to dysfunctional behavior in our relationship with others. Hypocrisy breeds hypocrisy. The channels of communication get distorted. The system does not grow. We keep exerting authority in order to preserve our positive self-image, at least in our own minds. However, the more we do this the more disconnected and ineffective we become. Consciously or unconsciously, we dissociate ourselves from information and relationships that might make us uncomfortable. We project our dark feelings onto others. Implicitly or explicitly, we say, "You were responsible. You have lost more games in two weeks than I have in two years." Needless to say, behaviors such as these undermine the probability of creating productive community.

The Relational Impact of the Hypocritical Self

Argyris (1998, p. 103) provides an analysis of a conversation between a professional change agent and a line manager. Jack, the line manager, was told to work with Tom, the consultant, whose assignment it is to empower his people. The program starts with a series of meetings where Tom talks about the importance of trust, openness, and honesty. As a result of the meetings, some people get hopeful, but after a month Tom decides that Jack has returned to his old management style. Tom decides that he needs to have a conversation with Jack. The exchange is presented in Exhibit 4.1.

This conversation captures what happens all too often in our efforts to bring about change. Here we see Tom, the facilitator, expressing a number of assumptions about Jack's behavior. Tom's assessment is that Jack's answering questions and solving problems for his employees is undermining the process of empowerment that Tom is trying to teach. Tom believes that Jack is not walking the talk. He lacks integrity because he is just "producing the numbers without upsetting people."

Because Jack is obviously not participating in the empowerment program that is Tom's responsibility, Tom decides that Jack is the problem. So he decides to confront Jack. Based on a single sentence from Jack, Tom says, "But I was wondering how well we're doing at getting people more committed to their jobs. How empowered do you think they feel?" This, of course, is not a question but an implicit judgment of Tom disguised as a question.

Jack gets the implicit message loud and clear. Consciously or not, he knew that Tom was judging him and in doing so was distancing himself from Jack. In fact, Tom is behaving just as Ray Carr did when he dissociated himself from our basketball team.

At the very least, Jack feels resentful. He may also feel that he is being blamed and that Tom simply doesn't grasp the big picture. Furthermore, Jack may instinctively feel that Tom does not have the skills to help him empower his people—and, of course, he would be right. Jack sees Tom as Tom sees Jack: as a fraud and a hypocrite. Although the empowerment program may be politically correct and cannot be challenged, it is doomed to failure with its present staffing. All Jack has to do is bide his time, be polite, and very soon it will all go away.

Doing the Natural Thing

This case seems like an impossible situation. You might think, "How could Tom ever hope to be successful?" Actually this impos-

Exhibit 4.1. An Analysis of a Corporate Conversation.

Tom's Unspoken Thoughts	What Tom and Jack Say
Tom: Things aren't going so well.	Tom: So how's everything going? Jack: Things are going pretty well. There's a lot of pressure from above, but we're meeting the numbers.
Tom: Oh great. All Jack cares about is the numbers. Empowerment isn't even on his agenda.	Tom: Great. Super. But I was wondering how well we're doing at getting people more committed to their jobs. How empowered do you think people feel?
	Jack: Well, I think we're doing okay. If there are problems, people come to me and we work it out. Sure, some people are never satisfied. But that's just a few people, and we can handle them.
Tom: Just what I feared. Jack's not "walking the talk." He just doesn't get it at all.	Tom: Look, Jack, if you solve all their problems, how are we going to empower our employees?
Tom: This is hopeless! There's got to be an easier way to make a living. I'll never get through to him. I wish I could tell Jack what I think, but I don't want to put him on the defensive. I've got to stay cool.	Jack: Well, to be honest with you, Tom, the signal I'm getting from above is that my job is to produce the numbers without, you know, upsetting people. To be fair, I think I am doing that.

Source: From C. Agyris, "Crafting a Theory of Practice," in *Paradox and Transformation,* edited by R. E. Quinn and K. S. Cameron, 1988, Ballinger. Used by permission of HarperCollins Publishers.

sible situation is quite normal. The assumptions are normal and the failure is normal. Tom could bring about change but he would have to take a transformational perspective. He would have to recognize that he is currently engaging in hypocrisy of the worst kind and would have to begin employing the principles of ACT if he wanted to enjoy any success in empowering Jack and others.

In his own mind, Tom has concluded that the change program is not working, but he refuses to acknowledge it. He talks as though everything is just fine with him, even though he knows, in his gut, that this is far from the truth. The person who truly is not walking his talk is Tom. He has actually chosen to create a hypocritical self, so he tends to have a hypocritical world mirrored back to him. Because he is modeling unauthentic behavior and communicating unauthentically, he presents to the world a self that is divided and unempowered.

For Tom to be successful, he would first have to reduce his own integrity gaps. If he did so, he would become an empowered person capable of empowering others. Instead of distancing himself from others, he would create a productive community and engage others in the dance of co-creation. Perhaps the most empowering act of all would be his ability to tell others exactly what he was experiencing.

Even as readers we may be doing something similar to Tom. Consider the fact that Tom is a professional working in the middle of an established hierarchy. If we are not presently in a similar situation in our own lives, we may dissociate ourselves from Tom. We may be feeling that this could never happen to us. We would clearly be different. The first chapter tells the story of the mother who could not get her daughter Erin to do her homework. Like Tom, she would have been most offended to be called a hypocrite, but that was in fact the case. The coach, the salesperson, the therapist, or the CEO, each of us is Tom the change agent. Each of us is Ray Carr, the frustrated coach. Each of us is Erin's mother. We become ineffective in our efforts, so we dissociate from the person or persons we are trying to change. In doing this, we do a very natural thing: we refuse to look at our own hypocrisy.

Hypocrisy and Emergent Reality

As the dynamics of personal hypocrisy unfold, we become divided within ourselves and we distance ourselves from emergent reality. When we are faced with evidence of failure and we deny it, our self becomes even more divided. When we feel ashamed of something we've done, we get more divided. We feel bad, in part, because we know that we have the potential to be more than we are, yet here we are choosing to behave in ways that increasingly diminish the self. The more divided we become, the more disempowered, worthless, and unlovable we feel. The divided self is the diminished self, the self in the process of deterioration and slow death.

Slow death begins when we are no longer connected to emergent reality. To be fully alive, we need to be engaged with what is really happening around us from moment to moment. But engaging emergent reality requires confidence. It can mean leaving the comfort of our present knowledge base. For example, we might be working within a well-established hierarchy, where we know exactly what is expected of us, how we are to relate to others who are also participating in that hierarchy, and what we need to deliver to be accepted and valued. But to engage emergent reality often means that we won't have all the answers, we will have to learn as we go. In the midst of uncertainty, we have to come up with creative solutions. Then, through trial and error, we have to mold the potential solution into something that will work. Some people call this *action learning*. Bill Torbert calls it "action inquiry" and suggests that regularly engaging in this process will result in an extraordinary form of confidence.

> Most forms of professional knowledge result in *conditional confidence*—confidence that we will act well as long as the situation does not violate our assumptions about it. The active, awakening attention described here results in *unconditional confidence*— confidence that we are capable of discarding inaccurate assumptions and ineffective strategies in the midst of ongoing action. [Torbert, 1987, p. 168]

The natural reaction, given our need for control and our fear of failure, is to avoid action inquiry, that is, engaging emergent reality. We would prefer to stay within the safe boundaries of what we already know, to keep operating where we feel secure in our expertise. We do not want to be in a situation that "violates our assumptions," that is, engage in situations that are outside our boundaries.

We need *unconditional confidence,* that is, confidence that comes from knowing that we can learn our way through virtually any situation. We see ourselves as "capable of discarding inaccurate assumptions and ineffective strategies in the midst of ongoing action." Here I think of people with a high level of mastery in their given fields. I watch Michael Jordan leading a fast break, and it seems to me that he has unconditional confidence that he can effectively adjust to any situation that emerges. Most people who are at the top of any given field—sports or elsewhere—have this confidence. They are the creators who attract the field to new levels.

How do we increase our confidence that we can learn in the midst of uncertainty and change? Torbert argues that we are most likely to be willing to engage in action inquiry after we have increased our integrity, and that we are most likely to increase our integrity when we engage our lack of integrity. Having unconditional confidence requires that we open ourselves up to really looking at our own hypocrisy.

Engaging Our Lack of Integrity: An Example

Given our natural defenses, as explored above, it is easy to see why it might be difficult to embrace our own hypocrisy. I think of an experience with my oldest child. In her early years, she was an excellent student. In her middle school years, she traded academic focus for social relationships. Her grades went down. Each year we told her that the next year would be more important. As she entered her junior year in high school, her grades continued to suffer.

At this point I, like Erin's mother, began to intervene. First, I explained that grades were critical. They would determine the university she would enter. The university she attended would determine the kinds of people she would meet, the kind of job she would eventually secure, and the kind of person she would eventually marry. Her entire future depended on her study habits right now. Of course, my argument fell on deaf ears. Her behavior did not change. I felt I had failed. I turned to forcing, setting up a variety of rewards and penalties. Still her study habits did not change. What did change was how we related to each other. We had increasingly frequent and intense confrontations. Our relationship was in trouble.

One day, deep in frustration, it finally got through to me that my efforts to change my daughter were failing completely. Furthermore, I was destroying my relationship with my child and feeling terrible about it. It was time to take a deeper look. I did not like what I found. Despite the theory of choice and accountability that I espoused, I was practicing domination and force. I was a hypocrite. Furthermore, while I was making arguments about her welfare, I was more concerned with looking like a good parent. The ends I wanted for her were just that—ends that I wanted. I was not particularly concerned with what she wanted. Our relationship was not productive community. I was a hypocrite. I would have to find a very different set of behaviors if I hoped to close my integrity gap.

After considerable agonizing, I decided there was no other choice to be made: I had to live what I believed. I went to my daughter and told her she was a bright person and I was confident that she could analyze the consequences of her own decisions; she was accountable to herself. I would say no more about grades. During the ensuing period, her grades got worse! She was sure that I could not live up to my new stance, that I trusted her to be accountable to herself. She was determined to test me. Although it was difficult, I did live my commitment. I trusted her to make her own decisions. The power struggle between us collapsed. Slowly her grades improved. When it became her honest responsibility, she made her own choice to improve.

The critic asks, yes but what if the grades had not improved? Then you would be a failure. Wrong! That mentality assumes that this is just a more complex form of manipulation. My acceptance of her as an inherently valuable human being with the right to choose is not a cause with a predictable effect. It is not a more clever form of control. If she had chosen to become a blue collar worker, that outcome would also have been acceptable. What I was doing was clarifying my deeper values, walking naked into the land of uncertainty, acting with unconditional confidence, and interacting with emergent reality in whatever way it chose to unfold. When I clarify my deepest values, my being state tends to change. When my being state changes, I tend to interpret the world differently and I tend to act in more healthy ways for me and for others.

People as Things

I often fall into ineffective patterns. The above case is an example. I started out by demanding a particular kind of behavior from my daughter: Get good grades! I had done a problem analysis, focusing on external variables, that is, studying harder to get good grades. I wanted and expected conformity to a certain set of standards that my daughter was not meeting, but I was ignoring the inner development that would, in essence, assure her that I believed she could and would handle the problem in her own way.

This is, of course, the way most of us approach problems with relationships. We look at the surface issues. We attack human issues just as we would repair a machine or refine a procedure at the office. We look for a logical, objective fix. If the car is hesitating, I replace the spark plugs. It is simple cause-and-effect logic. There's nothing wrong with approaching machines and simple technologies that way. Indeed, this is what our professions train us to do: to look for the technical fix. This fact leads Palmer (1998, p. 19) to comment: "That is why we train doctors to repair the body, not honor the spirit; clergy to be CEOs, but not spiritual guides; teachers to master techniques, but not to engage their students' souls."

Here we are at the core of ACT. As a parent, I had demanded committed behavior and got none. When I modeled committed behavior, committed behavior followed. I had to change myself in order to change my daughter. It was not a surface issue. It was a matter of productive community. It required recognition of my personal hypocrisy, followed by my doing something to change it. Personal transformation brought a transformation in the relationship.

The Ubiquity of Hypocrisy

The previous two chapters began with passages from Jesus. The first is about change, the second describes a change attempt. Let's revisit them:

> And why beholdest thou the mote that is in thy brother's eye, but perceivest not the beam that is in thine own eye? Either how canst thou say to thy brother, Brother, let me pull out the mote that is in thine eye, when thou thyself beholdest not the beam that is in thine own eye? Thou hypocrite, cast out first the beam out of thine own eye, and then shalt thou see clearly to pull out the mote that is in thy brother's eye. [Luke 6:41–42]

> So when they continued asking him, he lifted up himself, and said unto them, He that is without sin among you, let him first cast a stone at her. And again he stooped down, and wrote on the ground. And they which heard it, being convicted by their

own conscience, went out one by one, beginning at the eldest, even unto the last: and Jesus was left alone, and the woman standing in the midst. [John 8:7–9]

Both of these quotations tell us something about hypocrisy in the change agent. First, we are all quick to focus on the problem with the person who is the target of our attention. We tell that person about the mote in their eye and why it has to come out. Second, as we do so, we are almost always guilty of hypocrisy. It is somewhat equivalent to our stoning the wicked woman, without questioning our own worthiness to judge her or the part we are playing in her condemnation. In our mind, she has violated an important principle: She has sold her "self" for something of small value. Deep in our souls we know that it is wrong to denigrate the self in this way. Perhaps, when we see someone commit such an act—like choosing not to study in high school—it triggers our sense of moral indignation.

However, perhaps our moral indignation is stimulated by the fact that in the daughter who will not study, or in the adulterous woman, we see what we most hate about ourselves—the decision to be less than we might be. When a master change agent neutralizes our defenses and leaves us peering into our own dark shadow-self, we see that the uncommitted daughter or the adulterous woman is not only out there, she is also inside us! As the Pogo cartoon once proclaimed, "We have met the enemy and it is us!" At such a moment of realization, the stones drop from our hands and we slink away.

Accepting Our Hypocrisy

Over the years I have become focused on this notion of hypocrisy, and I have come to accept an unacceptable fact. I am a hypocrite. When I take this notion very seriously, it makes changing myself much easier. Carl Rogers had it right when he said, "We cannot change, we cannot move away from what we are, until we thoroughly accept what we are. Then change seems to come about almost unnoticed" (Rogers, 1961, p. 1).

When I accept that my behavior is hypocritical, I can usually commit to change. I exercise some form of self-mastery and I experience personal growth and increased insight. For a time I am euphoric. But then I make a terrible discovery. Even though I have taken a big step forward in reducing hypocrisy in one part of my life, I now have the eyes to see hypocrisy in other areas. After going through this process a number of times, I have discovered that my reservoir of hypocrisy is indeed quite deep. In fact, there is undoubtedly an unending supply. This awareness has helped me do one thing. I have internalized the story of the mote and the beam. Whenever I am in a change situation, I almost always ask the terrible question: How am I practicing hypocrisy in this situation? If I am working with another person who is trying to bring change, I try to help them embrace their own hypocrisy before they start pointing out the motes in the eyes of those who are the targets of change. This is not easy because in asking the change agent to embrace their hypocrisy, I must also embrace mine.

That we need to embrace our hypocrisy is a bad news–good news proposition. The bad news is that it is very difficult. The good news is that it is a choice that we control. We cannot control many of the variables in our external world. But we can control our own behavior. Closing our integrity gaps is a choice that always remains with us. We do not need permission from anyone to make such a choice. Each time we do make such a choice, we have a sense of victory. We begin to create a new self and we start to live in a new way. We see things that we could not see and we have options we did not have. We can access resources that we did not know existed. We feel empowered and we become empowering.

Transcendence Is Getting out of the Envelope

Transcendence is energy shifting from one form to another. The acorn is a seed that contains the script for an oak tree. Through the process of transcendence the acorn becomes much more than a tiny nut. Its shell (envelope) must open to the energy of the soil. This process of interaction includes the death of the acorn as a nut. The acorn transcends its shell to become an oak. Energy that was once held in the form of the acorn gathers new energy from other sources—the soil, the sun, the air, and the rains from the sky—and begins to take form as a tree.

People can be like acorns. Our consciousness can unfold, gathering energy from new sources, evolving into something much greater and more life-giving than we presently enjoy. Chatterjee (1998, p. 37) tells us that the word *development* shares the same root as *envelope*. "Development simply means de-enveloping or opening up the scripts of our lives."

Here's how this works: We are conscious of some things and react to them in predictable ways because previous learning and experience organizes and directs our consciousness. We might say that we have developed *scripts*. These scripts are like the scripts that actors follow. We have lots of scripts in our heads. These scripts tell us how to act in given situations. When my daughter decides that social life is more important than study, she is following a script. When I get upset with her choice and exercise coercion, I am following a script. At that point, neither of us can experience the other in a meaningful way. We have retreated into our shells. We are having a secondary encounter, based on past scripts, instead of a primary encounter in which we are enacting productive community.

Our scripts are envelopes. As long as we hold those scripts they define who we are. They give us comfort, but they also limit our growth and restrict how we experience and interact with the world around us. When we choose to look at our own hypocrisy, we enter unfamiliar territory. The experience is not always pleasant. What we discover is a place of negative emotion, and it is most uncomfortable. As we dwell in this painful territory, we are forced to make sense of it. We are usually driven to close our integrity gaps, and this expands our consciousness.

This kind of growth is transcendent and transformational. We are transcending our old scripts and transforming from an old self to a new self. When we grow we feel the consciousness expand. This is a profound experience because we are now engaging and creating current reality. We are also enacting a new and better self. When we are growing, we are more likely to put ourselves in the place of the change target, and think deeply about their feelings and reactions. We may get into their world and see how threatening we are to them and how helpless they feel when we approach them. We may begin to become "conscious" of why they do not want to study. In fact, we may see more meaning in the sentences uttered by the change target than they are aware of themselves.

As integrity increases, power increases. The transformational change agent has an expanding consciousness and a confident connection with emergent reality. This allows the agent to envision the difference between the actual and the infinite possibilities in the target of change. The transformational change agent communicates the potential of the other person to the other person. The other person is then more likely to change.

Transcending Hypocrisy Requires Surrender

Our transformational capacity takes root and grows the moment we embrace the possibility of transcending our own hypocrisy. Carl Rogers spoke of the "congruent self." When our experience, awareness, feelings, and communication are in alignment with one another, we become congruent, that is, we are no longer feeling one thing and saying another, or failing to communicate something we should. We are authentic in that we are the message we speak. Our relationships then have "a tendency toward reciprocal communication with a quality of increasing congruence; a tendency toward more mutually accurate understanding of the communications; improved psychological adjustment and functioning in both parties; and mutual satisfaction in the relationship" (Rogers, 1961, p. 344).

What this means is that change follows altered consciousness. When an individual, group, or organization develops a new awareness of reality, it also develops new patterns of behavior. Honest engagement of emergent reality leads to new meanings, and new meanings lead to transformation:

> Thus, the source of change and growth for an organization or an individual is to develop increased awareness of who it is, now. If we take time to reflect together on who we are and who we could choose to become, we will be led into the territory where change originates. We will be led to explore our agreements of belonging, the principles and values we display in our behavior, the purposes that have called us together, the worlds we've created. [Wheatley, 1996, p. 100]

Why is it necessary to reduce our hypocrisy before attempting to change others? Hypocrisy is ubiquitous. Gandhi tells us that when "modern, organized artificiality" and "true, simplicity of heart" do not correspond, there is "always gross self-deception or hypocrisy." King tells us that it is natural for the majority to let the conscience sleep. Jesus shows us that we tend to project our hypocrisy onto people we want to change. This leads to disconnection and violence, where there can be no productive community.

With the acceptance of our hypocrisy we begin to close our integrity gaps. The more we narrow those gaps, the greater our integrity becomes. With such increased integrity, our awareness and understanding of emergent reality tends to increase. We can see both the actual and the potential. We are more confident and more willing to let go of our old scripts and trust that we can, quite literally, learn our way into new systems, new beliefs, and new perceptions. In our relationships with others, we become more authentic, congruent, and empathetic, no longer separate from them but experiencing ourselves as equal members of a productive community. We attract those around us into the process of transcendence that we ourselves are experiencing. They change because we change.

CHAPTER FIVE

TRANSCEND FEAR

The Fourth Seed Thought:
Transcend Fear

JESUS   *When Jesus therefore perceived that they would come and take him*
         by force, to make him a king, he departed again into a mountain
         himself alone. [John 6:15]

GANDHI   *[E]very man has to obey the voice of his own conscience, and be*
         his own master and seek the Kingdom of God from within. For
         him there is no government that can control him. . . .
         [Iyer, 1990, p. 92]

KING   *First, we must unflinchingly face our fears and honestly ask*
         ourselves why we are afraid. This confrontation will, to some
         measure, grant us power. We shall never be cured of fear by
         escapism or repression, for the more we attempt to ignore and
         repress our fears, the more we multiply our inner conflicts.
         [King, (1968) 1986, p. 511]

Transcending Fears

Wherever we find people gathering together as a group we also
find a system of sanctions, that is, a network of formal and informal rewards and punishments that are assigned to different behaviors. In the passage above, Jesus hears that a group has come to
bestow a particular commendation upon him. He had just fed five
thousand people, and they wanted to make him their king. In light
of his ability to provide for the physical needs of so many people,

with but five barley loaves and two fishes, we can understand why they expressed such intense excitement and commitment. In fact, Jesus saw that their zeal was so great that they were ready to "come and take him by force, to make him a king."

Most of us would think of this kind of veneration as the fulfillment of an ultimate dream. In this glorious moment the world finally recognizes our genius and gives us the adoration we so deserve. It is heady stuff. For any normal human being, this would be an irresistible moment. But Jesus' reaction was not normal. What did he do? Instead of rejoicing, he "departed again into a mountain himself alone."

Why? When we learn the whole story we discover that he was committed to being internally and not externally driven. It was important to him that he remain very clear about who he was and what results he wanted. The next day he returned to the same people. Instead of performing another miracle, which would have fed their tendency to idolize him, he talked to them about their focus on the physical and told them about a deeper kind of focus. The listeners found the concepts too hard. They therefore departed.

Like Jesus, Gandhi understood how external sanctions can shape our lives or divert us from our true purpose. He saw that to be internally driven one had to listen to one's conscience. He was convinced that if he was deeply loyal to his conscience, his power would emerge and he would not be swayed from his path by external influences, not even at the risk of death. To a person living an externally driven life, this would seem incomprehensible or simply silly.

Like Gandhi, Dr. King understood that most of us, even though we might deny it, are driven by fears of what will happen to us if we fail to conform to the will of the system. He also understood that suppressing our fears only causes them to multiply. He argued that we need to bring those fears to the surface and face them head on. When we do, we will be filled with power. This is the same power of which Gandhi spoke and the same power Jesus understood. It is a power that is essential to the internally driven efforts of the transformational change agent.

In a seemingly invisible manner, socialization shapes what we believe about ourselves. We then act on those beliefs, and in doing so we co-create the world in which we live. In many ways, that world is a place of necessary comforts. In other ways it imprisons us.

Graham (1998, p. 43), for example, describes the training of elephants. The process begins by placing a huge chain around the leg of the young animal. The chain is then staked to the ground. The elephant begins by fighting this constraint but eventually gives up and accepts that it can only move within the radius of the constraining chain. The trainer then begins to reduce the size of the chain. The trainer eventually switches from a chain to a large rope. Finally, the constraint is reduced to a rope no bigger than one's little finger that the elephant could easily snap, except for his prior conditioning.

In our lives we often undergo a similar process. The normalized world teaches us that there are things we can do and things we cannot do. We accept these beliefs and act as though they were true. Our actions are then accommodated and reinforced. Like the elephant, we conform. This conformity serves many positive functions and is actually a good thing. Having routines makes life more efficient. We do not have to think about every decision. However, our routines tend to blind us to possibilities outside our belief systems. Unexamined conformity can limit our perceptions about life and its many possibilities. We may have a deep yearning to move on in our lives, to become something more than we are, yet we keep walking in the same circle, like the elephant, held by the shackles of our own beliefs.

Because conformity is usually discussed in its negative light, none of us wants to be thought of as a conformist. Yet even the most creative and rebellious among us are in fact conformists. We have been trained to behave in thousands of ways that we never think about. Why? What are the shackles that hold us? One of the most central is the need for social approval. In order to have a self, we must interact with others. Our sense of self arises out of our interactions with others. We instinctively seek acceptance by the group to which we belong. We feel a great need to be part of some group, even if the group is a destructive gang. By obeying the instinctive pull for social approval we willingly pay the price of conformity. The result is that we follow a set of routines. We not only do not look for the invisible chain that binds us, we may deny its very existence. We walk in circles and never think about why. In this sense, we all live the unexamined life.

Conformity in Organizations

The dynamics of conformity are found in families and small groups but are particularly obvious in large organizations. Most of the latter are held together by systems of fear. Too often the result is overly conservative decision making and employees from top to bottom who feel powerless. Insecure authority figures, trying to meet both real and imagined expectations, hand down directives and strategies that have been formulated mostly out of a desire to stay out of trouble. These often lead to a mixture of positive and negative outcomes—but one dares not discuss the negative ones. There is that invisible shackle again, making it clear that negative feedback is not acceptable. In fact, as fear continues to drive the organization, confrontation of any kind becomes taboo. In time, positive confrontation is as rare as the negative kind.

Any system that progresses into this level of fear gets cut off, to one degree or another, from emergent reality. Nobody dares make a choice based on what they are experiencing in the present. We no longer live on the cutting edge. We are forced to view the present through a lens developed in the past and based on other people's judgments. We become disconnected. Everyone knows this but no one dares to discuss it. To raise a voice of dissent is to risk rejection from the group. The emperor's nakedness goes unchallenged.

At this point we can describe the social environment as corrosive. Our fear-driven behaviors undermine progress. We become increasingly insecure and defensive. Honesty disappears. Back-biting, finger pointing, and scapegoating increase. If we feel any motivation at all, it is self-serving, motivated by a desire to stay out of trouble or take advantage of other people's fears to foster our own advancement. Because the real problems cannot be discussed, no solutions are even offered. A number of things begin to happen at the unconscious level. Individually we tend to get increasingly angry for selling ourselves so cheaply. We hate our increasing lack of authenticity. The real self, the self with the capacity for greatness, begins to die. We no longer nourish ourselves, nor can we even pretend that we are seeding the universe.

Upon first entering such an organization, many people, like tethered elephants, struggle to free themselves of the constraints. They may initially do this knowing that these constraints are not beneficial to them or the organization. But after a time they come to accept the radius in which they are allowed to move. Frustration grows, leading to power struggles with other people in the organization. This drains everyone's energy. People end up feeling tired, discouraged, abused, depressed, anxious, and powerless not because they are being productive but because they are not. These feelings then lead to more negative behaviors. Eventually, people come to be absolutely convinced that they are powerless. With conviction, they recite lists of the endless ways they are constrained.

Creativity Becomes a Destructive Force

Yet even those who are constrained, even those who are lowest in the organization's hierarchy, have an impact on the group. In working with change agents who work with union people, I have noticed that they often have deep insights about the dynamics of large organizations. I was in a room with a woman who is a change agent working with members of the United Auto Workers (UAW). A speaker was making the point that large organizations take away creativity. She became increasingly uncomfortable until she finally interrupted and said, "People always have their creativity, so when they are constrained, they simply reroute it to sabotage the organization that is sabotaging them."

Her point is well taken. Disempowered people get frustrated and then find ways to act out their resentment and anger with a system that seemingly robs them of their self-expression. Their acting out affects virtually everyone in the organization on a personal and collective level.

Slow Death

At the personal level, my frustrations over feeling powerless tend to turn into more serious problems. My self-image grows increasingly negative. I see myself as a person of little value. My behaviors reflect these feelings. I then attract people who also have a negative self-image and who need to feel superior. We form codependent and often abusive relationships. We commiserate, co-creating more negative self-images, and the process spirals downward, accelerating rapidly. I end up in other positions and roles in which I am treated as a person of little value. I then become still more convinced that I am a person of little value; in fact, my actual value to the organization rapidly evaporates the more negative I become. I am in the process of slow death.

The vicious cycle goes on and on. At this point, its course cannot be altered by superficial intervention such as telling or even coercing. It requires a transformation that literally gets inside me and alters my underlying self-image. This is important to recognize. When the downward spiral has progressed this far, there is only one thing that can bring about any real change: I cannot change until I actually experience the power that is inherently in me! This requires a fundamental choice, but one I am not likely to make because my life is so dominated by fear.

Creating the Toxic Context

At the collective level, people who feel powerless do look for ways to get even. They act out in negative ways. The irony is that this acting out certainly doesn't improve the system—to the contrary! And since the powerless people live within the system, they are essentially making things worse for themselves. Their negative behavior corrodes the organization even more. Management and labor stand pointing their fingers at each other, while both are literally losing their lives in a toxic environment that they have co-created. In such toxic environments, the normal assumption on the part of labor is that management needs to fix the problem. Management, meanwhile, blames the problem on labor. Similarly, in families, the children blame the parents and the parents blame the children; the father blames the mother and the mother blames the father. In athletics, the players blame the coach and the coach blames the players.

After a time, the implicit assumption is that the system cannot be fixed and no one expects it to be fixed. We accept that life is supposed to be toxic. We accept the fact that each person's role is to pretend to care about the system, while in the privacy of their own minds they tell themselves that their first priority is their own welfare. At this point we come to know for certain that the world is a Darwinian place where only the strongest survive.

Although the normal assumption is that no one can fix a system that has become this dysfunctional, Advanced Change Theory makes the radical assumption that anyone can fix it. Even so, the collective will not change by having one person come in and point out the problem. Telling and coercing simply perpetuate the current situation.

The individuals, groups, teams, and organizations will not change until they can identify and embrace their potential, that is, really grasp what they are capable of achieving. This will not happen until one person, somewhere, makes a fundamental choice and begins to demonstrate a new way of being. This will result in new actions, words, and commitment. This new pattern mirrors back the dysfunctional routines and transforms the organization through creating a new model and literally making it impossible for the old system to continue. It is only when this kind of cardinal change is initiated that individuals within the organization can embrace and transcend their fears of the external sanctions.

Impressing Authority Figures

We all experience fear—the dreaded encounter with dark anxiety organized around the sense that something bad either has happened or is soon to happen. Since there are so many bad things that could happen, it is quite natural that we would find ourselves full of fear. Because one of the four universals of professional life is to avoid negative emotion—which fear certainly is—we invest a great deal of energy repressing and denying that feeling.

Our social fears generally have to do with wanting to be perceived as competent and being accepted as a contributing member of the group. Within any organization upon which we are dependent for our well-being, we are naturally going to be concerned that the authority figures see us as competent. In fact, one of our greatest fears is failing to meet up to the expectations of an important authority figure. In the professional world we go to great lengths to impress such people. When we fail, it can be devastating. Two personal experiences come to mind:

In graduate school, I wanted to study under a particular professor. I arranged to take an independent study with him. He told me to read a particular book and then discuss it with him. I read the book several times. I took careful notes and organized them several different ways. When I was sure of myself, I arranged the meeting. He asked me to take him through the high points of the book. I proceeded. He seemed unimpressed. Then he started to ask me questions. He asked me about things that I had not even noticed. His face took on a look of disapproval although his words said I did fine.

I walked out of the professor's office and went into a deep depression. I was convinced that I did not really belong in graduate school. I did not have the tools. In fact, I could not think of any activity on the earth to which I could possibly contribute. I remember thinking that I was such a loser, that it was unfair for me to breathe the air I was breathing. That same air could have been used by a competent human being. As I write these words and recall those negative emotions, I can still feel the shame of failure. It was all very real.

On another occasion, I was attending a meeting just after receiving my doctorate. I was with two senior faculty members. We were meeting with senior executives from a large mental health agency. Within a few minutes the air was filled with the code words of mental health. Most of the time I had no idea what they were talking about. My own worst fears had come to fruition. My education was a waste. I did not know a thing. I was going to be a total failure as a professional. I excused myself and went quickly to the rest room. I thought I was going to throw up. Again, that memory is very painful.

The Common Secret

A few months after the above incident, we were working on the mental health project again. It just so happened that one of the senior faculty members was being pushed outside his area of expertise. The issue had to do with a problem in which I happened to have excellent training, so I stepped in. I saved the day and felt heroic. The senior faculty member had two reactions: First, he was deeply grateful that I was able to save him; second, he was deeply troubled. As we walked down the hall together, he said, "Sometimes I feel like my entire career is a fraud." This confession surprised me. I could not imagine him feeling the same sense of inadequacy that I had been feeling a few months before.

We tend to share a common secret: We are afraid that we simply do not measure up. We really are pretenders and it is only a matter of time until we are exposed. These fears may eventually be linked to an even more disturbing conclusion—that we are inherently bad people.

The Organization of Fear

In many organizations there are complex games that play dangerously on these kinds of irrational but universal fears. Because expertise is equated with competence and control, *effectiveness* is frequently defined as "being able to answer any question that may be asked." This perspective, combined with our fears, leads to extensive micromanagement; managers and employees alike generate a glut of essentially redundant and unnecessary data. In meetings, fearful managers carry in files bulging with information. Superiors then attempt to extend the dysfunctional game by asking questions that the lower-level managers are not likely to be able to answer.

Like the proverbial actors strutting and fretting upon the stage, great energy is invested in appearing competent and maintaining status. In environments such as this, people live in constant dread of being discovered, of being exposed for their deceptions. Since everyone buys into the game, virtually everyone ends up struggling with their own fears of incompetence. They feel insecure and behave in ways that lead other people to feel insecure.

For years I watched this process play out in the Big Three auto companies. Then came the great downsizings. As people started to do the jobs that had been done previously by two or three people, it was not as easy to play the expert game. One of the hardest adjustments people had to make was getting past the expectation that good management meant knowing and staying on top of every detail. Suddenly everyone had to risk trusting other people, not because they wanted to but because they had to. This same thing happened in many other companies during the 1980s. It was not an easy change.

The failure to impress the boss can cost a promotion, and this can lead to the loss of status and prestige. I recently met a man who worked in a large oil company and was a successful executive. At thirty-nine, it was clear to all that he was on the fast track. Then one day the impossible happened. The job that he was in line for, the job he was sure that he would get, was assigned to a thirty-seven-year-old. Someone had replaced him on the fast track. In addition to managing his own shock and disappointment, he had to manage his loss of status. Suddenly, his network changed. People that used to want to go to lunch with him no longer called. His jokes, which once brought much laughter at the water cooler, were not so funny anymore. His status had fallen and so did the quality of treatment he received. He was now an object of less transactional value.

Fears Are Undiscussable

Occasionally, I find myself in situations where someone challenges the validity of another person's fears. It usually happens when I am working with a group to approach the fact that communication in the organization is suffering from a lack of trust. As this discussion progresses, the senior authority figure will sometimes say something like this: "Why should there be any fear? After all, when was the last time anyone got fired around here?" A moment of uncomfortable silence follows. Everyone looks puzzled and they shake their heads. The authority figure smiles in triumph. He seems to be saying, "Don't you see that all your fears are unfounded?"

But the truth is far more complex than that. It is simply a fact of life that fears are greatly exaggerated. Not nearly as many negative things happen as powerless people believe. However, getting fired is not the only way that organizations dispense punishment, and every employee can list a half-dozen ways that authority figures accomplish this. Even so, while they might be able to list how punishment comes from management, the same people would be hard-pressed to list the ways that employees punish each other.

We find this same dynamic at work in families. Occasionally my older children will tell me some of the punishing things that I have done and how much I hurt them. I am always in shock at how they have distorted history. After all, I argue, mostly with myself, haven't I always behaved with their best interests in mind? Other times I may mention how one of them behaved so as to undermine the self-esteem of one of their siblings. This brings the same reaction. Surely their father has distorted history! It is always difficult to see our own punishing behavior, whether in the workplace or at home. Human systems are complex. Many painful dynamics emerge, no matter how much we try to deny it.

Engaging Our Fears

At the start of this chapter, Dr. King is quoted as saying, "We must unflinchingly face our fears and honestly ask ourselves why we are afraid." From this process, he tells us, we will find power. I suspect that the power he is talking about is the power to transcend ourselves and transform the world. However, we are reminded that, "We shall never be cured of fear by escapism or repression, for the more we attempt to ignore and repress our fears, the more we multiply our inner conflicts."

Notice that Dr. King does not tell us that we should be without fears. The myth that we might be able to do that is created from our own sense of inadequacy. To admit to our fears is forbidden, particularly in professional circles. Surely, we tell ourselves, all those other competent-looking people are fearless. It is only the inadequate me that is a coward inside, a fact that we carefully avoid revealing. Real heroes have no fear. All this, indeed, is a myth. Transformational people have many fears and they are willing to admit to them. The story of one experienced leader provides us with a good example of this.

David was in the midst of spearheading an important transformation within his organization. At a critical moment in this journey he was slated to give an important speech. He prepared well for it, but when he got to his key point, he expressed himself poorly. The message he stated was the exact opposite of the one he intended. He was inundated with negative feedback. Most of it came through informal and anonymous channels; some brave souls gave it to him directly. All were upset. He had not only bombed, he had lost credibility and precious support at a critical time.

David scheduled a meeting with me soon afterward, describing everything that had happened to him. I listened, then told him, "When that happens to me, I become paralyzed!" He looked up in shock and said, "You have had this happen to you? You get paralyzed? That is exactly what happened to me. I could hardly function for a week. I just withdrew and became self-absorbed. I tried to look unflustered and carry on as normal but I was paralyzed. It has happened to me in the past. In fact, it has occurred enough times that at least now I know that I am going to get through it when it does happen. I just have to wait and live with it. But that does not make it easy. In fact, it is awful. It is good to know that it also happens to you."

As humans we all have an endless supply of fear. I recently tried to make a list of the ones that I regularly experience. I found it very difficult to make the list. I kept telling myself that I did not have any fears. I find it very hard to share the list. It feels shameful and makes me fear that the reader will reject me. But here are just a few: In presenting my research in the university, I fear exposing my ignorance to my peers and having them see me as less than expert. They may then reject me and close me off. When I have to deliver in a new and challenging corporate consulting situation, I fear doing the wrong thing and causing a corporate disaster. In corporate situations in which it is clear that people are not telling the truth, I am often fearful to reveal what is really going on, afraid they may become angry. When I need something from people I do not know well, I fear offending them and often avoid asking for or getting what I really need. In writing this book, I am sometimes fearful of revealing my innermost thoughts. I am afraid they may be rejected by the critics. I fear getting to the end of my life and discovering that I got the entire agenda wrong and have not used my time wisely.

The above fears are just the beginning. I have quite a supply, and the list could go on and on. I suspect that the same is true for my readers, since none of us escapes being afraid. Just as we must embrace our hypocrisy, we must embrace our fears. We need to experience them so that we can know them. We need to contemplate and come to understand them; only then can we begin to outgrow them. We do not kill them or forsake them forever, we simply start to outgrow them. They no longer fully imprison us. Note the comment of the above executive. He had been paralyzed by a sense of failure in the past. It had happened often enough that he at least knows he will successfully live through those fears when they raise their ugly heads again. He knows the key is not to overreact. He just needs to wait and his shattered world will reorganize itself.

Negative Emotions as the Engine of Growth

Advanced Change Theory suggests that we need to change continually. But that doesn't mean change just for the sake of change. It means change that allows us to become not only more effective people, but also more in alignment with our true selves. Real personal change always means experiencing some kind of negative emotion. We know this and we fear this. We therefore try to deny the signals that emergent reality is different from the reality we have already experienced and with which we feel comfortable. We insist on the validity of our past scripts. We want no cracks in the shell of our acorn. We start to rationalize the need for change. We point fingers and blame others. We start hoarding seeds and preventing forests.

It is difficult to think about negative emotions as essential elements of our personal development. An example may be helpful. Mark Youngblood (1997) provides a graphic account of having his business fail. He spent a year trying to launch a company. He spent his life savings, went into debt, and exhausted himself trying to make the business successful. Finally, he had to admit what all the data had been telling him. The business was not going to make it.

> With it went everything that defined who I was to the world. I could no longer say that I "was" my job, because I had none. I couldn't rely on my wealth to create a sense of worth and identity, for I had no money and loads of debt. I could not look to social standing, for a failed entrepreneur has no social standing. And the failure of my love relationship, a month earlier, ensured that I could not find myself through the love of another. I had nothing, therefore I was nothing. I had died. [Youngblood, 1997, p. 208]

This episode seems much worse than a failed speech, of course. As we read Youngblood's words we can feel his emotion. We clearly understand and empathize. No one would ever want to enter such an emotional space. Yet one of Youngblood's single greatest lessons emerged from living through those negative emotions. Consider his observation:

> Until that point, I had lived my life through the eyes of other people. I had defined myself through object-reference—my sense of identity and my feelings of self-worth were tied directly to the outer circumstances of my life—all of these external references were stripped away. When I looked in the mirror, I did not know who I was. For me, the ego-death and subsequent "rebirth" was a wonderfully and powerfully transformative event. I experienced a sort of "awakening" in which I realized in a flash of insight that "I" was not my ego or the external trappings of my life. "I" was still all that had ever been, my true self. Nothing that was real and certain had changed, just superficial aspects of my environment. [Youngblood, 1997, p. 208]

I find his statement breath-taking. He had learned that he had lived his life through the eyes of others. We all do this. We constantly ask, How do they see me? What image must I portray? Who must I pretend to be?

Mark learned that he had been defining himself through object-reference, that is, his assessment of himself was always dependent on how people in the transactional world responded to him. Honors and objects were of exaggerated importance in his world. He was constantly asking, "Am I impressive? Are they willing to give me more status? Am I managing my status? Do I own the right things? Am I ready to buy things that convey a higher power and status? Do the objects around me carry status and create the kind of reactions I want? Am I transacting well in the social realm?

When we reach this point of external referencing, which I have been describing above, we have created scripts in which people are not inherently valued as people. They only have value insofar as they contribute to the transaction. Everything is now situational. Loyalty is conditional. To feel successful in this world, people must perform as I expect and must return the social rewards I desire.

The world of external referencing is a world where a thirty-seven-year-old gets moved ahead of a thirty-nine-year-old in the hierarchy, and the jokes of the thirty-nine-year-old are no longer funny. It is a world where the thirty-nine-year-old becomes a less useful object. When we reach this point, everyone is a prostitute, selling themselves out, denying their own lives, in return for the rewards of a paycheck and a little prestige.

Once Mark Youngblood's sources of status and power dried up, he discovered what he had always feared. He was a nobody; he was a zero. This, of course, is what we all fear. Underneath it all, perhaps we are of no value. We all, therefore, greatly fear what Youngblood experienced: the stripping away of all the external props. What could be worse than the death of the ego? Yet his ego death is followed by an event of greater revelation. He says his "subsequent 'rebirth' was a wonderfully and powerfully transformative event."

Youngblood does not report consciously doing anything to make this rebirth happen. It just occurred in an instant. What was it? He awakened to the fact that his life was much more than external honors and the accumulation of material objects in the world. He was not an object. Other people are not objects. The "real world" is not transactional. Underneath it all, he had a lasting self. The only things that had really changed were the "superficial aspects of his environment." Here a great reversal had occurred. What he was sure about was this: What had seemed to be the most important thing in his life, the foundation of his life, had turned out to be inconsequential and artificial.

To someone in the transactional being state, of course, Youngblood's discovery of another reality would seem impossible. But to Mark Youngblood it was very real, indeed. When we change our being state, we change our reality.

The Fear of Failure

I recall a young man who was having some trouble being effective in his assigned role in an organization. Stan (not his real name) wasted time in a number of pursuits that were unrelated to what he most needed to do, that is, the work that would satisfy his own inner prompting. He knew he needed to change, but he was avoiding the work of change. His life orientation was based on a rationalization that was usually expressed as follows. "I could do it if I really wanted to; I just do not want to."

After establishing a relationship with him, I eventually challenged Stan to become more effective. He seriously contemplated this challenge, but instead of accepting the challenge, he found a number of new excuses. I kept at him and felt that I was making progress. I thought he was on the verge of making the necessary commitment. We scheduled a meeting and I went into it with positive anticipation. The discussion was long and serious. After several hours, the question of commitment again moved to the forefront. I asked him to make the required decisions. He sat quietly for several minutes and then tears flowed. Finally, he looked up and he asked, "What if I tried, with everything I have, and I failed?"

His question still rings in my ears. I have contemplated it for years. Stan's question provides a powerful insight about his thought processes. Behind the mask of his flippant rationalizations resided a deep fear. He was afraid to try because he was afraid he would fail and discover that the person living inside his body was really a zero. This was the reality he suspected, and he did not want to engage it. Driven by this fear, he did not act but chose instead flight from emerging reality, stagnation, and slow death. This is the state of being in which many live. In contrast, some, like Youngblood, engage risk. When they succeed, they enter another state of being and another reality. When they fail, they enter still another state and another reality. In both the state of success and that of failure (like Youngblood), they discover a common reality. They are not zeros but people of transformational power. Action is a central element of ACT.

Transcending Object Reference

Like Stan we all tend to fear failure because we have become adapted to a state of being that is driven by object-reference. We come to believe that the real self only exists in the eyes of others and that reality is transactional, dependent on our ability to make compacts and swing deals with people who matter. We strive for power and objects of status. We judge other people as means to our ends. Our level of moral reasoning is quite conventional. To enter the transformational state of being, we must surrender object reference. Chatterjee states it well:

> We can practice the law of transcendence by progressively letting go of our urge to hold onto things, objects, addictions, and our urge to be important or powerful. Letting go does not in any way diminish ourselves, it does not make us less influential or less powerful. On the contrary it extends our human capacity for action in infinite ways. [Chatterjee, 1998, p. 180]

We all want to be important and powerful. We all want to possess things of external value. Note that the problem is not having them, but holding onto them. Being important and powerful is a potentially good thing. The honors of men and things of the world are to some degree necessary. Holding onto them is not.

The paradox is that if we hold onto the scripts that got us to our present level of wealth and status, we will loose wealth and status. Wealth and status are not the ends for which we are on the earth. We are here to seed the universe, to contribute to the emergence of the larger systems in which we exist. That requires that we transcend our old scripts. If we seek to seed the universe in accord with our unique mission, the necessary resources will emerge. If we fear failure and stop taking risks, we will fail. If obtaining wealth and power become the ends that we seek, we may obtain them, but we will probably then exchange our capacity to seed the universe for the capacity to preserve our wealth and status. It is only by letting go of our desires for wealth and power that we grow. To become transformational we have to become inner directed and other focused.

Transcendence means engaging the soil and letting the shell of the acorn crack—allowing the oak tree to be born. When we let go of our old scripts, when we stop trying to serve ourselves and seek to serve others, the new self emerges. We do not have to do anything. It happens in an instant. It simply requires a fundamental choice to allow ourselves to become the oak tree that the universe has already programmed us to become.

Chatterjee says that when we let go of object reference, "We let the intelligence of pure consciousness manifest in us and through us." When we let the old self die, the new self immediately emerges and it is in perfect alignment with emerging reality. We become one with our environment. We co-create.

Becoming an oak tree is an exhilarating experience. It increases our capacity to further seed the universe because we can now produce thousands of new acorns. We can now make the contribution we are supposed to make. The self is no longer divided. We are both creating and living in a world of infinite potential. We now feel and know that potential, and we learn that we are not zeros. We become creators.

When we create, we claim the role we attribute to God. In most traditions, God is defined as the great creator, the original cause of the process from which we emerge. Now, as inner-directed and other-focused originators, we become one with the great source.

This is a radical statement, I know, but I believe that this is the natural outcome of choosing transformation. It is an increased awareness of where the evolutionary process is taking us. The normalized world conveys the fear that we are zeros, and we tend to internalize the fear. Regular, personal transcendence of fears, constant effort to step outside our scripts and engage emerging reality, continuous struggle to live an inner-directed and other-focused life, leads to the opposite conclusion: We are not zeros. We are of infinite potential. Perhaps this possibility gives rise to still another deeply held fear. I find it most interesting that Nelson Mandela, the man who transformed South Africa, would include in one of his speeches the following quotation from *A Return to Love* by Marianne Williamson:

> Our deepest fear is not that we are inadequate. Our deepest fear is that we are powerful beyond measure. It is our light, not our darkness, that most frightens us. We ask ourselves, Who am I to be brilliant, gorgeous, talented, fabulous? Actually, who are you not to be? You are a child of God. Your playing small doesn't serve the world. There is nothing enlightened about shrinking so that other people won't feel insecure around you. We are all meant to shine, as children do. We were born to make manifest the glory of God that is within us. It's not just in some of us; it is in everyone. And as we let our own light shine, we unconsciously give other people permission to do the same. As we're liberated from our own fear, our presence automatically liberates others.
> [Williamson, 1994, p. 165]

Importance of a Unique Mission

Practicing transcendence by progressively letting go of object reference is no easy task. For most of us, it is impossible until we find a unique mission. It is often then that we are able to transcend the external sanctions that seem so pressing and real in our lives.

I once completed a workbook designed to increase personal insight (Redfield and Adrienne, 1995). In the exercises, it asked me to list all good and bad things that had happened in my life. Then, instead of telling me, as I expected, how to resolve all the conflicts associated with the bad things in my life, the workbook asked a very startling question. It went approximately like this: "Based on all the good and bad things that have happened in your life, what unique mission have you been prepared to serve that no one else can serve?" I thought that this was a brilliant question. It suggests that I can find value in every aspect of my past. All of our past events have prepared us to add value in the future. From this perspective, each one of us has been prepared to make a contribution no one else can make. When we succeed in answering this question, we are more ready to enter the transformational being state.

Knowing our unique purpose in life leads us to be more internally driven and gives us the will to overcome the challenges of the external world. This in turn allows us to more effectively engage the external world and add value to it. Victor Frankl lived through the Nazi concentration camps and wrote a book about his psychological observations (Frankl, 1963). He noted two points that are relevant here. First, that people are always free to choose. Second, having a sense of purpose gives us the strength and the capacity to transcend even very abusive and even life-threatening situations.

When I discuss the leadership of organizational change with executives, I usually go to a place they least expect. The bottom line is that they cannot change the organization unless they first change themselves. At first they think I am just making one more cute point. They come to this conclusion because they know I could not possibly be serious about such a silly position. As I continue, however, it becomes clear that I really do mean it and I provide enough support for my argument that they usually begin to squirm. The logic of starting on the inside is radically different from the comfortable, external logic that they commonly practice.

The pressure mounts, and then comes the inevitable objection. "But you do not understand . . . " They then list all the insurmountable constraints in their environment. The basic message is, We cannot live with integrity because we are not free to do so. Here is where Frankl's first point comes to bear.

> We who lived in concentration camps can remember the men who walked through the huts comforting others, giving away their last piece of bread. They may have been few in number, but they offer sufficient proof that everything can be taken from a man but one thing: the last of the human freedoms—to choose one's attitude in any given set of circumstances, to choose one's own way. And there were always choices to make. Every day, every hour, offered the opportunity to make a decision, a decision which determined whether you would or would not submit to those powers which threatened to rob you of your very self, your inner freedom; which determined whether or not you would become the plaything of circumstance, renouncing freedom and dignity to become molded into the form of the typical inmate. [Frankl, 1963, p. 104]

The choice to be inner directed is always available. Surely the corporate setting, the public agency, or the dysfunctional family is not more constraining than the Nazi concentration camp. There, as in other settings, the majority descends to the level of the transactional context. Hence the statement made to me by a discouraged executive, "We desperately need leaders with voice, but our company is full of organizational prostitutes, people whose bodies are for sale." This extraordinary statement reflects the fact that most of us follow a very ordinary level of moral reasoning. In the concentration camps, ordinary citizens, dragged from their homes, learned within hours to lose their humanity and behave abusively. The critical point, however, is the exception to the rule, that a minority of the people chose their own way. They kept their inner freedom and chose not to become a plaything of circumstance. If one person can do this, it destroys the credibility of the universal argument, "But you do not understand . . . "

Frankl's second point is also important here. He argues that purpose gives power. He describes two men who had begun to talk about suicide. He worked with them and they both chose to live. In both cases, Frankl's challenge was to get the person to see that life was still expecting something from them. They had a role to play in seeding the universe. One had a child who was waiting in another country. The other had written a series of unfinished books. There was a unique mission for each one. No one could fully take their place. Frankl writes:

> A man who becomes conscious of the responsibility he bears toward a human being who affectionately waits for him, or to an unfinished work, will never be able to throw away his life. He knows the "why" for his existence, and will be able to bear almost any "how." [Frankl, 1963, p. 126]

When we find a unique purpose, life takes on greater meaning. We can transcend the actual because we envision the possible. There is a way that the universe needs to be seeded and only we can make that contribution. We have a reason to live that is internally driven and other focused. Having such a purpose provides intensity of effort and gives us the courage to confront external sanctions and fight for survival. There are many examples.

The Power of Purpose

Here I am reminded of a story told by Joseph Jaworski. He was a successful lawyer who gave up his practice to establish an institute that would increase ethical leadership. He called it the American Leadership Forum. Once he made his courageous decision, his sense of purpose intensified. One night he had a terrifying experience. He walked to a parking lot and slipped into his car. As he was about to shut the door, he felt a hard object pressing against his body. He looked up to see a young man with a fierce look. He was pressing hard with a huge knife. Through clenched teeth the man said, "I don't want to hurt you, but I will. Now you move over from behind that steering wheel."

Jaworski held up his key and told the man to take the car, but to leave him alone. The man pressed the knife harder and said, "I don't want the car, I want you."

Jaworski noticed that there was a second man outside the car. He felt an intuition that, if he cooperated, he would die.

I remember thinking for an instant, I'm not going to let this man kill me. I'm doing something too important, and I've got to finish it. With that, I grabbed his wrist with both hands before he could shove the knife any further into me, and I pulled it away, slamming his hand against the door jamb, and causing the knife to fall on the ground. In that instant I was able to swing my feet around outside and hold them up as barriers. By that time, he had the knife again and began thrusting and trying to slash through my feet. I remember kicking him in the face, landing a powerful blow. He backed off with the knife in his hand and was ready to come at me again when I began yelling at him at the top of my voice. He had the knife in his hand, thrust out toward me, and he was ready to come at me, and I screamed at him, "You dirty son of a bitch, you touch me again and I will kill you, I will kill you with my bare hands, God damn you! Come on, come on, just try it."

He took a step backward and looked. I screamed even louder, "Come on, you filthy son of a bitch." I felt like a crazed animal. He stood there and looked at me for what seemed like a long while and then turned away and ran, and his partner ran with him. As he ran away, I was still screaming at him at the top of my lungs. [Jaworski, 1996, p. 132]

After the men ran away, Jaworski says the adrenaline wore off and he began to shake uncontrollably. He was amazed at his capacity to defend himself against that knife. But he knew that his power to do so was a function of his commitment to his purpose. He recognized that bringing about the American Leadership Forum was not an external intention. He and his purpose were one.

Over time, he came to consider this incident a defining moment in his life. It was then that he had realized a primal part of himself. He had experienced a form of pure energy unlike anything he had previously felt and he began to understand the kind of commitment that is necessary to bring about the "unfolding generative order."

Aspects of Commitment

Jaworski says there are two aspects of commitment. First, there is action. Committed people are acting. They cross the line from the zone of comfortable certainty and begin the adventure of creation. During that adventure, they must learn in the land of uncertainty and persist in the face of opposition. They are committed to see things through to the end. They will drive through the external sanctions and institutional barriers.

There is also a second aspect to commitment. Jaworski says it has to do with the "ground of being" for taking action. This concept takes us back to Frankl. It has to do with having a unique mission that will seed the universe. It is knowing that what we are doing is something needed at a higher than normal level. It is something no one else can do. We become internally driven and other focused. As we proceed, we enter a state of higher consciousness. We become open to a higher purpose, and we turn ourselves over to it. Our actions then help co-create it.

Recognizing the Greatest Punishment

As we have seen, organizations, groups, and families develop patterns for allocating rewards for people who conform to their collective expectations, and punishments for people who deviate. In this way, routines are maintained and equilibrium is preserved. Based on assumptions about what normal people want and need, sanction systems reward and punish through acceptance, status, power and money, and all that is associated with these.

Over time, it is easy to buy into a transactional mindset, to come to believe that we cannot survive without the collective's resources. An inversion happens. I am very prone to these temptations. The resources become the end for which I live. I begin making compromises. I accept and enact the transactional reality. Nevertheless, I am often frustrated. I resent the negative thing that I sense is happening to me, and I spend much time complaining about "those people" who are doing this to me. The thing I sense is that I am no longer being true to my own life. I am allowing myself to be led. Since I am not able to lead myself, I am not able to lead others. I can exercise authority. I can tell and coerce. I cannot entice people to power, because I do not have it. I cannot be a transformational change agent. I cannot seed the universe.

But the truth is, I am not a helpless victim. I have co-created my world. I have been an active participant in scripting my own slow death. I have colluded with the collective in creating the me that now exists. Although I vehemently deny it, I have both control and accountability. The chances are great that I will not recognize or exercise either until I make a fundamental choice. Yet given the rewards and punishments involved, why would anyone ever overcome their fears so as to make a fundamental choice such as I've described here? Usually the answer comes with some kind of crisis. Yet it can come from disciplined contemplation as well. When it does come, it brings a powerful realization that transforms the interpretation of punishment and my relationship to the collectivity.

The courage to live divided no more, and to face the punishment that may follow, comes from this simple insight: "No punishment anyone lays on you could possibly be worse than the punishment you lay on yourself by conspiring in your own diminishment. With that insight comes the ability to open cell doors that were never locked in the first place and to walk into new possibilities that honor the claims of one's heart" (Palmer, 1998, p. 171).

Here I am reminded of an executive who chose to live divided no more. One day he was faced with having to downsize his unit. One of the people he had to fire was a man who had worked for him for years. He considered the employee to be a good friend and saw the task of firing him as the most difficult of his life. After being fired, the employee went home and committed suicide. He also left an audiotape for his former boss and friend. The executive told me that he listened to the tape and then he made a decision. He said, "I decided from that day forth, there would never be a day in the company when I would fail to tell the truth."

In making this decision, he assumed he might be fired. To his surprise, he found that he became much more influential. His peers started coming to him, asking him to go tell senior people some uncomfortable message. He would answer, "Why don't you go tell them yourself?" They would explain that he was the only one who could get away with such forward behavior. He would try to explain otherwise, but they would assure him he was wrong.

This man made the decision to live divided no more. His painful experience had made it clear that he had been incorrectly interpreting the notion of punishment. Choosing to sell himself, colluding in his own diminishment, was far more costly than anything the organization could ever impose. This realization led to his fundamental choice. In transcending his fears, he chose to step outside his scripts. He found the ability to "open cell doors that were never locked in the first place." Once he stepped outside his scripts, the organization was forced to respond to him. He was creating a new self and a new context. His fundamental choice made him a transformational change agent and people were drawn to his integrity and his power.

The normalized world does not recognize the power to make such decisions. We are not encouraged to lead our own lives. We are taught to be responsive, to follow. We are not taught to be prime movers. Robert Fritz (1989) suggests that we can each see our lives as a creation separate from ourselves. When we take this perspective, we become less apt to spend our time trying to flee negative emotions. We gain the capacity to mold our lives as separate creations, and we can do it without experiencing the identity crisis that most people experience when they undergo deep change. He argues that people in the reactive mode tend to make emotions the centerpiece of their lives. Emotions become the measurement system for assessing the immediate situation. People are then forever fleeing from or searching for the "right" situation, the one that will make them happy. Internally driven people have a different perspective. They know that their emotional states keep changing. They pursue their intended result no matter what their temporary emotion might be.

The Consequences of Fundamental Choice

Earlier we considered Jaworski's account of warding off the knife attack. He indicated that his fundamental choice at that moment, and the presence of a unique mission, created a will to live and transcend obstacles and threats that he had never before confronted. As we turn to the personal consequences of fundamental choice, we might consider another reflection. After changing his life, Jaworski reflects back on his career as a lawyer in the normalized professional world:

> Looking back at these years, it's difficult for me to understand how I could have maintained such a fragmented existence for so long without caving in to its incoherence and lack of central commitment. Life was an absolute blur—I was popping from one activity to another without a moment's hesitation to reflect and consider my overall life direction. At the time, I considered this to be a great

life, but in fact, I really didn't know life at all. Mine was a Disney World sort of life—inauthentic, narrow, utterly predictable, and largely devoid of any real meaning. [Jaworski, 1996, p. 31]

There are important personal ramifications involved with making a fundamental choice. Our entire life pattern changes. Once we commit to live by a new set of principles, we see our lives differently. We often begin to envision a unique life purpose and become deeply committed to it. As we act on these commitments, we sense that we are making an important contribution. We are seeding the universe. Interestingly, the desire to do this thing is not driven by the desire for honor or for things. Although we still acknowledge the transactional world, it becomes far less consequential for us. We make the contribution for its own sake. We do what we are doing out of love. When we act is this way, we are inner directed and other focused.

Our lives are no longer determined by the scripts assigned by the group. We become the authors of our own stories. In doing so we violate the key assumptions of the social sciences and the key assumption of the people around us: We are transcending our own culture. There is now a new sense of freedom, giving rise to new excitement and enthusiasm about our own lives and what we are doing with them. Moreover, our enthusiasm is infectious. People around us are moved in ways that are subtle but powerful. We become living symbols of a new vision. We send out new signals to everyone around us, and if we are in an organization, our very presence disrupts old routines. It can repel and even infuriate some people even as it inspires and draws others to us. Those who are drawn to us are magnetized to us because we symbolize and embody the potential that virtually everyone senses within themselves. A new dialogue is born and the culture in which we are participating begins to change. The transactional system gets transformed.

The Organizational Payoff for Choosing

Since the external world is always changing, the organization, group, team, or family needs to change as well. Yet the opposite tends to happen. Collectives of people do everything they can to preserve what is familiar to them. Under those circumstances, pro-ductive community withers and dies. The organization becomes less and less effective. Given that reality, one would reasonably think that a change agent would be welcomed. Guess again!

From the vantage point of a change agent, we may announce our transformational intent. People laugh, attempting to deflect the anxiety they are feeling. If we persist, they use rational argu-ment. They list all the reasons that the thing we propose cannot be done. If we persist, they shift to moral indignation and begin to interpret our intentions as destructive, or even evil. At that point, the collective will likely try to isolate, humiliate, eliminate, or assas-sinate us.

This leads to an interesting paradox. To be effective, the orga-nization needs us to care so much about rescuing it that we would risk dying for the same system that would kill us for caring enough to propose the effort. When we make a fundamental choice we do just that. We care enough about the system to risk dying for it (Quinn, 1996). When we declare that the emperor has no clothes, we are risking our identity, our role in the organization, and our life as we have come to know it. We have stepped outside the self-focused, transactional model.

I was once sharing my views on the empowerment of employ-ees within an organization. When the message sunk in, a woman in human resources responded in shock: "You mean really empower them! How would we control them?" In asking this ques-tion, she was exposing an assumption that most people make who are enmeshed in the transactional model. The unspoken logic goes like this: (1) It is important for me to be politically correct; (2) I may need to pretend to involve people, maybe even do it; (3) but in the end I cannot really trust any of them. I must be sure I am really in control. Whatever I am pretending on the surface, I need to be clear about the real nature of this Darwinian game. Other-wise, there will be chaos, and bad things will happen.

What this particular woman could not understand was that truly empowered people do not need to be controlled because they are more loyal to the organization than she is. She is con-cerned first with preserving what she is and what she has. The transformational change agent is "empowered and empowering to the community." They are willing to sacrifice for the community that would punish them for doing so. She is not. She is at a conventional level of moral reasoning and sees a conventional reality.

The real benefits of a productive community are created by people who make fundamental choices. They bring the vision, courage, and commitment for change. They are the seed of adhocracy that allows the hierarchy to transform and survive. Transformational thinking is the heart and soul of productive community.

Transformational change agents have two characteristics that provide the inspiration and the foundation for building productive communities:

1. They take risks. In their study of real change leaders, at the middle levels of organizations, Katzenbach and his colleagues (1995) found that such change agents had the courage to speak out. In their successes, there were always two or three extraordinary risks they had to take. Sometimes they surprised themselves in their willingness to step forward and take these risks. They had to go beyond the authority of their formal role, and they had to put their jobs on the line. Why did they take such risks? They did so because the success of the project was more important to them than their own status quo. They had become internally driven and other focused. In my words, they were "willing to die for the company that would kill them for caring."

2. The real change leaders also challenge existing traditions and verities. This second characteristic particularly holds my attention. In hundreds of conversations, in every imaginable organizational setting, I have listened to executives express their helplessness, saying that while they agreed that things needed to change their hands were tied by their boss. They felt that no one understands them because no one understands how constrained they are by forces outside their control. It is not easy living in an organizational concentration camp. I do not want to make light of these arguments. In fact, it is important to recognize that they are made with honest conviction. The speaker is certain of his or her position and can argue it eloquently. Many even lie awake nights attempting to figure out ways to escape from these constraints, yet are unable to find the opening to leverage their life-giving changes into place. That is why this second point is so critical.

Katzenbach finds that real change leaders are willing to challenge their bosses. They do so not in an arrogant or offensive way but with conviction that everyone can benefit by following through on this challenge. Katzenbach says: "They do, however, develop higher levels of confidence that enable them to speak out when it matters, much more readily and effectively than their counterparts in normal managerial roles." They ask higher managers questions that others believe cannot be asked, questions with high impact, thus challenging traditions and changing existing behaviors. For the normal person in the transactional phase of an organization's life, such statements are incomprehensible. It is not unlike the claim made by Frankl when he said there was a very small minority of people in the prison camps who held to their own truths in the face of impossible challenges. Frankl's world was more extreme, of course. The prisoner is challenging the guard. In Frankl's mind the exceptions were important because they disproved the excuses of many. The same might be said here.

Having noted the extremity of the claim made by Katzenbach, however, it should be recognized that he extends the claim even further! In observing the way real change leaders challenge management, he states that they are seldom closed down by management but, perhaps surprisingly, they are actually "listened to and appreciated." Real change leaders strengthen rather than weaken their relationships with senior leaders! Since this happens in a visible way, they also provide a role model for others. They are changing the culture because they increase the likelihood that others will engage in the patterns of productive community in the future.

As incredible as the above claims may seem, they are within the capacities of anyone with the willingness to step forward and take action. Any organization, be it a small family or a mega-corporation, that has such people in their midst will stand a much better chance than most of staying in touch with emerging reality. Any organization that can boast having such people is more likely to become a productive community.

Breaking the Rope

At the beginning of this chapter, I mentioned the training of elephants. In a public presentation, I once told the story of the elephants trained and constrained by the small rope. A member of the audience came up afterward and told me an interesting sequel.

He said that occasionally something happens that leads an elephant to break the thin rope. When this happens, the elephant is no longer willing to collude with the institution in limiting its freedom and potential.

We need to be transformational change agents, and we need transformational change agents in all our communities. We become transformational when we transcend the sanctions of the normalized world. I will be the first to say that this requires much of us. We must be willing, even when the world is seeking to destroy us, to "unflinchingly face our fears and honestly ask ourselves why we are afraid." It requires, at all times, that we listen for and obey the voice of our "own conscience." It is only then that we become what we know we were meant to be.

CHAPTER SIX

EMBODY A VISION OF THE COMMON GOOD

The Fifth Seed Thought:
Embody a Vision of the Common Good

JESUS   *This is my commandment, That ye love one another, as I have loved you. Greater love hath no man than this, that a man lay down his life for his friends. [John 15:12–13]*

GANDHI   *Fundamental to Gandhi's thinking was his belief in the goodness of the individual. He believed that individuals want to work for the common good. That is why he called on people to make sacrifices to achieve independence and uplift the poor and why he appealed to the sense of honor and conscience of those who opposed him. As a result, many heeded his call for sacrifice, and his opponents, though skeptical at first, always treated him with courtesy and respect. [Nair, 1994, p. 98]*

KING   *I still have a dream. It is a dream deeply rooted in the American dream that one day this nation will rise up and live out the true meaning of its creed—we hold these truths to be self-evident, that all men are created equal. [King, (1968) 1986, p. 219]*

Embody the Common Good

In Chapter One I talked about the necessity to envision productive community. In this chapter we explore a concept that is crucial to bringing about productive community, the necessity for the change agent to embody the core values and common good of the productive community. Let me briefly review the notion of productive community.

Productive community is a synergistic community, made up of groups of people who are becoming more inner directed and other focused. In this community the common good and the individual good greatly overlap. There is clear purpose and structure. There is high cohesion and responsiveness.

These notions seem far from the realities of the transactional world. Many will argue it is silly, even dangerous to advocate such ideas. I would have to agree that these systems are not normal. Yet we are surrounded by evidence that such systems can work and that they are anything but foreign to our understanding. For example, we throw eighteen-year-old strangers together to fight our nation's wars. Within weeks, these people make decisions to die for one another. Fifty years later, the survivors still hold reunions to celebrate both the worst and best time of their lives. Similarly, most parents on the verge of divorce get divorced, but a few confront their mutual crisis, find a higher purpose that they share, and bring the family together stronger than ever. Girls or boys from diverse neighborhoods, and with little in common, find themselves playing on the same athletic team. Certainly it is true that in many cases there is no commitment to a common purpose or to building relationships within that setting. But in a few cases those same boys or girls do come together, find themselves working for each other's benefit, and experience a synergy they never forget.

Can this kind of synergy work in the world of business? It not only can, it does. I have seen different factories within the same parent company whose experiences were radically different: In one, they may experience total lack of cooperation among their members, whereas in another, people are not only working toward shared goals but are producing exemplary achievement records. One characteristic that differentiates them is that they are committed to each other and to a higher good. Take another example: Engineers regularly complain about dysfunctional project teams. Even though several teams from the same company may be working to develop the same project, they fail to cooperate with one another. Yet in one case, engineers from competing divisions join a project team, charged with building the project that will make or break the company. These people make a commitment to the company and to the team. They work twenty hours a day and make enormous sacrifices for each other. After the job is done and the product succeeds, putting the company back on top, they report that the experience of working together for the common good was the most exciting and significant experience of their careers.

Productive communities are exceptions. Because they are outside the transactional reality that we so commonly experience, we deny they are possible. Yet they do come together. Given the fact that there is so much negativity around people's expectations about building such organizations, how do such systems ever get created? There are clues in the above quotations.

Jesus tells us, "love one another, as I have loved you." Note that he does not refer us to a vision statement written at a management retreat and then distributed to everyone on a plastic card. His message is much more grounded. He is saying, "to understand the needed behavior, look at me; the core value is love and if you do as I am doing, we will all become more than we are." A transformational change agent, be it child, parent, coach, engineer, consultant, or CEO, must understand and embody the core values, not just give them lip service. Jesus, Gandhi, and King all understood this concept. Each was striving to be a living symbol of what the collective needed to become. Gandhi believed that people want to work for the collective good and he "called on people to make sacrifices to achieve independence and uplift the poor." He not only made this call in words but at every turn he embodied the values. He became a living symbol of what he envisioned. Dr. King called for a country in which each person had the courage to embody the value of equality. At every turn he tried to embody the courage necessary to bring that value to life.

Why is it necessary to embody the common good? Becoming the personification of the vision inspires others. They are lifted to new behaviors by our behavior. In witnessing our courage, they take courage. As they engage in new patterns of behavior, a new community begins to arise. When the transformational change agents embody the vision, they attract productive community into being. Just as individuals enter new states of being and discover new realities, emergent collectivities represent new being states and discover new realities. Such communities reinforce those individuals who seek to live in the transformational reality. The individual and the community become synergistic. All this must start with an individual who becomes the living symbol of the desired future.

The Importance of a Living Symbol

Here is a surprising twist. It seems to me that everyone has a vision and everyone embodies his or her vision. This is true even for those of us who have never contemplated the concept of vision. We all behave in accordance with how we perceive the world, and that's our vision. Our behaviors, which are shaped by our visions, tend at least partially to contribute to the world around us being as it is.

The manager who sees the world as adversarial will predictably act in an adversarial way. Any organization this person directs will mirror back his vision in the relationships at work. In the manager's mind, the behavior of employees validates his or her perception of the world, though the truth is that the employees are only responding to the manager's adversarial vision and behavior. There is a saying that perception is projection, meaning that the world we perceive is one that we have molded by projecting our beliefs onto it.

Over time, these behaviors get locked into the culture. It becomes a culture that expects and even demands adversarial relationships and behaviors from its members. What each of us sees, we enact and what we enact gets reinforced and repeated over time.

I have visited many companies and noted the unique characteristics of the CEO. I often find these same unique characteristics mirrored throughout the culture of the company. Sometimes the characteristics are positive, sometimes negative, but often they are both. Charan and Tichy (1998) have made a similar observation. They refer to the organizational culture as the "genetic code," and the leaders as the genes:

> The genetic code embodies the leaders' ideas (or lack of them),
> the values they hold, the emotional energy they create (or fail
> to), and the edge they bring (or don't bring) to the tough calls.
> How they see the world and act on it is translated into everyone
> else's behavior in thousands of ways, both visible and invisible. The
> code the leaders create governs all transactions and interactions.

It dictates how everyone thinks, acts, and behaves. It determines choices and actions: what courses are set, which ideas fly and which ones sink. It determines how people communicate with and treat each other; it determines who gets rewarded and promoted (and sometimes who gets fired), and who gets brought in from the outside. [Charan and Tichy, 1998, p. 155]

The above statement suggests that the senior authority figure's real vision—how he or she sees the world—"is translated into everyone else's behavior in thousands of ways, both visible and invisible." The cultural expectations that emerge from this eventually come to govern "all transactions and interactions." What I am, what I embody—my vision of the world and how it works—really does matter. This is critical to understand if we are to be empowered and create a productive community. It is critical because I do, in fact, have some control over what I embody.

I believe this notion applies in all collectives. Think about families. What is embodied in a parent, both good and bad, gets carried on for generations. I recently saw the movie, *The Joy Luck Club*. It is a wonderful portrait of family dynamics followed through several generations. Three young Chinese-American women, born in America, struggle with conflicts in their lives. They seem to be normal problems. Yet the movie shows how the problems actually are rooted in conflicts that started decades before in China. These earlier conflicts took place between some people the young women did not know. Conflicts unconsciously embodied by their parents and grandparents were implicitly transferred to the youngest generation. As the movie ended I sat in tears, thinking about the conscious and unconscious conflicts that I embody and how I must pass them on to my own children. What we are matters. What we choose to be matters even more.

Anyone Can Be Transformational

Before moving on, I want to go back to Charan and Tichy's statement about CEOs (above). I think that it accurately captures an important dynamic. However, I am concerned about the statement because it is top-down. It makes an assumption that nearly all management literature makes: It begins with the premise that the chief authority figure sets the culture. This is partially true, but it is not the whole truth. First, the culture also has an impact on any authority figure who comes in from outside the organization. Just as individual people attract, and are attracted to, certain others for friendship or love, so a corporate culture will attract one kind of person more than others. Moreover, once that person is in the door, the culture will also mold them to behave within its rules.

Second, anyone within the culture who chooses to be transformational—not just top management—can choose to become a transformative figure. The book we have occasionally cited by Katzenbach and his colleagues, *Real Change Leaders,* identifies many such people. This notion of minor players transforming the companies where they work flies in the face of the common assumption that only a powerful CEO can determine the course of a company. Similarly, the dysfunctional parent is not the only "gene" that will affect their children's growth. Nor is the inspiring athletic coach the only "gene." Everyone we encounter is a "gene." Virtually every one of us has unlimited potential. This potential is tapped by choosing to break the external cultural rules and embodying a future that reflects the common good.

The Son Who Changed the Culture

I am reminded of a story told by a friend of mine. During his entire life, my friend's relationship with his mother had been one of constant conflict. That script was deeply etched in the culture of the family. Bill could tell you how his mother was going to challenge him before he even entered a room where she was present. He could foretell his reaction and her reaction to his reaction.

Even though Bill fully understood the underlying rules of this little choreography, he could not change the dance. Then he spent a week at a retreat. During the week his relationship with his mother became a focal point for him. A professional helped him work through many of his own feelings toward her. The results excited him. For the first time in his memory, he had positive feelings toward his mother. He described his next visit:

> I took a deep breath and walked into the kitchen. I saw her before she saw me. I thought about the sacrifices she made and how much

I loved her. She turned and looked at me. She opened her mouth.
My stomach tightened and I thought, "Here it comes." She paused
and smiled. Then she went on with what she was doing. I was
stunned. That was not what she was supposed to do. I was different
and now she was different. From then on the relationship totally
changed. I never said a word, but I was different and she somehow
sensed it.

As children, we can change the culture of the family. Children,
parents, teachers, supervisors, or CEOs, we are all genes. We can
all carry the code but we can also choose to change the code. We
can all be transformational. It does not happen often, but it can
and does happen.

The Common Good Versus Personal Interest

I believe that everything I have learned about the problems of
organizations can be stated in a single sentence: In organizations,
individuals often choose personal good over the collective good.
In organizations, some choices are simultaneously good for the
individual and for the organization. There are also choices that are
good for the organization but not good for the individual. There
are still others that are good for the individual but not the organization. The latter category is particularly important. When faced
with the choice between organizational and personal good, it is
natural to choose personal good. This natural pattern is the root
cause of a vast number of collective failures.

According to the transactional model, it is natural for people to
be self-serving. In organizations, we witness many people choosing
personal good over collective good. Although we seldom see ourselves doing this, it's easy for us to recite legions of cases where others have chosen personal good over collective good. When someone
above us in the hierarchy does this, it is particularly troublesome.
Everyone at our level knows. Yet the issue cannot be discussed.
Emergent reality cannot be recognized. We have to pretend.

In families, we live with this dynamic every day. Father says he
is killing himself at work for our sake. We know this is not true but
would not dare raise the issue. Mother says that anything we decide
is fine with her. We know it is not, but again we dare not raise the
issue. If we do go ahead and decide, we incur her sense of injustice.

In every group there is an implied or unspoken contract. The contract suggests that we all contribute because we value the collective outcome. When someone in the group chooses personal good over collective good, we sense that we are all being cheated.

When the boss chooses personal good over collective good it has an impact on the organization much like father's disloyalty to mother would have on the family. In both cases, distrust and cynicism spread like wildfire.

In an organization, when someone chooses personal good over collective good, trust begins to wither. Commitment and cohesion begin to disintegrate. Every transaction takes more time and costs more because the tendency for people to make spontaneous contributions, which we have within ethical environments, atrophies and eventually disappears altogether. The need for management to exert control escalates. Coordination among work groups no longer happens naturally, and whatever coordination does exist requires constant monitoring. This strained condition is the normal version of human organization.

The same deterioration occurs when the organizational good is chosen over the good of the larger society. When the automobile company calculates the potential money to be lost in legal suits due to the deaths of children on defective school buses, versus the cost of exposing and repairing the flaw, cynicism spreads throughout society. And the same cynicism spreads throughout the organization. People in the organization do not like how they must now see themselves. They practice denial. Everything becomes more transactional. The same is true for people who work in government when leaders violate ethical standards behind the scenes.

Productive Community: The Path to Collective Fulfillment

The transformation model calls for a social order different from what I have described above for the transactional model. In the transformational model we look for change agents who are inner directed and other focused. We look for people who can bring together a group, help it get organized, and then pursue a unique vision. Such people can help the group monitor emergent reality and make hard decisions. They can facilitate commitment, cohesion, and trust and can build productive community. They literally embody the vision of the common good. But that's a tall order. Is it really possible to find such people? To many people experienced in organizational dynamics, it seems unrealistic because such a person would have to transcend the transactional scripts they've come to expect. For this reason we might want to better understand the notion of transactional and transformational scripts.

Spreitzer, Quinn, and Fletcher (1995) did a study of how people see themselves when they are performing at their very best. They argued that we all have implicit theories of successful performance and that we all strive to get into our own success script. It is likely that we are unaware of these scripts; we follow them unconsciously and actualize them whenever we can.

In studying a cross section of professionals, they identified four basic success scripts:

- The Journey of Responsive Service (other directed and other focused) (8 percent)
- The Journey of Independent Task Pursuit (other directed and inner focused) (28 percent)
- The Journey of Intense Achievement (inner directed and inner focused) (46 percent)
- The Journey of Collective Fulfillment (inner directed and other focused) (18 percent)

The Journey of Responsive Service

Eight percent of the people held this script. Here is an illustration.

> I am at my best when I am given an assignment that allows me to serve others. I can do something that matches my ideals. As I start, I minimize planning, structure, and intensity and engage in action. I learn by reflecting on this action. I stay flexible and open and look for intuitive insights. When the task is completed, the world is a better place. I then move on, looking for a new opportunity to serve.

These people tend to be idealistic and dedicated to the service of others; they are reflective, open, and intuitive. They have a desire to serve and are very much other focused. Yet they are somewhat unsure of themselves and often wait for direction. They are less likely to take initiative. They tend to be other directed.

The Journey of Independent Task Pursuit

Twenty-eight percent of the people studied were trying to construct this journey. An example follows:

> I am at my best when I am given a task or assignment that is specific. I organize in a careful, analytical way. I clarify objectives, plans, and schedules. I work alone, making an intense individual effort with no regard to feedback. I am fulfilled when the task is complete and I receive approval. I stay connected to the activity or product.

These people tend to be highly structured. They want personal control as they work intensely toward the completion of their assigned tasks. They tend to be quite inner focused and show limited interest in relationships. They strive for high levels of independence. The researchers first thought that these people were inner directed. Further examination, however, led to the conclusion that whereas they tend to be obsessed with independence, they are not inner directed but highly dependent on authority for vision, direction, and approval.

The Journey of Intense Achievement

Note that the majority of the people studied (46 percent) were trying to construct this path to high performance. Here is an illustration:

> I am at my best when I can create a situation in which I am challenged to demonstrate my ability and obtain appropriate rewards. I take charge of a collective and provide vision and direction. I take an intense action focus, overcoming barriers and emphasizing goal achievement. I am fulfilled when the goal is achieved and the accomplishment recognized. I then turn things over to another.

These people want to take charge, provide direction, overcome barriers, and achieve goals. They have high achievement needs and usually feel fulfilled when they have accomplished their goals and received recognition. These people tend to hold strong opinions and be inner directed. They know what they want. Yet they can often take on the role of the ruthless hero discussed earlier in the book. There tends to be an inner-focused drive to obtain rewards and recognition.

The Journey of Collective Fulfillment

Only eighteen percent of the people were trying to enact the Journey of Collective Fulfillment. An illustration follows.

> I am at my best when I can do something that fits my values. I am not reward but purpose driven. I serve others. I bring together a collective and help them develop and embrace a unique vision. I nurture commitment and cohesion through participation and trust building. I stay open to feedback and new alternatives. I feel fulfilled when the group begins to mature. I value the relationships in and the products of the community and stay connected to them.

These people tend to be inner directed and other focused. Their goal is productive community. They are interdependent and seek to co-create an involved community with commitment, cohesion, and trust. They are open to feedback and new alternatives. They embody a vision of productive community.

Taking the Script of Collective Fulfillment

In the study from which these scripts were drawn, the researchers were not examining movement from one script to another, but it is interesting to note that people with the inner directed and other focused script tended to be older. It may be that we move from one script to another, that we can and do change as we mature. I suspect few if any of us are born with an inner directed and other focused script. I suspect we have to grow into this worldview.

In Chapter One I cited Csikszentmihalyi's (1997) story of Keith. Keith was on the Journey of Intense Achievement. He spent a decade trying to impress superiors. He worked long hours, neglecting his family and his personal growth. He sought achievement and credit for his efforts, and was not averse to walking over others to get it. Yet in the end, his career advancement reached a ceiling. He was finished. It was then that he gave up. He became more relaxed, less selfish, and more objective, turning more of his attention to the good of the company. He transitioned into the Journey of Collective Fulfillment. Ironically, once he made these changes he was given the promotion he had been seeking.

Moving to the Journey of Collective Fulfillment, however, does not ensure that we will stay on that path. We may fall back. In fact, it may be natural to do so. Consider the following example.

In the last chapter, we considered the experience of Jaworski (1996), who gave up his law practice to found a leadership forum. As this happened he clearly moved into the transformational mode and enacted productive community; then something happened to him. Here the reader should note that in our society, the most dominant leadership script is the Journey of Intense Achievement. In this script, leaders are dominant and responsible. They take charge, provide the vision, the intensity, and the drive. This is the leadership script most frequently sought by society and most readily accepted by people in authority. Jaworski was on the Journey of Collective Fulfillment and he enjoyed being there. But then he began to experience fear. Soon he noted a change in his behavior as he shifted to the Journey of Intense Achievement. He comments on this point:

> I began to feel I was indispensable to the whole process, that I was responsible for all the people involved, and that everyone was depending on me. The focus was on me instead of on the larger calling. In this state, the fear factor began multiplying. I reverted to the "old" Joe—clamping down, working twelve, fifteen, and eighteen-hour days all week, and eventually on weekends as well. I would wake up in the middle of the night dripping with sweat, thinking of all the people whose jobs depended on me, and worrying about where the necessary operating capital would come from. I felt overwhelmed, overworked, and overstressed, and eventually, my obsessive worry led to panic and anxiety attacks. [Jaworski, 1996, p. 122]

Even when we experience the inner-directed and other-focused script, we can be pulled out of it. Yet as we more and more frequently experience the script of collective fulfillment or productive community we can, like Jaworski, learn to stay in it for longer periods. The more we do so, the more we evolve. Our intent changes. We do not care so much for wealth and status. We get very centered. We do not ask what people will think of us or what reward or punishment we will get. In this sense, we are temporarily free from fears. We simply ask, What is the collective good? What is good for the system that supports us all? How can we better seed the universe?

The answers to these questions are not always to our liking. Sometimes we have to sacrifice our own needs to the common good, as when an employee-owned business makes the decision to take across-the-board cuts to weather a slump in the market. The pain, however, can be endured because we are clear that we are not acting only in our own behalf. We are acting in behalf of the larger system in which we are participants, and people in the system are willingly committed to the pursuit of a greater purpose.

The Actual and Potential

In transactional systems, people put themselves first. When the common good is not fulfilling their self-interest, they turn their backs on the common good. By contrast, in the productive community we want and expect individuals to behave as individuals, that is, to have varying opinions, expertise, temperaments, and skills in which they believe and for which they even have passion. We do not want clones.

The productive community needs diverse perspectives; individual expression is essential. This can only happen when there is a shared vision of an important purpose, a commitment to the disciplined pursuit of that vision, and rich, trusting relationships. The productive community is both differentiated (each individual is respected for her or his unique contribution) and integrated (working together in common purpose). The transformational change agent understands this fact. By focusing on the common good, this change agent becomes more authentic, and others are attracted and integrated into the pursuit of the common good. The change agent is simultaneously self-authorizing and loyal to the whole. He or she is "empowered and empowering to the community."

One of Gandhi's most quoted statements is, "I must first be the change I wish to see in the world." The question is, Why? The answer is that self-changing people go outside the boundaries of the normal and expected experience. They recognize the difference between their actual and potential selves and they are motivated toward fulfilling the latter. They have increased consciousness of the difference between the actual and the potential at both the individual and the collective levels. Self-changing people become empowering to the community because they can now see the potential they could not see when they were in the normalized state. Because they are self-changing, they are self-organizing. They understand that the universe offers infinite possibilities.

In a self-organizing universe, the group can reorganize itself into something more differentiated and more integrated. Furthermore, people within such groups become living symbols of the potential. They embody the transformational process. I love the following observation about such people: "They are indeed the symbolic seeds for inside-out transformation of the organization—metaphors that bring about metamorphosis" (Chatterjee, 1998, p. 126). Such people embody the envisioned collective good. Self-changing, transformational change agents engage in behaviors that symbolize the change. They become the seeds of transformation. They reflect the potential they see.

Seeing Potential

Some years ago I had the opportunity to teach a group of teenagers. I conceived an object lesson. Since most of my six children were teenagers, I decided first to experiment on my own family. One night I called them together for a trial lesson. I said I had a common object in my possession; I wanted each person to handle the object and describe it without saying its name. I pulled an old basketball out of a bag and passed it around the room. Since all six children were basketball players, this was a familiar object. The first one said it was round and brown in color, then handed it to the next child. Each of my children was forced to work a little harder to come up with a unique description. Each had to pay attention to more fine-grained characteristics of the object.

It just so happened that the last child to get the basketball was my son Shawn. Shawn has always been more introverted than extroverted and has never been particularly verbal. He is tactile and tends to express himself physically. Playing basketball was a perfect medium for him. His position was point guard and he tended to play it with great creativity. That night, he picked up the ball and looked at it. We expected him to struggle to come up with a word or two and then pass it on to his mother. Instead, he picked up the ball and slowly started to talk. He said the ball was an object that can bring people together and make them more than they are individually. His rhythm of expression increased in intensity. Soon he was waxing poetic about the object as the rest of us sat dumbfounded and inspired by all that he had to say.

Shawn's performance had a powerful impact on all of us. I went to bed thinking about what he had said and the next morning I was still thinking about it. I decided to keep the object lesson but change the topic of my planned lesson. When the time came to teach the group of teenagers, I repeated the exercise. When they finished describing the basketball, I told them about Shawn. I asked them to explain why he behaved as he did. They told me that he loved the basketball. I asked why he would love such an object. They gave a number of reasonable answers. I then asked them to take two minutes and list the objects about which they had similar feelings. Then I asked them to talk about their objects.

A young lady raised her hand and said, "That is how I feel about my flute." She went on to describe sitting in her room and playing. She talked about her feelings and how she could express them. She talked about creating her own music. The teenagers in the room were unusually reverent in the face of this self-revelation.

A boy raised his hand and talked about his computer. He said that when he used it he had a sense of enormous potential, yet he knew his knowledge of how to use the machine was limited. He was very willing to learn because he saw a direct connection between his learning and his capacity to perform. He could feel himself grow.

Soon there were many hands in the air. The next girl talked about her ballet shoes and after that a boy talked about his martial arts uniform. The list went on. The expressions continued to be unusually self-revealing, yet did not elicit the typical teenage derision. Each person listened with reverence to the story of every other student. It was a sacred experience for everyone, including me. Why?

The people in that room were talking about and experiencing reverence. *Reverence* is the feeling we get in the presence of greatness. We feel respect, admiration, veneration, deference, awe, wonder, affection, and esteem. Why does Shawn feel this way about a basketball when others do not? Why does the girl feel this way about her flute and the boy about his computer? They see beyond the surface of the objects! They see deeply into the objects and what the objects offer.

With these objects, they have learned that they can co-create a greater self than the one that exists. With these objects they can contribute, seed the universe, and make it a better place through a unique contribution. In these objects, they see the greatest potential of all, and this engenders reverence. The experience is so powerful that they are willing to reveal themselves. It is so powerful that their teenage peers feel the love and transcend their own scripts, thus allowing them to listen with reverence.

Seeing Deeply

It is possible to learn to better see potential. I am reminded of the old statement that we should read a book as we would read a love letter. If we receive a love letter, we do not read it and put it down. We read it very carefully. We look at the nuances of every sentence. We search for meaning in every word. We are focused and very conscious. We look deeply into the love letter. With this notion in mind, consider a Chinese parable translated by W. Chan Kim and Renee Mauborgne entitled, "The Sound of the Forest."

> Kin Ts'ao sent his son Prince T'ai to the great master Pan Ku to learn the basics of good leadership. When the Prince arrived before the master, he was advised by the master to go alone to the Ming-Li Forest. After one year the Prince was asked to return to the master and describe to him the sound of the forest.
>
> After spending months in the forest, when Prince Ta'i returned, Pan Ku asked him to describe all that he could hear. Replied the Prince, "I could hear the cuckoos sing, the leaves rustle, the hummingbirds hum, the crickets chirp, the grass blow, the bees buzz, and the wind whisper and holler." Even before the

Prince could finish, the master told him to go back to the forest
and find out what more he could hear.

Puzzled by the master's whims, Prince Ta'i returned to the
forest again. For days he heard no sounds other than what he
had heard before. Then one morning as he sat silently beneath
the trees, he started to be conscious of faint sounds he had never
heard before. The more keenly he listened, the clearer the sounds
became. Slowly a new light of wisdom dawned on him and he
decided to return to Pan Ku.

The master asked him what more he had heard. The Prince
responded with reverence, "I could hear the unheard—the sound
of flowers opening, the sound of the sun warming the earth, and
the sound of the grass drinking the morning dew." Pan Ku was
delighted that his disciple had found the secret of the forest and
said: "To hear the unheard is necessary to be a good leader."
[Quoted in Chatterjee, 1998, p. 169]

To be a transformational change agent, I must see my circumstances in a transformational way. I must deeply understand the
world around me as it is and as it can be. If I am transcending my
own scripts, I am likely to be far more conscious of my environment
as it is and as it can be. I can see things in it that others cannot see.
The vision I have is unique. I am not trying to get my family, group,
team, school, or company to mirror or copy my vision so that everyone is just a clone of me. I am aware of something that only I can
do, something that is my unique contribution, my way of seeding
the universe. Such a vision requires a deep sense of the system as it
is. I cannot have such a sense unless I am able to hear the voices in
my organization. I must understand the frustrations and the
dreams, even the unspoken dreams of the people. I must be able
to read the organization like a love letter, understand the nuances,
and "hear the unheard." It is only then that I will have reverence
for the organization, as the teenagers had for the basketball, flute,
computer, and martial arts uniform.

Seeing the Potential in Organizations

These days, we read much about the "vision" of organizations.
Since there is so much uncertainty in today's business environment, people clamor to know the vision of their company, and this

pressure drives uncomfortable executives to provide a vision just for the sake of having one. Typically a top management team goes off for three days. They hole up in a room with lots of flip charts and go to work. They begin by exploring the purpose of the organization. They argue and they wordsmith for several days and finally return home with some noble sounding words. The words are reproduced on small cards, laminated, and distributed to the workforce. Typically, the cards are then ignored and things go on as before. Why? What's all this activity about?

The above process for "finding a vision" follows the transactional model. At the outset, someone answers honestly as to what they think the vision is. Someone else always disagrees. "That is not what our unit is about." The conflict drives the group to a higher level of abstraction. Eventually, what emerges is a statement about motherhood and apple pie. No one objects, but no one cares.

Others envision the future by asking planning questions. What resources do we have? What objectives do we seek? What tactics should we adopt? This results in incremental adjustments, but the company has still not come up with a transformational vision.

Why is it so difficult to come up with a vision? Fritz (1989) gives us a clue. He claims that people in the transactional world of organizations are simply not visionary. They don't know how to differentiate between the actual and the potential. They keep making compromises within the transactional realm and never experience the transformational realm. The product that then emerges cannot engage the human spirit. The human spirit is not evoked by a compromise.

Reading the Context

One of the best examples of reading the collective context and engaging the human spirit is embodied in a story related in my book *Deep Change*. Given its relevance here, I would like to repeat it. It is about a global company that had a long record of financial success. Suddenly, the world changed. The company faced a significant financial challenge. Everything that had made them successful was now in question. They were in the midst of a crisis, and people were frustrated. They were looking for a new vision from their new CEO.

Given their deteriorating situation, the company's top management decided that an immediate intervention was necessary. Several professors, including me, were brought in to design a program. There would be a series of four one-week meetings. Each meeting would be held with one hundred of the company's top four hundred executives.

Our top priority was to see that this company confronted and resolved their real issues. The first roadblock we had to overcome was the company's cultural tradition of being very polite. There was seldom any kind of public conflict. This made the design of our intervention difficult. Whatever we did would have to follow this tradition of politeness.

The intervention would begin with introductory presentations on finance and strategy. Next, I was to direct a session designed to move the executives toward the identification and analysis of other issues, beyond finance and strategy, that were facing the organization. In preparation for my part of the program and to better understand the culture of the company, it was suggested that I interview some of the people who would attend the session. I conducted the interviews and subsequently found myself putting my insights in writing. Portions of the document follow:

The Inner Voice of the Organization

During our life we often experience periods when we seem to lose our sense of meaning and purpose. There is no longer a feeling of alignment between our inner values and our tasks in the external world. We find ourselves working harder and harder and receiving less satisfaction from our efforts. We struggle through every day, lacking the vitality, commitment, and initiative we used to have. After much inner reflection and contemplation, we begin to realize that we need a new focus, a new vision, but it is difficult to uncover. By way of illustration, consider the following story.

I have a young friend whose life was in great turmoil. She was intensely focused on the accomplishment of a few key tasks. Her intensity was often a source of difficulty. She frequently found herself at odds with both her family and her employer. Her confrontations with these people escalated until she reached a state of continuous, intense anger. Her productivity declined and she sensed that she was becoming less functional.

One day, instead of going to work, she went for a hike on a nearby mountain. After several hours of climbing, she reached the peak. Exhausted, she sat down to rest. She was there only a few moments when she realized she was not alone. Three people stood nearby, preparing to hang glide. One by one they pushed off the edge and leapt into the wind currents. She watched as they gradually descended to the floor of the valley. When they landed, she could barely see them.

This overview caused her to do some reflection that had a great impact on her future. She thought about her own conflicts, and how insignificant they were in the scheme of life. She wondered if perhaps she had lost her perspective. As she stood there, she concluded that her confrontations were more destructive to herself than to others. This insight was particularly potent and she resolved to confront her problems in a different way. She returned home with a new outlook and a sense of relief. She believed that from that day forward her life had turned around.

The interesting thing about this story is that my friend's resources for change were all internal. Her stimulation came from viewing the vast panorama, but the actual resolution to her dilemma was already embedded within her. Her inner voice was telling her that she was not acting productively and that her actions were becoming self-destructive. Her inner voice led her to extricate herself from the logic of task pursuit. It led her to climb a mountain and put herself in a position where she could clearly hear her inner voice.

After viewing the vast panorama, she began to take on a larger perspective of her surrounding environment. She could, for the first time, confront the reality that she had been denying—that her coping strategies were failing. She realized she could not survive and thrive unless she did things in her life differently. She needed to adjust the alignment between her inner values and her external realities. [Quinn, 1996]

This realization came because she was finally listening to her inner voice.

Listening to the Inner Voice of the Organization

An organization also has an inner voice. Like a person's inner voice, the organization's voice calls for continuous realignment of internal values and external realities. Since a realignment usually implies deep change, the inner voice may seem like a threat to the existing organizational culture. This culture's central impulse is to preserve itself, so it works to silence the inner voice, and it usually succeeds. What nearly every person in the organization knows is true cannot be openly discussed or even acknowledged.

Unlike the inner voice of the organization, the individual voice always maintains self-interest. The organizational voice, in contrast, wants the organization to succeed, so its voice will ultimately bow to truth, paying little homage to power. It seeks to expose painful realities. In seeking the collective good, the inner voice does not distort the needs for sacrifice and change by deferring to the preferences of a particular individual. The inner voice of the organization is often a threat to those in authority.

Interestingly, the inner voice is the most potent source of power in the organization. It leads to realignment and an increased flow of resources. Its roots are in the moral core of the organization. The vitality of the organization, which depends on individual effort, can only be maintained as long as people stay connected to the inner voice. When they become disconnected, energy is lost and commitment dies.

The articulation of the inner voice of an organization is often the first step toward revitalizing a company and uncovering a vision filled with resonance. It will provide direction if people have the courage to listen and commit to change.

The following takes us through the process of articulating the inner voice of a company. It was the result of interviewing members of the global organization discussed above. Although it is my own interpretation, I have integrated the messages in the hearts and minds of many individuals in the company, since it is in their hearts and minds that we find the true inner voice. By paying attention to the themes running through the interviews I conducted, I uncovered an underlying structure. Bear in mind that what follows is not the voice of any one person but the collective voice we call the *inner voice of the organization.*

An Interview with the Inner Voice of the Organization

[In the original document, this section contained eight questions and answers. Each answer described a key issue facing the company and was illustrated by a concrete example. Each of the answers represented an undiscussable issue. Each undiscussable issue represented a weakness or a need within the company. The list is as follows:]

- The company is characterized by loyalty and considerable unused human potential.
- The organization must make deep change in order to become more viable and thus be able to survive in a rapidly evolving world.
- There is an unconscious conspiracy of silence, and an inability to confront issues and identify needed adjustments.
- There is extensive "group think" and an absence of models for constructive conflict.
- There are authoritarian figures who have "chosen" individual good and self-interest over collective good, and they have been reinforced.
- There are transparent issues everyone would like to believe are successfully kept secret. Individuals try to save face by pretending that no one knows what everyone knows—and the process works as long as no one listens to the organization's inner voice.
- There is not a cohesive leadership team.
- There is no clear, believable, and moving vision.

Summary and Implications for Action

Note that even though the inner voice spoke frankly about the top of the organization, it did not place the responsibility for its problems on the top management group. The voice recognizes that responsibility for deep change belongs not only at the top but with every person in the company—that everyone is really the CEO. However, the hierarchical culture doesn't like this truth, and frightened people try to rationalize it away by projecting responsibility to the authority figures.

Once we have heard the inner voice of the organization, what is the next step? Do we dare reinvent the culture? Does the company dare let truth speak to power? Does it dare have constructive conflict? On the surface, everyone involved will answer that they want to hear and speak the truth. But if we're honest, we find deep resistance within ourselves. A part of us shrieks a warning against any message that suggests that we might have to sacrifice or change. Nor do we want to take any foolish risks with those in authority.

If we are in a position of authority, we see no reason for our subordinates to be fearful. We tell them that our door is always open, that they should be empowered. Occasionally, they take us seriously and act on their own, momentarily becoming responsible adults, and these acts of independence and power make us uncomfortable. Of course, we let them know how we really feel. No matter how good our intentions, our discomfort with our employees' expressions of empowerment do not go unnoticed. The fact is, our expressions of discontent put fear in the hearts of those who would speak the truth and act on it.

So it is that any organization that has reached this critical juncture finds itself in a quandary, wanting to change, knowing it must, but stalled by a million undiscussable fears. We would like nothing better than to have a charismatic CEO step in, erase all this ambiguity, and lead us safely into the promised land. However, the chances are that this isn't going to happen. And since we are all CEOs, we all must face the difficult questions, such as

- Do I care enough to do this myself, providing my own charisma and erasing ambiguity?
- Am I courageous enough in my senior roles to listen, to give subordinates permission to ask about my contribution to existing difficulties?
- Am I brave enough to ask myself whether I am choosing slow death for the corporation?
- Can I recognize when it is time to leave?
- In my subordinate roles, am I courageous enough to be the CEO?
- Am I willing to take charge of the company by assertively pursuing the collective good, even if I have to enter the danger zone of a senior person?
- Am I willing to take real risks for the good of the company?

Designing the Intervention

The document captured painful reality. In this particular company, the document describing the inner voice of the organization, and the list of questions that grew out of it, were distributed throughout the company. Over the next few weeks, we scheduled a series of meetings that opened an honest dialogue. The CEO attended the first week. We advised him to listen to everything, but to say very little, even when he knew that certain statements were not factual. It was a time for others to speak and feel safe. He needed to listen to the inner voice of the organization, and he agreed.

During the week the exchange of ideas and opinions was intense and constructive, and with some encouragement people spoke candidly. In the beginning, the CEO was blamed for nearly everything but soon the tone of the sessions changed. People were beginning to look closely at themselves and to assume some responsibility for the organization's undiscussable issues.

Close to the end of the program, I asked everyone to rewrite the description of the company's inner voice. What was the inner voice of the organization now saying to them individually? Each person was to consider a vision and strategy for their own stewardship and share it with other members of the group with whom they were working. This exercise indeed proved to be rewarding. Most people discovered that they really did have a sense of direction for themselves and their organization.

In the final session the CEO spoke for an extended period with unusual candor and passion. There had clearly been a breakthrough for everyone: The organization shared a vision of how they could become a productive community. At the conclusion, of his speech, the CEO received a standing ovation. One person walked up and hugged him, an act that was sincere and that was symbolic of what most people in that room were feeling. As the CEO left the room, another senior person said, "I would walk through walls for that man. I'm going home and I know exactly what I need to do to carry out the vision that's been expressed here."

Soon afterward, the CEO cleared his calendar and allotted three weeks, over the next two months, to attend the three remaining follow-up sessions. He was getting in touch with the core of the organization.

At end of the third week he announced that he now knew what the company needed to do, and he presented his vision for the company. This vision required enormous sacrifices on the part of nearly every member, yet it was accepted enthusiastically, and with a sense of thorough commitment.

Over the next few months, deep changes occurred within the organization. There was enormous progress and tremendous political conflict. Many suffered, especially those at the top. In the midst of this chaotic period, they were slowly but unequivocally resolving their undiscussable issues. The organization had begun to move forward, with vitality and commitment that it hadn't experienced for some time.

Embody a Vision of the Common Good

In the above example, the CEO heard the unheard. He felt the frustrations and the dreams of the organization's members. He understood the past and the present. And in the process he developed reverence for the organization. He saw it in the way the teenagers I spoke of earlier saw the basketball, the flute, the martial arts uniform, and the computer. The company had suddenly become for him not just a means to an end but a way to contribute, to seed the universe, to make it a better place through a unique contribution. This reverence did not go unnoticed by others in the company; indeed, it became infectious. The CEO was now providing the model of change that would influence others.

Although this story may seem unusual—and it is—the empirical data suggest that this is the kind of metamorphosis that transformational change agents can actuate. Katzenbach and his colleagues (1995) found that the real change leaders they analyzed do not engage in formal vision exercises. Instead, they work with people at every level, looking for the language and imagery that has a potential for energizing and aligning people: They know that the real value of vision will rise out of intense and informed dialogues with many different people about why they are doing what they are doing. These conversations bring to the surface what is already lying dormant in the minds of the people. When the transformational change agent articulates the voice of the organization, the people respond.

None of these achievements can be accomplished if we are locked into an expert role where we strive to stay in control. The organizational voice will not respond to self-interested authority. Yet it cannot resist expressing itself to those who are committed to the common good.

Sincere listening is a key element of the co-creative effort described here. The sincere listener is not separate from the speaker.

Together they make it possible to articulate the undiscussable issues. They make emergent reality more clear. As speaker and sincere listener engage in honest dialogue, the change agent is transformed, becoming increasingly committed to a more productive community. A vision emerges wherein people are so committed to each other that they are willing to sacrifice for one another. They share an image of an organization. There is "full self-realization and self-expression for the benefit of all." They see a community in which all people are treated with justice and respect. They envision a synergistic community in which the collective good and individual good are one.

As people hear the organizational voice and articulate it, they allow themselves to change. As they transform, they come to embody the common good. To use Chatterjee's (1998) words, they become the "metaphors for metamorphosis." They move from the conventional and transactional level of moral reasoning to the highest levels of moral reasoning. When the people ask how, the change agent responds, "If you do as I am doing, we will all become more than we are." A transformational change agent, be it a child, parent, coach, engineer, consultant, or CEO, embodies the collective good and becomes a living symbol of productive community.

CHAPTER SEVEN

DISTURB THE SYSTEM

The Sixth Seed Thought:
Disturb the System

JESUS   *[T]hey shall lay their hands on you, and persecute you, delivering*
         you up to the synagogues, and into the prisons, being brought
         before kings and rulers for my name's sake. . . . And ye shall be
         betrayed both by parents, and brethren, and kinsfolks, and
         friends; and some of you shall they cause to put to death.
         [Luke, 21:12;16]

GANDHI   *I know that in embarking on non-violence I shall be running*
         what might be termed a mad risk. But the victories of truth have
         never been won without risks, often of the gravest character.
         [Payne, 1969, p. 385]

KING   *In any nonviolent campaign there are four basic steps: (1) collection*
         of the facts to determine whether injustices are alive, (2) negotiation,
         (3) self-purification, and (4) direct action. [King, (1968) 1986,
         p. 290]

Risk and Transcending Our Scripts

Throughout this book, I have emphasized that to bring about
change we need to transcend our scripts. But going outside our
scripts involves risk. Risk means stepping forward into uncertainty,
danger, or even peril. Two kinds of risk are involved in transcending our scripts:

First are the psychological risks, discussed earlier in the book, reflected in personal fears associated with letting go of an old self or a familiar way of working.

Second are the social risks. Jesus points out what will happen if people assess emergent reality and behave with increased personal integrity. To do this is a transformational act that will disturb the social system, which may react violently in defense of its way. Gandhi understands that transformational change agents are often sabotaged, humiliated, fired, or assassinated. Yet he still advocates taking such risks.

Dr. King shares four steps in his change strategy. He tells us that after engaging in the normalized processes of data collection and negotiation, we must move to the transformational processes of self-purification and direct action. This is important. Self-purification is the essence of the transformational process. Direct action in Birmingham and other cities of the South was a high-risk proposition. The actions King initiated required greatness of purpose and high self-trust. King had to be very sure of himself, sure enough to overcome the fear of adversity and even death that he would have to confront in order to succeed. That, of course, is what he meant by self-purification. Being sure of his data and then going through the self-purification process greatly increased the probability of his performing effectively on the edge of chaos.

Chaos: The Intuitive Attraction

Many professional change agents have developed an intuitive understanding of the role that chaos can play in the transformational process. Kurt Lewin, for example, argued that we cannot really begin to understand a system until we try to change it. He understood that individual as well as collective scripts would stay hidden until the normal way that the organization operates is challenged. As soon as a change agent introduces a variation to that system, he or she will quickly learn about the scripts that are holding that system together. Once the scripts are brought to the light they tell us a lot about how that system handles variations. This is what led to Lewin's statement about the connection between changing a system and understanding it.

Many change agents see great potential in chaos because these situations demand that we relinquish our scripts and directly encounter emergent reality. This leads to transcendence of the existing system, which in turn gives rise to radical change. In chaos we find the power to reinvent ourselves and our communities. William Bridges, for example, suggests that chaos is not a "mess," but rather "a primal state of pure energy to which the person returns for every true new beginning" (Bridges, 1980).

In math, the radical sign ($\sqrt{\ }$) is the sign for locating the square root. *Radical* literally means "returning to the root." From this perspective, chaos and radical variation become our vehicles for identifying the root of any system. It is good to keep in mind that all of our efforts to create systems of "meaning," which includes all of our scripts for holding any system in place, have emerged from our efforts to bring order out of chaos. The very fact that we go to so much effort to create and maintain systems shows how little tolerance we have for chaos. We strive to prevent or avoid it. This orientation is often counter productive. Consider the example in the next section.

Chaos in the Developmental Process

In the social sciences some people are trained as professional group facilitators. Their job is to keep groups both cohesive and productive. These facilitators often argue that when new people come together to form a group they go through four stages: forming, storming, norming, and performing. The group meets and begins the forming process. This often gives rise to tension and conflict. As the group moves through the tension and conflict stage, norms or expectations about how to operate will usually evolve in a natural way. The emergence of this order is energizing and increases the probabilities of high performance. Unfortunately, authority figures who lack the training of professional facilitators see the tension and conflict and they immediately rush in to cut it off. They deem it their duty to impose order. In doing so they often cripple the very outcomes they seek. In contrast, the professional facilitator welcomes the conflict and occasionally even helps stimulate it. The chaos is seen as a necessary step in the developmental process. The facilitator who knows the powerful role that chaos can play wants the group to experience it—to be destabilized so that it can restabilize at a higher level of functioning.

It has also been noted that chaos serves an important role in individual development. Virginia Satir, a particularly gifted psychotherapist, identified five stages in the deep change of individuals: (1) status quo; (2) entry of a foreign element; (3) chaos; (4) implementation; and (5) relapse (Gross, 1994, p. 103). She believed that chaos is necessary, that it is a kind of "molting" period that ultimately leads to greater openness. As parts of a system are put into disarray, there is often a search for new possibilities. When a "changing person risks moving into unknown territory via the expression of shameful pain, vulnerability, and/or frailty," that person can begin to reconfigure their personality in a more aligned, healthy, or whole way. Coping with chaos, however, requires that we remain centered, aware of reactions and resources, open to seeking support, and able to develop strategies for tolerating confusion:

> The capacity for coping with chaos is often associated with high self-esteem, self-efficacy, ability to reframe meaning systems, faith in positive outcomes, clarity of one's reality, and the ability to access personal resources. It means bringing energy to an effort under stress, personal flexibility, accepting uncertainty and change, and developing inner strength. [Gross, 1994, p. 103]

Internal resources matter, both for the individual and for organizations. Without inner resources it is difficult to engage chaos. I tend to assume that healthy people are more likely to initiate changes than people who are not healthy. The same principles hold true for healthy organizations. And conversely, the sickest people and organizations are sometimes the least willing and able to face reality and are the least willing to seek help.

From Chaos to the Edge of Chaos

One of the fastest growing areas of change research is complexity theory, which emerges from research on dynamic, nonlinear systems. This field of study grows out of interdisciplinary work in math, physics, and economics and is explored by scholars associated with the Sante Fe Institute (Waldrop, 1992). The concept is being incorporated rapidly into the study of change in groups and organizations.

Complexity theory suggests that all living systems, including individuals, organizations, groups, and families, are maintained by negative feedback. According to this theory, any phenomenon that is outside the normal range of action or thought is a variation or problem to be solved. The problem then needs to be brought under control by negative feedback.

A simple example of how negative feedback accomplishes this can be seen in how we react to a change in temperature. Let's say I am sitting in a room and I feel it is getting cold. I get up and put on a sweater. As I monitor the changing temperature, I define the cooling of my body as an undesired variation. I take control and counterbalance the variation of temperature by putting on a sweater. If the room heats up, I reduce the variation by taking the sweater back off. My body temperature is maintained at its "normal" level by the function of negative feedback loops.

It is important to see that the negative feedback loops are based on the presence of a desired norm—in the above case a specific body temperature that is comfortable and presumably healthy. We experience a variation outside that norm and decide that it is not something we want. We reject it and then do what we can to correct the problem so that we can return to the established norm. Negative feedback loops tend to hold systems in equilibrium. By contrast, positive loops amplify variation. They bring movement, expansion, or growth. They encourage people to move outside the norm. It works like this: (1) Something I do meets with the approval of others; (2) their positive feedback reinforces me and (3) encourages me to repeat or pursue that action. If I continue to get reinforcement I will continue to repeat what I've done, thereby garnering further positive reinforcement.

Individuals, families, groups, and organizations function in the same way. They have beliefs or scripts that define the norm. They then measure, monitor, analyze, and judge behavior within their system, neutralizing variations that might threaten it. In organizations, in particular, the first reflex of most managers is to assume that any variation in the system is a problem, and then launch into solving that problem. The normalized view, the one we are all socialized to accept, calls for continuous problem solving that is based on assumptions around negative feedback. This is, of course, a very linear, cause-effect logic: I am getting cold, so I will put on a sweater. I know the cause (putting on the sweater) will bring the desired result (warming of the body), so I implement the logical cause-and-effect process.

From the perspective of complexity theory, every living system is a congregation of elements that are connected through a network of constantly changing patterns. The outcomes of these interactions are rarely linear. The more agitated and disturbing the environment in which they occur, the less linear and predictable are the outcomes. One of the most interesting contributions of complexity theory is a notion called *the edge of chaos,* or *bounded instability.* To understand this concept we need to recognize that a system can take on at least three typical states (there are actually many):

First, a system can be chaotic. That means it has too little structure, so that it is overly sensitive to changes in the environment. The various parts of the system behave independently of one another, and in an uncontrolled and uncoordinated way. There is no continuity between past and present. All patterns of action become random, and the system disintegrates.

Second, a system can be stable. Here there is too much structure. All the parts of the system are tightly controlled and interdependent. The patterns of action within it become completely predictable and the system does not respond to environmental changes affecting it. It moves toward complete stasis, where it finally becomes stagnant and dies.

Third, a system can move far from equilibrium but not all the way to chaos. Such a system has a boundary or structure, but within the structure there is a good deal of instability. *Bounded instability*—that is, instability with specific limits—occurs when there are both negative and positive feedback loops. The negative loops provide stability, while the positive loops introduce new elements into the system, providing opportunities for new direction and growth. The system is constantly moving back and forth between these two kinds of feedback.

An Example of Self-Organization

A system based on bounded instability has the capacity to self-organize, and thus to respond to the changing environment and move naturally to higher levels of complexity and integration. Self-organizing processes tend to be transformational. The system makes a radical shift to a new form. The behavior of the new form can be forecasted in a general way but cannot be specifically predicted. We can recognize the general patterns of such a system, but not the specific path.

By way of example, let's return to the notion of the group facilitator in the training group. Training groups are different from normal groups because the experience is designed to help people learn about dynamics that occur in all groups but that most people cannot see. Here is a typical scenario: The people arrive at an appointed time, enter a room, and sit in a circle. They sit quietly and naturally look to the facilitator for direction. However, the facilitator does nothing, thus creating a leadership vacuum. The people grow uncomfortable, unable to tolerate the uncertainty and ambiguity. People try to relieve the tension by asking questions or proposing actions. These usually go nowhere. At this point let's imagine that someone (let's call her Sharon) suggests that they appoint a leader. Others in the group feel this is premature. Cynthia suggests that they get to know each other a little better by going around the circle to introduce themselves. For Sharon, this is negative feedback. Her proposal has been rejected. She sits back quietly for an extended period. Eventually Jim comments that he is worried about Sharon. He wonders if Cynthia's proposal to do introductions has hurt her feelings.

At this point, several members of the group have gotten involved, questioning what is happening and why Sharon is upset. Sharon denies that she is angry or that she is withdrawing. Ned, who is task-focused, starts pacing the floor, complaining that he is growing impatient with this game of interpersonal cat and mouse, and if things do not change he is leaving the group. He did not come to waste time. The tensions continue to climb.

About now, George pipes up, pointing out that the group is not taking responsibility for what it has done to Sharon. Tempers flare. The group is surely plunging toward the abyss of total chaos. Tom then voices agreement with Ned and suggests that they have all been sidetracked. Expressing considerable anger, he calls for a more productive agenda. As the seeming chaos grows, everyone becomes deeply uneasy.

In the normalized worldview this is what we fear, that the group will get out of control. We operate on the assumption that there always has to be a control system to maintain order. There must be a leader and a clear agenda or we will plunge into chaos. *Although this logic may be normal, it is wrong*. Let us return to our group and analyze the dynamics.

How did the group become so unstable? Initially the group was working on normal task issues: Why are we here? What is our agenda? Do we need to appoint a leader? Should we introduce ourselves? When Jim expressed his concern for Sharon, there was an important shift. The group turned its attention to the nature of the feedback it had given Sharon. There was now assessment and feedback on the feedback in the group. The group was beginning to learn about how it was learning. More was at stake and more people were expressing more feelings. Each person's comment opened up other issues, and feedback expanded exponentially. Frustration kept increasing.

When this happens people usually panic and look to the facilitator for help. Yet the experienced facilitator does not try to reduce the tension. An inexperienced facilitator, acting with the normalized worldview, might see this as a potential disaster and try to impose control. In contrast, the experienced group facilitator continues to do or say things that tease conflicts to the surface. He or she knows, at the general level, that under these conditions of bounded instability, some unpredictable act, at the specific level, will take place and become the stimulus for transformation.

The unpredictable act that will transform the system may come in the form of a statement, a question, or a symbolic movement. It is impossible to predict. In one case, a frustrated group had been locked into patterns of increasing tension for nearly two hours. It was nearing the time for dinner. The members began to argue about whether or not they should adjourn to the dining room. Someone suggested that instead of doing that, what about having a picnic. That was a switch! Suddenly a stunning change had been introduced to the pattern. In less than a minute people were volunteering, organizing everything from the menu to the entertainment. There was no leader or director—just a spontaneous discussion that resulted in a high level of order. The picnic was a spectacular success. From that point on, this previously quarreling group of people was transformed. The people went on to have a most productive learning experience.

How can a single act, such as the picnic suggestion, suddenly change the course of an entire group? Complexity theory proposes that harbored within any state of bounded instability is a "sensitive dependency on initial conditions." This means that the system is capable of responding to and making use of events that might be completely outside the central structure.

An illustration commonly given by complexity theorists is the butterfly and the hurricane. A butterfly flaps it wings in Asia, and the result may be a hurricane in Florida. This is not to say that the flapping of butterfly wings is the cause of all hurricanes but that in this particular case the conditions existed for this to occur. In a state of bounded instability, tiny factors that would normally have no impact whatsoever can escalate and transform the system. Change becomes easier at the edge of chaos because small stimuli can set in motion profound transformations. The picnic suggestion would have had zero impact earlier. At the point it occurred, however, the seemingly insignificant suggestion was transformational.

In normal groups we never see or even imagine the emergence of self-organization. The experienced facilitator, however, trusts the transformational process because of past experience with other groups. The facilitator does not know exactly what will take place, or how the process will unfold, only that the group will make a radical shift to a higher level of order. The group will form a new script and suddenly become more cohesive and productive. When the transformation takes place, it will be a dramatic and almost sacred experience that few of the participants will ever forget. It becomes a reference point in their lives, allowing them to learn their way through uncertain situations in the future while performing at a level beyond normal expectations. However, this capacity is only bestowed upon those who have experienced the process of transformation for themselves. Learning begets learning. The facilitator knows all this from the experience of walking at the edge of chaos with other groups.

An Important Differentiation

Note that the edge-of-chaos concept is different from the notion of chaos suggested by the intuitive change agents at the outset of this chapter. They saw chaos, extreme confusion, and disorder as the root of transformation. The precision of scientific complexity theory, however, suggests something different. In a state of bounded instability, at the edge of chaos, there is order. It is just that this order cannot be seen through a normalized lens. It requires a customized lens. The customized lens—which includes the awareness of what we have been discussing in the above paragraphs—allows the change agent to recognize the underlying order of the system and accept that a specific developmental path cannot be predicted. If we're to successfully facilitate change, we will have to understand the system deeply and trust the natural process of transformation that applies. These notions of trust and letting go fly in the face of our natural need to be in control. It is not an easy concept. But perhaps it is sufficient to know that it is available to us. One of the major hindrances to our capacity to understand and apply the principles of complexity is our own desire for control.

Control and Emergence: The Warehouse Inventory Case

Since we all have been taught to worship at the altar of control, the above illustration is hard to accept. The cynic argues, "This stuff is theoretical, it has no application in the real world." Actually it does. Consider another example:

> The time was midnight, and the scene, a warehouse in Dallas. A team of people was swarming over the building counting inventory for a system conversion scheduled for the next day. I was the Big–6 consultant leading the effort; Sally was the client manager. I knew this project was going to be a challenge when I first learned that the warehouse had never been fully inventoried. We had no way to know what to expect, so our planning document could serve as a rough outline at best. The counting was going to be chaotic and the reconciliation was a nightmare. Because of the number of problems we could expect to encounter, I knew that the only way to get through the effort was for all team members to think for themselves. We would have to improvise and learn as we went.

The project had started out well enough, but before long we
ran into our first problem. Sally, who had been uncomfortable with
the approach all along, used this opportunity to step in and seize
control. Her method was to control all the activities, telling each
person what, when, and how to do each task. She was responsible,
so all problems came to her. Individual team members were nothing more than physical extensions of Sally. This was classical management at its best.

At first, things seemed to run smoother with the centralized
control. But then the number of problems started to multiply.
Because the problems were unfamiliar, each took a substantial
amount of time to analyze and solve. Delays built up as people
sat around waiting while Sally solved another person's problems.
She was overwhelmed by a never-ending stream of interruptions
and demands on her time. After several hours of this, the project
had come to a standstill, and Sally had collapsed in exhaustion.
Her attempts to control the process and to separate intrinsically
related activities into discrete parts had only made matters worse.
After she relinquished control, team members stepped in and
followed the original approach. Soon the effort gained momentum
and the team's collective learning led to increased productivity.
By morning, the project was complete. [Youngblood, 1997, p. 13]

What I like about this story is that it illustrates the notion of
emergence in a concrete way. There is also something mysterious
about it. As with the picnic story, the cynic will say that it doesn't
make sense. Who ever heard of order emerging from chaos without some form of centralized control?

It is tempting to criticize the cynic. Yet the story causes me to
ask a fundamental question: Under the same circumstances, would
I have trusted the emergent process? In the story, Sally comes off
as a kind of villain. Uncomfortable with what she perceives as
chaos, she seizes control and begins to tell people what to do. She
imposes a structure: All problems must come to the responsible
person (her) to be solved.

When Youngblood labels this "classic management at its best,"
he is right. The term *classic* means that something is timeless, pro-
totypical, archetypal, or standard. For most of us, being "accountable" means being in control, of having a clear picture of what will
happen next. When we are the person who has the assignment of
being accountable, we feel great pressure to respond to normal-

ized expectations. The result is that unless I wear my customized lens that allows me to see a bigger picture, I tend to act exactly as Sally acted. To do otherwise requires an understanding of the emergent process and the courage to trust it. This is not such an easy thing to learn.

Control and Emergence: An Exercise

Learning to understand and trust the emergent process is not easy. Let me describe an educational exercise that I run with some regularity: You are among forty other people who have come to a seminar at the Executive Education Center at the Michigan Business School. Everyone there is a stranger to everyone else. I break the group up into four smaller groups and have the group arrange their chairs in four circles. I pass out blindfolds, and you put one on.

I tell you that in a few minutes I am going to assign a destination point somewhere else in the building. Your job is to find your way there as a team—but with your blindfolds in place at all times. There will be a set of materials on the floor of your assigned room. As a team, you must find all the materials and assemble them into a single object. With blindfolds in place, you must figure out what that object is and build it with quality. When you are done, you will return to the room where we are now meeting. When everyone on your team is sitting in the correct chair, you may then take off your blindfold. You have three minutes to plan your strategy.

When the three minutes are up, each team is assigned its destination point and is told to begin. Your team members join hands and arms and begin groping their way toward the assigned destination. Uncertainty is rampant. Progress is slow and messy, but eventually you do arrive at your destination. Your team now confronts a number of complex problems:

- How do you find the materials?
- How do you figure out what the object is?
- How do you assemble a complex object you cannot see?

For the next hour, you engage in a chaotic process. At last your team concludes that the object is assembled with quality. You join hands and grope your way back to your starting point. At last, with everyone in the right chair, you remove your blindfolds. You and everyone else on your team stand up and begin slapping high fives. I tell your group to go back to the room where you previously met, and see your product for the first time. As a group you race off to the place where you built the object. There your team circles the object in reverence. There are more high fives and excited talk about what has occurred over the past sixty minutes. Each of the other teams has the same experience.

I now ask the forty people in the room to reconstruct the history of their teams and list what they believe are the keys to their success. Your group reports the following:

"We talked about our assignment and then developed a plan. We appointed a leader. We executed our plan and then returned successfully. We had a common goal; luckily, we had a person with some expertise on building such objects; we had a good plan and an effective leader; we stayed within our plan; we had a sense of urgency; we had communication, trust, and teamwork; we listened well; we were persistent."

Most people going through this process will interpret the experience as being a really good team-building session. They don't fully appreciate what actually happened. In the debriefing, I typically make the following three points:

1. The claim about expertise is wrong. There are groups that end up with no expert, yet they also complete the task. Expertise is not a prerequisite because human groups know how to learn.
2. The claim about appointing a leader is accurate but misleading. In fact, the leadership was not centralized. It moved constantly from person to person as was appropriate; no one controlled the process.
3. The claim that you all knew what to do and then went out and did it is a distortion. The process was very messy and you made endless mistakes. All you had was a directive, a set of strangers in a trusting relationship, and a set of feedback loops that emerged once you started to move. Through trial and error you created the future that is now part of your past.

In most cases, these observations confuse participants. But as we go on, nearly everyone concurs that what I pointed out was true:

There was a very messy process that went unreported, a process that was just the opposite of planning, control, and execution. As you and your group honestly look at the reality of what occurred, you see clearly that you did plan, control, and execute but not in the linear way you claimed. A key point is that even when we experience self-organization we distort our reports. We report that we planned and executed a linear process when it is only true in the smallest of ways. Consider a statement from Wheatley:

> We don't have to look beyond ourselves to see self-organization. Each of us has frequent, personal experiences with this process. We see a need. We join with others. We find the necessary information or resources. We respond creatively, quickly. We create a solution that works—but then, how do we describe what we did? Do we dare to describe the true fuzziness, the unexpected turns, the bursts of creative insight? Or do we pretend that we were in control every step of the way? Do we talk about surprises or only about executing plans? Do we brag about our explorations or only our predictions? Our analytic culture drives us to so many cover-ups that it is hard to see the self-organizing capacity in any of us. [Wheatley, 1996, p. 37]

Even when we get outside the bounds of the normalized worldview and experience the exhilaration of the self-organizing universe, we tend not to be able fully to appreciate it. We are so caught up in the scripts, language, and expectations of the normalized worldview that we are blinded to the creative process that actually occurred. Even when we experience productive community we tend not to understand or appreciate what really happened. To understand better what actually happened, let's turn to the work of Van de Ven and his colleagues.

Holding Two Worldviews at Once

For decades, researchers have studied the inner workings of innovation, that is, what is going on in a person's head or within an organization when innovation is at its peak. They observe people in the midst of these processes and then generate theories about what they think they see happening. Like the participants in the above exercise, they report that innovation happens in definable and orderly stages. Then they design neat little flow charts, with boxes and arrows, showing how one neat step follows another. But does innovation really work that way?

In recent years Professor Andrew Van de Ven and his colleagues have found that innovation involves processes within processes, and these cannot be reduced to a linear model. Instead, the researchers suggest that "the innovation journey is a nonlinear cycle of divergent and convergent activities that may repeat over time at different organizational levels if resources are obtained to renew the cycle" (Van de Ven, Polley, Garud, and Venkataraman, 1999, Chapter 7). The journey can be described in terms of initiation, development, and termination, but these are rough stages, not neat boxes. Here is Van de Ven and colleagues' description of this messy process:

1. Innovations are not initiated on the spur of the moment, nor by a single dramatic incident or a single entrepreneur. In most cases, there was an extended gestation period lasting several years, in which seemingly random events occurred that preceded and set the stage for the initiation of innovations.
2. Concentrated efforts to initiate innovations are triggered by "shocks" from sources internal or external to the organization.
3. Plans are developed and submitted to venture capitalists or top managers to obtain the resources for innovation development. However, as noted below, when the innovation development begins, repeated efforts at restructuring and refinancing the innovation unit are often necessary to transform innovation ideas into practical realities for adoption and diffusion.
4. Soon after developmental activities begin, the initial innovative idea proliferates into numerous ideas and activities that proceed in divergent and parallel paths.
5. Setbacks and mistakes are frequently encountered because plans go awry or unanticipated environmental events significantly alter the ground assumptions of the innovation. As setbacks occur, resource and development timelines diverge. Initially, resource and schedule adjustments are made and provide a "grace" period for adapting the innovation, but with time, unattended problems often "snowball" into vicious cycles.
6. To compound the problems, criteria of success and failure often changed, differed between resource controllers and innovation managers, and diverged over time, often triggering power struggles between insiders and outsiders.

7. Innovation personnel participate in highly fluid ways. They tend to be involved on a part-time basis, and high personnel turnover rates occur. During the course of their involvement, personnel tend to experience euphoria in the beginning, frustration and pain in the middle period, and closure at the end of the innovation journey. These changing human emotions represent some of the most "gut-wrenching" experiences for innovation participants and managers.

8. Investors and top managers are frequently involved throughout the development process and perform contrasting roles that serve as checks and balances on one another. Seldom were major innovation development problems solved without intervention by top managers or investors.

9. Innovation units typically engaged in relational contracts with other organizations to obtain the resources, competencies, or proprietary assets needed to develop their innovations. These dyadic relationships operated independently of other inter-organizational relationships for a while, but with time and changing conditions, they were spun into complex webs of interdependent networks where actions in one dyadic relationship cascaded in a domino effect on other relationships in the web.

10. Entrepreneurs were often involved in activities beyond their immediate innovations by working with competitors, trade associations, and government agencies to create the industry or community infrastructure necessary to gain support and legitimacy for their collective innovation efforts.

11. Innovation adoption and implementation efforts did not wait until innovations were completed; they often occurred throughout the developmental period by linking and integrating the "new" with the "old" or by reinventing the innovation to fit the local situation.

12. Innovations stop when they are implemented or when resources run out. Investors or top managers make attributions about innovation success or failure. Although these attributions are often misdirected, they significantly influence the fate of innovations and the careers of innovation participants. [Van de Ven, Polley, Garud and Venkataraman, 1999, Chapter 7]

As I read these twelve items describing the messy, non-linear, innovation process, it reminds me of the process of blindfolded people building a complex object. The same kind of learning is involved, but just what kind of learning is it? The researchers provide us with an insightful model of the cyclic learning processes in the innovation journey (Figure 7.1).

The underlying dynamic of convergent and divergent behavior is found throughout the spectrum of human life. We find it in the development of society, in teams of all kinds, in leadership, in investing, in all developmental activities. This means that anyone whose life is affected by innovation is continually experiencing shifts between divergent and convergent cycles. When the cycle is convergent, the normal assumptions we have around planning and control make sense. They work. But when the cycle is divergent, behavior must change. The normal assumptions cease to work well. Here, as Van de Ven and his colleagues suggest, there must be a "divergent search, learning by discovery, pluralistic leadership, and running in packs with others to create new relationships and institutions for collective survival" (Van de Van et al., 1999, Chapter 7). This is what Sally, the woman who was responsible for the warehouse inventory, could not understand, what most of us cannot understand, and what my students in the blindfold exercise grapple with every time they attempt to describe what they have experienced.

Moving from Cycle to Cycle

What does all this mean for change agents? When we try to bring change to an organization, most of us are socialized to look on the surface of the problem. We do not really see the flesh-and-blood child, parent, family, employee, team, organization, or society in a deep way. We see only the problem to be solved. We do not see the potential that each person who is part of the system can bring in the way of new perspectives and actions. Nor do we see our own role in the system. There's a folk saying that goes something like this: "Ask a carpenter's advice and he will look for some nails to drive; ask a surgeon and he will look for something to cut; ask a preacher and he look for the fault in your soul." Like the carpenter, surgeon, and preacher, we tend to see only the problem that our expertise can presumably solve.

Figure 7.1. Cycling the Innovation Journey.

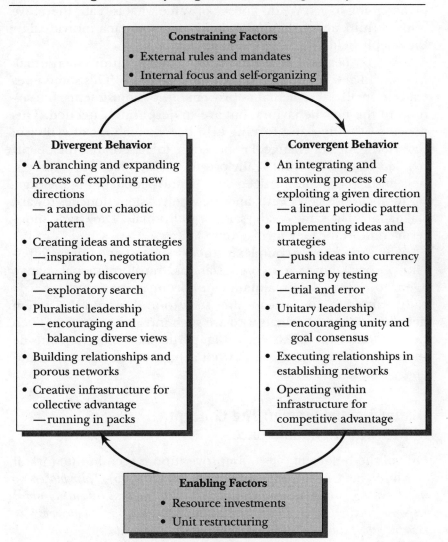

Constraining Factors
- External rules and mandates
- Internal focus and self-organizing

Divergent Behavior
- A branching and expanding process of exploring new directions
  — a random or chaotic pattern
- Creating ideas and strategies
  — inspiration, negotiation
- Learning by discovery
  — exploratory search
- Pluralistic leadership
  — encouraging and balancing diverse views
- Building relationships and porous networks
- Creative infrastructure for collective advantage
  — running in packs

Convergent Behavior
- An integrating and narrowing process of exploiting a given direction
  — a linear periodic pattern
- Implementing ideas and strategies
  — push ideas into currency
- Learning by testing
  — trial and error
- Unitary leadership
  — encouraging unity and goal consensus
- Executing relationships in establishing networks
- Operating within infrastructure for competitive advantage

Enabling Factors
- Resource investments
- Unit restructuring

Source: From Andrew Van de Ven, D. Polley, R. Garud, and S. Venkataraman, *The Innovation Journey.* Copyright 1999 by Oxford University Press, Inc. Used by permission of Oxford University Press, Inc.

The problem organization is our target, an object upon which we are going to act. We do not see or value what is really there. We seldom think about the deeply held scripts of each individual or the deeply held culture of the collective.

We may begin by trying to impose change within the normalized worldview. First, we tell, and then we force. This sometimes leads to small, incremental improvements or adjustments, but seldom to the new behaviors that are so desperately needed. This process of telling and forcing also breeds feelings of cynicism toward the idea of change. People come to believe that the deeply needed changes are not really possible, which leads to hopelessness. Instead of choosing deep change, the people within the organization choose slow death, and the whole system slouches toward stagnation. The same can be said for individuals. They trade short-term comfort for long-term agony.

The principles of complexity theory suggest an entirely different approach, however. In organizations, transformational change agents do not seek to maintain equilibrium as managers are typically trained to do. Instead, they seek to understand the system deeply and the individuals who are such integral parts of it. Then they try to disrupt the system so that participants must step outside their scripts, pay attention to what is happening right now, and engage in new behaviors.

Disturbing the System: The Concept of Provocative Competence

One of the best examples of improvisation is seen in the work of jazz musicians. According to Barrett (1998, p. 605), *"Jazz players do what managers find themselves doing: fabricating and inventing novel responses without a prescripted plan and without certainty of outcomes; discovering the future that their actions create as it unfolds."*

The reader might consider highlighting Barrett's sentence, since it describes what parents, teachers, salespeople, and everyone is called on to do. In playing the various roles of our lives we are all jazz musicians. Life calls on us to fabricate and invent "novel responses without a prescripted plan and without certainty of outcomes; discovering the future that their actions create as it unfolds." Most of us, however, do not want to let go of control. We do not accept the call. Instead of inventing, we stay in our routinized scripts and our music begins to die.

In his work on the subject of innovation, Barrett claims that jazz musicians have a skill he calls "provocative competence"—the ability to interrupt habit patterns. He writes:

> Many veteran jazz musicians practice provocative competence; they make deliberate efforts to create disruptions and incremental re-orientations. This commitment often leads players to attempt to outwit their learned habits by putting themselves in unfamiliar musical situations that demand novel responses. Saxophonist John Coltrane is well known for deliberately playing songs in difficult and unfamiliar keys because "it made [him] think" while he was playing and he could not rely on his fingers to play the notes automatically. Herbi Hancock recalls that Miles Davis was very suspicious of musicians in his quartet playing repetitive patterns so he forbade them to practice. In an effort to spur the band to approach familiar tunes from a novel perspective, Davis would sometimes call tunes in different keys, or call tunes that the band had not rehearsed. This would be done in concert, before a live audience. "I pay you to do your practicing on the band stand," Hancock recalls Davis' commitment to "keeping the music fresh and moving" by avoiding comfortable routines. "Do you know why I don't play ballads any more?" Jarrett recalled Davis telling him. "Because I like to play ballads so much (Carr, 1992, p. 53)." [Barrett, 1998, p. 609]

The Paradox of Provocative Competence

Barrett reports on the work of group leader Miles Davis and notes that the disruption must not be toxic, that is, disruptions must be challenging but not overwhelming. How we disrupt matters. The concept is not a license to behave in impulsive patterns—quite the contrary. The paradox of provocative competence is that it requires both a disciplined focus on achievement and a disciplined sensitivity to the needs of other people. The change agent must see and treat other people as "competent performers able to meet the demands of the task." It involves believing that each player can feel uncomfortable and still perform successfully. Yet unlike many suggestions in the management literature about assigning "stretch goals," we are not talking here about just asking people to extend themselves beyond their present reach. It requires more than authoritarian request on the part of the group leader. Miles Davis, for example, helped group members by creating alternative paths to action: "He imported new material that opened possibilities and suggested alternative routes for his players."

I believe that transformational change agents recognize and meet the challenge of being in a learning relationship with the group. The transformational change agent says, "Here is the standard, which I know is impossible, so let's stand together and learn our way into a higher level of performance." This is not the stance assumed by the authority figure in the normal model, whose success depends on others conforming to a specific behavior that he or she prescribes. Neither is it the work of an impulsive person introducing confusion to the system while calling it chaos. The chaos here is much more sophisticated. This disruption produces chaos that is bounded. The change agent disrupts the system so that positive feedback and negative feedback loops can work together. A small stimulus can then move the system to radically higher levels of performance.

A Master of Provocative Disruption

Another example I'd like to offer comes from group facilitation. Earlier I used the example of a group being run by a professional process facilitator. One of the best process facilitators I have ever seen is David Bradford. He was the founder and, for several years, director of the Organizational Behavior Teaching Society. The OBTS is a professional society dedicated to the improvement of teaching in the field of organizational behavior. Each year, the OBTS would hold a three-day conference. The last day would end at noon. For the rest of that day and evening, the board of directors would meet. This was usually a group of ten or twelve people. The number of tasks to be accomplished always exceeded the bounds of the time available. Particularly demanding was the nomination and selection of two new board members. This was always the last issue on the agenda. The group always felt driven by time.

We would start the long session in the early afternoon. David would start us on the agenda. We would drive for results, but then, just as the task-focused group was about to close on a decision, David would disrupt us. "Let's take some time and reflect on the process and how our process is unfolding," he would say.

Even though I understood what he was doing, that he was intentionally disrupting us, my frustration would soar. I had an intense need, given the time pressure, to get the task completed. Instead, we would process our feelings. We would just about arrive at a very "warm and fuzzy" place, and David would take us back to the task. We would thus slowly zigzag our way through the agenda items. Finally, in the late hours, we would come to the complex issue of selecting two new members. David would continue the same disrupting rhythm. Tempers would flare and the situation would seem hopeless. Then suddenly, there was a solution, not merely an acceptable one but a very impressive one that everyone felt proud of and to which everyone was deeply committed. Each year this process and the magical outcome would repeat itself.

How did this magic happen? In disrupting the processes, David was pulling us outside our scripts. We had to become, like the jazz musicians, more mindful. As he moved us back and forth from task to relationship and back to task, he was creating space. There were more contribution opportunities for every individual, whether they were left-brained, right-brained, shy, angry, or frustrated. Each person could act independently, and in so doing the group was drawn into unexpected territories. These territories, in turn, required more exploration and created more feedback and more opportunities to contribute.

As the process unfolded, we were becoming more emotionally aware, more sensitive to how each person contributes to the emergent dance. We could better predict what we were going to do next, we could thus better adjust the course of our own actions. This knowledge and behavior then led to a richer network and a higher level of performance.

The more we experienced improved performance, the more we trusted each other. The more we trusted, the more honest we became, and this further increased trust. This exponential increase in trust made it possible for each individual to risk making more daring and more exploratory statements. Sometimes these were powerful contributions and sometimes they flopped. Yet having abandoned normal experiences, it was now acceptable to flop.

There was no punishment; people simply adjusted their steps and carried the dance into the future. The risk-taking individual was safe and able to come back and try again. Therefore, the trust climbed still higher. The number of positive feedback loops kept increasing exponentially.

By the time we approached the final big decision of the night, we were approaching what jazz musicians call the "groove," a level of performance wherein the organization of that moment takes on a life of its own. We were fully extended at the edge of chaos. The task was challenging. We were deeply committed to it and fully absorbed in the feedback loops. As individuals, we had the desire and the courage to give up our everyday sense of self. Ego investments diminished. We felt safe and competent and were not worried about being on stage. We experienced a transformation. We moved to a higher level of complexity and performance. It was indeed an exhilarating night. We were functioning at the highest level of productive community.

The normal administrator who lives through endless task-oriented meetings has no access to the theory or the tools used by David Bradford. The meeting described above defies normal logic. Normal logic assumes there is a script and seeks the prescription for action that the script provides. That way of operating is based on negative feedback loops and staying within specified parameters. It is about abolishing uncertainty. Transformational power is found outside that logic. It resides at the edge of chaos. It is a process of improvisation. It means creating the script as we go. We might paraphrase Barrett's (1998) sentence we highlighted earlier to say, *David Bradford contributed by helping the group in the process of "fabricating and inventing novel responses without a prescripted plan and without certainty of outcomes; discovering the future that their actions creates as it unfolds."* He was effectively disrupting the system, moving into bounded instability, and trusting the process of transformation and higher-level functioning.

Facilitating Adaptive Work

Learning to move an organization back and forth between divergent and convergent processes is a part of what Heifetz (1994, p. 22) calls "adaptive work." Adaptive work is about learning. It is the kind of learning that a person or a group must do when there is a gap between their script and emergent reality.

The role of the change agent in adaptive work is to nurture deep, fundamental change. This requires that we get outside the normalized expectations. Heifeitz suggests five principles to help people do adaptive work:

1. Identify the adaptive challenge. Diagnose the situation in light of the values at stake, and unbundle the issues that come with it.
2. Keep the level of distress within a tolerable range for doing adaptive work. To use the pressure cooker analogy, keep the heat up without blowing up the vessel.
3. Focus attention on ripening issues and not on stress-reducing distractions. Identify which issues can currently engage attention; and while directing attention to them, counteract work-avoidance mechanisms like denial, scapegoating, externalizing the enemy, pretending the problem is technical, or attacking individuals rather than issues.
4. Give the work back to people, but at a rate they can stand. Place and develop responsibility by putting the pressure on the people with the problem.
5. Protect voices of leadership without authority. Give cover to those who raise hard questions and generate distress—people who point to the internal contradictions of the society. These individuals often will have latitude to provoke rethinking that authorities do not have. [Heifetz, 1994, p. 128]

The Role of Resistance in ACT

The above five steps are logical but, admittedly, not easy. Distorting the system brings a reaction. That reaction can be potent. In the normalized worldview, we expect resistance and look for ways to prevent or control it. In that worldview, resistance is where the change process often ends.

ACT suggests another perspective. Resistance is not where transcendence ends or even where it stops off for a while, but where it begins. We need to think of resistance as an essential part of gestation. The oak emerges when the shell of the acorn cracks and the seed and the soil begin to interpenetrate. Palmer (1998, p. 165) tells us that the resistance itself calls for variation. Our encounter with resistance is the signal that we need still another pattern of behavior, another choice, as it were. The resistance requires more mindfulness. As long as the change agent maintains commitment to his or her purpose, the resistance will require the agent to imagine still new alternatives.

Think of resistance as a feedback loop in which the change agent and the resisting system are joined in creative tension. One is the acorn and one is the soil. As they interpenetrate, they gain the potential to move to still another level of complexity and integration. A self-organizing system is in place. Those who know how to facilitate significant change not only don't avoid resistance, they seek it, knowing how essential it is for the transformational process to be successful.

ACT recognizes that tension drives a system forward. The change agent is immersed in a nonlinear process of improvisation. All efforts at deep change are efforts in improvisation: There is a commitment to an important purpose, but there is no prior knowledge of how to get there. In organizational change efforts, this is seldom understood. If it is understood, it is not something that can be discussed. Everyone must pretend that they know what they are doing, when in fact they do not. The normal expectation is to appear to be in control, but now we know that this kind of posturing prevents the vital dialogue that is so necessary to the successful collective learning process.

Transformational change agents recognize the improvisational process. They are not afraid to admit that they are improvising and that they are behaving in ways that facilitate it. Van de Ven and his colleagues cite a passage from a speech by Dr. William Coyne, a senior vice president from 3M, probably the most innovative large company in the world of business:

> Innovation . . . is anything but orderly. It is sensible, in that our efforts are all directed at reaching our goals, but the organization . . . and the process . . . and sometimes the people can be chaotic. We are managing in chaos, and this is the right way to manage if you want innovation. It's been said that the competition never knows what we are going to come up with next. The fact is, neither do we. [Quoted in Van de Ven, Polley, Garud, and Vendataraman, 1999, Chapter 7]

This claim about the improvisational process is confirmed by the empirical literature. From the study of transformational actors in the middle levels of organizations, researchers report that real change leaders recognize the need to disturb the system and practice improvisation (Katzenbach and associates, 1995). They understand that after implementation, there is a need to increase the "mass and velocity" of the process, and after a certain point there is no turning back. The system is at the edge. It becomes necessary continually to improvise and experiment, striving to keep the momentum by working "a constantly changing mix of initiatives." The real change agents use whatever tools are available in whatever way they can. They learn their way forward, hovering at the edge of chaos.

So in the end, systems move to new levels of complexity because they are disturbed. Yet there is a basic irony about all this, since systems are designed to prevent disturbances, that is, to help each person within the system maintain a steady course. Even so, human collectives can never transform until someone cares enough, and dares enough, to deviate and disturb them. Remember, disturbing a system normally triggers resistance. And here we encounter yet another underlying irony, that as long as we are guided by normal assumptions, resistance marks the end of change, raising the specter of fear and dampening any enthusiasm for taking further action toward change.

The sacred servants understood all this. Jesus and Gandhi warn us how severe the risks can be. Dr. King tells us that direct action requires self-purification, something the other two also advocated. Only after we have purified ourselves can we be clear enough about our purpose and our commitment to go forward with all that the transformational entails. Only then can we see the wisdom of disturbing the system and ultimately joining others in the dance of resistance and transformation. Only then do we learn to trust a process that is far bigger than any one of us.

CHAPTER EIGHT

SURRENDER TO THE EMERGENT PROCESS

The Seventh Seed Thought:
Surrender to the Emergent Process

JESUS   *But beware of men: for they will deliver you up to the*
             councils, and they will scourge you in their synagogues;
             And ye shall be brought before governors and kings for my
             sake. . . . But when they deliver you up, take no thought
             how or what ye shall speak: for it shall be given you in
             that same hour what ye shall speak.
             [Matthew 10:17–19]

GANDHI   *History teaches us that men who are in the whirlpool . . .*
             will have to work out their destiny within it.
             [Iyer, 1990, p. 89]

KING   *Heraclitus argued that justice emerges from the strife of oppo-*
             sites, and Hegel . . . preached a doctrine of growth through
             struggle. It is both historically and biologically true that there
             can be no birth and growth without pains. Whenever there is
             emergence of the new we confront the recalcitrance of the old.
             [King, (1968) 1986, p. 135]

The Disturbed System and the Emergent Process

In the above statements, each of the sacred servants describes a disturbed system and an emergent process. Dr. King recognizes that improvement can only emerge from the interplay of oppositions. He indicates that growth emerges from struggle and from pain.

Pain is a part of development. Almost any experienced coach has used the phrase, "No pain, no gain." Youngsters of every age understand what this means. Yet because growth is painful and because our normal assumption is to avoid pain, we sometimes avoid the path to growth.

Gandhi understood that fundamental decisions create a tumultuous whirlpool and that it is within such a whirlpool that people grow the most. Living in a turbulent system requires that people become mindful of the emergent realities. He understood that when we have to work out our destinies within a disturbed system, we can, like the jazz musicians discussed in the last chapter, become more conscious and more creative.

The sacred servants suggest that we should trust the emergent process. Jesus tells his disciples that their behavior will disturb the system and they will be brought to stand before authority figures. He then advises them to not worry but to trust the process: "Take no thought how or what ye shall speak: for it shall be given you in that same hour what ye shall speak." To someone operating within the normalized reality, this is an incomprehensible notion. If you tell me I will know what to say at a moment of great challenge and high risk to my personal well-being, when my fears are the greatest, I become skeptical at best. In fact, my own experience seems to tell me that Jesus' advice to his disciples is not true. Too often when we are challenged by authority figures, especially those who do not have our best interests at heart—we do not find the right words. Yet the sacred servants tell us that if we change our state of being, we can transcend the shackles of fear, and in such a state we will enter the transformational reality and accomplish transformational deeds.

Inviting Others to Transcend Their Scripts

Helping others see what is possible is a great service. I sometimes refer to this as the *bold-stroke capacity*. When someone is in a transformational state, they see things with a simplicity that is conferred only to those who have transcended complexity. They have a view of the system that is both profoundly deep and profoundly simple. Because they have a deep understanding, they can offer an image, make a statement, or ask a question and the world changes. By using these tools, they get others to reframe their assumptions. When the assumptions or meaning system changes, the behavior changes.

From Asia come stories of transformation in which a single sage changed the world with a simple action. Consider the example of the old Zen master who sits eating in the public diner. Several thugs enter and begin to harass people. They approach his table where the old man sits peacefully. They begin to harass him as well. He says nothing, but picks up his chopsticks and, without looking, captures a bothersome fly. The thugs watch this action, conclude that such a man should not be disturbed, and then quietly leave. With a single act he has transformed their meaning systems and altered their behavior.

From the Judeo-Christian tradition, we get many such stories. One of the most famous is the episode of Solomon giving a single instruction, "Cut the baby in half and give half to each woman who claims to be its mother." One woman is pleased and the other horrified; the dilemma is thus easily resolved. Solomon awards the child to the woman who values the child's life. In an episode we have already covered, a crowd taunts Jesus about an adulterous woman, and he replies, "Let he who is without sin cast the first stone." The crowd quickly disperses. Each of these stories is about a person who understands deeply and can therefore move the group from one reality to another.

The cynic will argue that although these are cute stories illustrating spiritual beliefs, they have little application in the real world. This is true—or partially so. We seldom see transformational change agents such as these in our everyday lives. Yet they are there. When this kind of change does occur, the results are dramatic. Consider some examples.

A Bold Stroke at Coke

Ram Charan and Noel Tichy (1998) wrote a book entitled, *Every Business Is a Growth Business*. Their perspective is decidedly transformational. They argue that no organization is healthy unless it is growing, and there is no excuse for not growing. They claim there is no such thing as a "mature" industry. There are infinite opportunities for growth and change. Further, they argue that any organization that is not growing robs individuals who are participating in that company of opportunities for growth. By default, anyone who stays with such a company has chosen slow death.

Once a company falls into the no-growth rut, the better people leave, further reinforcing the lack of growth. A healthy organization is a growing organization. The problem is that organizations, like people, have scripts that restrict adaptation and growth. The leaders of such organizations cannot get into the "creative mode," nor can they determine what "they truly want to create; thus, in essence, becoming true to themselves."

Charan and Tichy's book begins with a story about Roberto Goizueta, who transformed the Coca Cola company in the early 1980s. The entire transformation of that organization begins with a distortion in the collective script. This happened because a change agent with a transformational mindset asked a bold-stroke question:

> By now, most people have forgotten just how bad Coca Cola looked when Goizueta took over. The company dominated the U.S. soft drink market with roughly a 35 percent share, and everyone knew the market was mature. The game they were engaged in involved fighting for tenths of a percent of market share—at exorbitant cost to the bottom line—or defending each tenth of a percent, since PepsiCo was kicking Coca Cola's can in marketing. Security analysts and business writers were all but composing its obituary.
>
> Goizueta didn't buy it. But how does one break the mindset of a mature business and jog loose the deeply ingrained set of beliefs that curbs everyone's thoughts and hopes, dulling their minds and slaying their imaginations? Goizueta recognized that Coca Cola was full of talented people butting their heads against a stone wall—the inexorable logic of squeezing out drops of market share in a zero-sum game.
>
> Goizueta had a simple but stunningly powerful insight that he shared with his senior executives in the 1980s. He asked almost casually, what was the average per-capita daily consumption of fluids by the world's 4.4 billion people? The answer was 64 ounces. And what, he asked, is the daily per-capita consumption of Coca Cola? Answer: Less than 2 ounces.
>
> Finally, he asked, What's our market share of the stomach? Not Coca Cola's share of the U.S. cola market or the world soft drink market but what is the market share of all the fluids that everyone

in the world drinks on a given day. Coca Cola's share was scarcely measurable.

Coca Cola's people had invested a lot in the idea that PepsiCo was their enemy. But Goizueta led them to see that the enemy was coffee, milk, and tea. The enemy was water.

With a few simple questions, Goizueta redefined Coca Cola's market to be larger than anybody had imagined. And he changed the psychology of its people. They saw that their company was not a large fish constrained to a small pond which they shared with PepsiCo, but a small fish in a huge pond shared by every possible source of fluids that the world population consumed on any given day. Rather than facing the depressing chore of struggling to not lose more fractions of their small potential market to PepsiCo, they began setting their sights on winning a larger share of the total consumption of fluids that people drank each and every day.

Obvious? Maybe. But it wasn't quite so obvious until Goizueta pointed it out. It was the beginning of Coca Cola's transformation from a threatened leader in a mature business to the greatest market value creator ever. (Goizueta's stock holdings at the time of his death were worth over $1 billion, making him the first "hired hand," or non founding head of a company, to become a billionaire.) [Charan and Tichy, 1998, pp. 4–5]

As I read this story, I am most impressed with Goizueta. "What is our market share of the stomach?" This is a wonderful example of a bold-stroke question. In a single statement, he distorts the collective script and puts the company into a divergent cycle. This question is not at all obvious. This is genius. This is a human being that is "empowered and empowering to the community."

As an administrator or consultant reading the above story from a normalized worldview, my first reaction to Goizueta's statement would be to admire the power of the metaphor. Then I would ask, how can I use this creative notion? How can my organization find its version of water? This would be a powerful question with potentially transformational results. It is, however, not likely to be transformational. This may sound like a contradiction, but I believe that the transformational challenge is not to think like Goizueta.

I have known many CEOs of large companies. Most of them show brilliance in one or more areas of analysis. Yet few of them operate in a transformational way. Transformational power is not a function of high IQ, or complex, strategic analysis. Transformation is not about thinking, per se. It is about our state of being, who we are, how we view the world and our own lives. Transformation tends to be stimulated by a person in a state of committed service to a significant purpose! When we have Goizueta's commitment, the chances of articulating a transformational image, of providing the correct bold stroke, will dramatically increase. The state of being we are in determines the reality in which we operate.

Transformation begins with a state of being, not logical analysis. The most important part of Goizueta's story is unwritten. To do what he did in our own context, we should not try to imitate his technique but his commitment. Imitation seldom brings transformation. What we need to replicate is the personal agony that got him to his bold stroke. When we replicate his journey of personal transcendence, we will truly understand his capacity for distorting the collective script and be able to come up with our own version of it. We will come up with our own metaphor, or some equivalent bold-stroke tool. Above all, we will not be imitating anyone's idea or technique.

If we truly grasp this concept of the bold stroke we will totally refocus how we think about change agents. Right now, the transformational leadership literature is like the literature on innovation (last chapter). It is about boxes, arrows, and flow charts. Leadership, like innovation, is a messy process. It is not captured in lists of behaviors connected in causal diagrams. Those lists will not bring extraordinary results in our context.

Let's return to the list of the twelve messy processes of the innovation journey, listed in Chapter Seven. Imagine that we could actually have access the story of the personal journey that brought Goizueta to the moment when he asked his momentous question. Suppose that we documented the story as Van de Ven and his colleagues documented the innovation journey (last chapter). What we would have is a complex story in which convergent and divergent processes were unfolding at multiple levels of analysis. We would have a story with many interrelated butterflies flapping their wings. We could hypothesize that Goizueta transcended his own scripts in order to survive the "whirlpool." Yet the whirlpool is an important part of the story. Goizueta and the whirlpool became one. My hypothesis is that he trusted the process; the key image emerged at the right moment. It was "given in the same hour."

Norma Rae in the Moment of Truth

The above case has a troubling aspect that begs our attention. When the change agent in a transformational story is the CEO, it makes people wary, me included. We read a story like Goizueta's and we say, "He was the CEO. Of course he got transformational results! That's what CEOs do. But that story does not apply to me, a normal person."

I contend that we do not have to be a CEO or a consultant to be a change agent. On the contrary, we all need to have the capacities for being transformational. So let me share a story with you, dressed in the garments of a frustrated, working-class woman.

The woman in this story had no formal authority and only a high school education. She would never have described herself as a heroic type but as an average person caught up in all the normalized transactions of small-town, factory life. Yet she enters the whirlpool, transcends her scripts, and comes to the moment of the bold stroke. She transforms her organization in the same way Goizueta transformed the Coca Cola company.

This story is portrayed in the movie, *Norma Rae*. The tale begins in a nonunionized textile mill where conditions are very poor. Our heroine is an attractive young woman with a feisty personality. She has two children: one from a former marriage, the other from a short-term affair. She is also in the process of ending a relationship with a married man. Her mother and father both work at the same mill where Norma Rae works. After all, this is the largest single employer in this small southern town.

Like the rest of us, Norma Rae lives in a transactional world. She lives with her parents, and her father worries about how her inappropriate behavior will affect the family. The implied transactional exchange is that he provides a home for her and, in return, she should behave in a way that reflects well on the family.

When Norma Rae tells her lover she is breaking off her relationship with him, he recites the litany of all the meals, gifts, and sexual satisfaction he has provided for her. He becomes enraged that she would cut off the sexual favors he expects in return. He then physically abuses her.

Meanwhile, Norma Rae is causing all kinds of problems for her employers. She continually complains about conditions at the factory. To stop her constant complaints, the boss proposes an exchange. He promotes her from machine worker to spot checker, where she monitors the work of the other employees. He expects that giving her this more responsible position will stop her complaints, but this distortion sets into motion another set of transactional expectations. Among her coworkers, there are norms of loyalty and equity. When she becomes a spot checker, her coworkers reject her because in their eyes Norma Rae has become part of management. Because she puts a high value on social acceptance she gives up her promotion and returns to her machine. Her peers immediately welcome her back.

Norma Rae begins dating someone new. When he proposes marriage to her, he points out that he does not owe anyone anything; he eats anything that is put in front of him; he can fix anything electrical; he just got a new job at the gas station; he hands his paycheck over to her every week; and he comes straight home at night. He tells her she has two children but no one to take care of her. He has one child but no one to take care of the two of them. Maybe they could help each other out. Norma Rae thinks about this and replies, "It has been a long time between offers." She accepts. Later, tensions grow between them. He points out that she is not meeting his expectations in terms of the meals, the laundry, the kids, and his physical needs. These are normalized expectations, and she is violating them.

As the story unfolds, nearly every interaction she has with a man has sexual overtones. The transactional expectations are traditional expectations for a young, single woman living in a small factory town. The transactional expectations help form her personal script. They teach her who she is. As she meets the expectations, she becomes what is expected. Where she strays from the norm, she is punished. Many times she is willing to pay the price of defiance. Many times she is not. Like the rest of us, she is a normal person pursuing hopes and fleeing fears.

Into this Southern Baptist town comes a Jewish union organizer. His name is Ruben. He is dedicated to the cause of unionization and has years of experience. He has a passionate interpersonal style and a great compassion for people and for living on the edge of chaos. In every relationship, he disturbs the scripts. He has a talent for pushing people up to the edge, but not over it. He has a clear sense of who he is and a courageous commitment to progress. As his relationship with Norma Rae develops, he conveys no sexual expectations. He does not treat her as an object. He does communicate strong expectations around her commitment to the union cause.

She responds to his expectations and begins to work hard to improve life at the factory. When her father dies in the plant, her efforts in the cause of unionization intensify. At this point, she too begins pushing people. Her efforts, however, become noxious. She pushes too hard and relationships are endangered. She does not know how to hold the edge. Here Ruben, the demanding mentor, urges her to soften. He wants people to be hovering at the edge, not tumbling over it.

In the meantime, the two of them create disruptions that stimulate both negative and positive feedback loops. Many of the institutions and centers of power push back on them. Many people complain and renounce their behavior. In spite of the resistance they are experiencing, Norma Rae and her friend hold to their purpose and the resulting tensions push everyone outside their scripts. Soon the whole town is in turmoil.

The turbulence peaks when the company posts a letter designed to splinter the workforce. It suggests that the black workers are all joining the union and will then dictate what all the white workers can do. This racist ploy provokes physical violence. Ruben tells Norma that the letter is against the law and that they now have management where they want them. Ruben, however, must have a copy of the letter and he is not allowed in the plant, where the letter has been posted.

Norma tries to copy the letter, but is only partially successful. It is made very clear to her that if she doesn't cease her efforts to unionize the workers, she will lose her job. Frightened, she confronts Ruben and tells him that she is going to stop her efforts. She argues that she has three kids and needs a paycheck. Ruben, however, will hear none of her fears, pointing to the bigger stakes. Convinced that he is right, she walks back into the plant and conspicuously copies the letter. The plant manager shows up and confronts her. She continues to copy the letter. When she finishes, he orders her to his office. After another confrontation, he orders her out of the plant.

She leaves the office, followed by a security guard. Instead of leaving the plant, she walks back to her machine. He grabs her arm and says, "Come on Norma Rae." She pulls away and screams that she will not leave until the sheriff comes to take her out. At this point she is at an emotional peak. She pauses for a moment, and then Norma Rae becomes Goizueta, a transformational sage.

She jumps up on a table, bends over, picks up a piece of cardboard, and writes *Union* on it. She then stands with the sign over her head and turns slowly around and around. This goes on for several minutes with all the workers watching her. Finally, one woman turns off her machine. After a time, so does another, and then another. Eventually all the machines are shut down. The factory comes to a complete halt. A few days later, the workforce votes to unionize.

An Analysis

Norma Rae engaged in a bold stroke. The bold stroke reframed the way all the workers thought. She, like Goizueta, transformed her organization. From where did the strategy come? Did she reason out the cause-and-effect relationships? Did she assume that copying the letter would lead to being ordered out of the plant, that on her way out she could stop at her machine, be pulled away, and then jump on a table and hold up a sign? Did she know that holding up a sign in that situation would stimulate people to turn off their machines? Did she assume that turning off the machines would galvanize the vote for unionization? No. None of that. She did not understand any of these causes and effects. She could not predict even a minute into the future. Norma Rae was in the whirlpool, and she did the only thing she could think of doing. She pursued her commitment in a turbulent system. At the critical moment, she simply stood in her truth. She got up on that table because she was committed, not because she knew the result.

Now here is a heretical thought. Leadership is not about results. It is about commitment. The entire management literature fails to understand this. Leadership authors do not understand that leadership means "Go forth to die." If they did understand it, they would not be enticed to write about it—because people do not want to hear this message. Most people want to be told how to get extraordinary results with minimum risk. They want to know how to get out-of-the box results with in-the-box courage. These are the questions of the normalized world. Most management authors do their best to deliver what they perceive that most readers are looking for. They tend to adhere to the basic assumption that if we examine the leadership of someone who is currently held up as a model, we can work backwards, and find the secrets of their success. Then all we have to do is copy the behavior of the successful person and we will meet with similar success.

Although profiling our heroines and heroes in this way can be helpful, it misses the key point—that the successful person got the result he or she desired because that person went forth to die. That is, the change agent held to fundamental commitments throughout turbulent and uncomfortable processes. The protagonist did not consciously and deliberately create the results we see. The transformational result emerges when commitment meets resistance. Goizueta learned his way to the great question just as Norma Rae learned her way to the sign on table. Analysis and planning did not play a big role. Each of them learned what they had to know in real time, risking a great deal and not always knowing what results their actions would bring.

The bold stroke is usually unique. It is not something we can imitate because it arises from a complex network of events and interactions that in most cases would be impossible to predict. The bold stroke requires extraordinary commitment, comparable to a soldier leading a charge. IQ and authority are largely irrelevant. Integrity is indispensable. Transformational change agents behave according to the highest level of moral reasoning. This behavior leads them to create an original self and an original world. In this sense, they are profound creators.

Some will argue that Norma Rae was hardly a moral giant. In fact, her sexual behavior suggests that she had loose morals. Some of us might consider such acts a justification for stoning. Others of us might simply consider it justification for differentiating ourselves from her. The fact is, when she reached the level of commitment wherein she was totally inner driven and other focused, she reached a state of perfect integrity. Reaching that transformational stage changed who she was.

Interestingly, after she stood on the table, she was arrested. Ruben made bail and took her home to her husband. In a discussion with Ruben, the husband complained that Norma Rae had changed. Ruben replies, "She stood up on that table, and now she is a free woman. Maybe you can live with that, and maybe you can't." The husband considers this, struggles with the concept, but finally makes the commitment to support her in her efforts for as long as she lives. Norma feels the depth of this commitment and reacts to it by drawing closer to her husband. Their marital relationship is thus lifted to a higher level of fundamental commitment.

Ruben's statement about Norma being free is insightful. Jesus taught, "If ye continue in my word, then are ye my disciples indeed; And ye shall know the truth and the truth shall make you free" (John 8:31–32). This suggests that commitment brings action in the face of uncertainty, action brings learning, and learning makes us free. When the cause to which she was committed met resistance, Norma Rae had to stand in her truth. She had to live by principle in the face of fear. When she did this, her state of being changed and she entered a new level of reality. In that reality she found a new view of the world. She also had a new view and a new definition of self. She had increased self-esteem and increased cognitive complexity. She was free because she increased control of her own co-creation. She was more internally driven and other focused. She could make choices that were not available previously.

Was Norma Rae perfect in a final sense? No. Was she at a higher level of moral reasoning than are we who would have dissociated ourselves from her? Yes. Will she stay there? No. Can she get there again? Yes. Will it be easier? Perhaps.

Life is a journey. As we saw in an earlier chapter, we can obtain the path to collective fulfillment, and then return to a much more self-focused mode. History is filled with destructive people who took the hero's journey and then became obsessed with self-interested and destructive domination of others. The journey is complex and it is never over.

Saving a Software Project

Kurt Wright (1998) tells of working as a consultant for a huge software project. It involved a $100 million government contract. The 400 engineers were thirty-eight months into a sixty–month schedule. The technical requirements were very complex, and the schedule slipped every month. The project was already eighteen months behind. Anxiety was reaching a peak because of a clause in the contract. There was a $30 million penalty if the contract was 18 months behind at the forty-eighth month milestone. Disaster thus lurked a mere ten months into the future.

As a reader, you might pause and ask yourself how you would approach this situation. If you are operating in the normal model, your list of ideas reflects a single underlying assumption: There is a problem that needs to be solved. This, of course, is the underlying assumption in every action that is being taken in the current system. Every discussion is designed to identify and solve the problem. In fact, the single question that drives the system is, "What is wrong?"

Wright says his objective was to change the foundation of the meaning system. He believed that if he could change the underlying question, he could transcend this seemingly impossible challenge. What was needed was to get every person operating on the same positive vision. He needed to galvanize everyone's efforts. Wright believed that the key was a new question. From the perspective of the normalized world, he made an absurd assumption: If he could find a bold-stroke question, the system would correct itself without further effort. This is the same strange assumption that Youngblood made about the warehouse inventory process that we discussed in Chapter Seven.

The bold-stroke question had to be outside the established norm. It had to be engaging enough to "capture everyone's imagination and lead to *wholehearted* commitment." Such a question would not come from his thinking about it. It required that he engage in and trust the interactive process. To get things started, he held a series of two-day retreats with eighteen to twenty engineers in each one. In the second week, the question he was seeking dawned on him: "What will it take to finish this project a week early?"

On the surface, this was a ridiculous question, and it was not well accepted. After a time, angry managers began to summon Wright to their offices. They would explain that he was losing his credibility and was going to get himself into trouble. Each time, he thanked them for their concern. Then he went back into the halls and asked the same question.

What was the outcome? Wright finished his work in six weeks, using only $90,000 of his $150,000 budget. Months later, the project finished on time and was $15 million under budget. Since the penalty was also avoided, Wright claims that his silly question was in fact worth $45 million.

Wright's question, like Goizueta's question and like Norma Rae standing on the table with her sign, disturbed the collective script and captured the imagination. It invited people to join him on a journey of common commitment. Once that commitment reached a critical mass, the project was like my blindfold exercise. It was like the warehouse inventory. It was self-organizing and transformational.

Trusting the process means more than what I just described. Transformation requires the change agent to become a metaphor for the metamorphosis. Wright did exactly that. Notice that he did not do a complex analysis. Instead, he simply searched for the right question. Yet how did he search? He held some retreats and engaged in dialogue until he knew. He surrendered himself to the process. He practiced action learning. He modeled what he wanted the system to do.

It is important to note that in later cases he never uses the same question. In each intervention that he goes into he becomes at one with the system, and then waits for a new question to emerge. He does not try to repeat his own thinking or the thinking of anyone else. He searches for the unique question that will give rise to shared vision and self-organization.

Transcending the First Law of Nature

The critics will ask, "But what of the risks? Trusting the process can be disastrous. What if Norma Rae had been fired or even killed? What if Wright's question had no impact? Many people take risks and fail. Isn't this perspective dangerous?"

The answer is yes, it is dangerous. Failure is a high probability. Leadership means go forth to die. Normal people do not do it because they have nothing worth dying for. The transformational person will argue, "Until we have something worth dying for, we have nothing worth living for." Transactional people often live lives of "quiet desperation." It was Maslow who pointed out that a transformational person has a vision, and death is an acceptable alternative, because if the vision lives, the transformational person lives. The transformational person is focused on something bigger than self. One of the most incomprehensible aspects of the transformational perspective is that personal survival is not the first law of nature. In this sense the transformational change agent becomes different from all other animals.

Self-Organization and the Role of Shared Vision

ACT suggests that when a critical mass of people internalizes a shared mindset, centralized leadership becomes unnecessary. The system will self-organize. This is difficult to comprehend and threatening in its implication. Yet understanding this notion can greatly increase our capacity to facilitate transformation. Consider an example.

One of my favorite parts of the movie *Gandhi* is a series of scenes that occur near the end of his life. At one point, he has all of India moving toward revolution against Great Britain. There are, however, acts of violence on the part of the Indians. Gandhi finds this unacceptable. His strategy is to provoke or disturb the system and then absorb the painful reaction. The change agent must not retaliate or compromise his purpose. The violent acts violated the high standard of nonviolence for which he stood. He declares that the violence must be stopped. His colleagues think this is impossible. Many argue that the people are inflamed and will not stop. Gandhi says he will repent for his part in the loss of life. He promises that he will fast until he dies or until the violence stops. And so he does fast for days and nearly dies. Remarkably, all of India comes to a halt. Many Indian politicians, thinking in transactional terms, consider this tragic. India deserves to be free, and the British deserve to die, just as many Indians have died. The process is just and fair.

Fairness is at the heart of conventional, moral reasoning. Such notions of justice are at the heart of the transactional model. Gandhi was operating at a higher level of moral reasoning.

Shortly after he has recovered from his fast, Gandhi is sentenced to prison. He goes willingly and serves for several years. When he comes out of prison, he determines again to provoke the system. He announces that he will march 200 miles to the sea.

There, in violation of British law, he will make salt. He sees salt as an important symbol. The sea belongs to India and yet Indians are not allowed to make salt. They must buy it from the British. During the march, he calls on all Indians to raise the flag of free India. The British decide to ignore the entire process.

Gandhi begins the march from his ashram. A reporter named Walker accompanies him. Walker writes for the *New York Times*. There are some British officers standing nearby. Walker asks whether an arrest will end the process.

"Not if they arrest me and a thousand others. It is not only generals who can plan campaigns," Gandhi replies.

Walker then asks, "What if they do not respond?"

Gandhi replies, "It is the function of a civil resistor to provoke, and we will continue to provoke until they respond or change the law. They are not in control. We are."

Here we might stop for a moment and think about this exchange. Is Gandhi correct? Is it possible for a process such as this to continue without its leaders? This would seem counterintuitive at best. How does Gandhi's theory of provocation align with complexity theory? Finally, and what is most important, how is it possible for one old man in India to be in control when his foe is the entire British Empire?

Gandhi is in control. The British are trapped in the assumptions of transactional thinking. They do not have the cognitive complexity to match Gandhi. Gandhi sees more deeply. The British mind operates within the system of exchange, that is, within technical and political reality. Gandhi transcends the system of exchange. He operates from the assumptions of transformational reality. He is empowered and empowering to the community. His world is co-created by the application of a higher level of moral reasoning. He is inner directed and other focused. He understands and trusts the transformational process. By being the metaphor for metamorphosis, the vision has now been widely internalized. The process does not need leadership. It will unfold as a self-organizing, emergent system.

The march to the sea is successful. World reaction embarrasses the British, and the viceroy meets with his generals. The generals report that salt is being made everywhere. The leaders of congress are selling salt on the street.

The viceroy orders the process stopped. He wants everyone but Gandhi arrested. The theory is to cut Gandhi's support out from under him and then deal with him later. In the scene that follows, a general reports that they have arrested nearly 100,000 people. All the leaders and all their families are in jail, and yet the process goes on. The enraged viceroy asks, "Who is leading them?" The baffled general answers that he does not know. He shakes his head and says, "We have even arrested Nehru's mother." At this point the British are experiencing but cannot comprehend the phenomenon of self-organization.

In the meantime, Gandhi has announced that the next day he will lead a march on the Dharasana Salt Works with the expressed purpose of closing it down. The viceroy orders Gandhi's arrest and demands that the salt works be kept open at all costs. In the next remarkable scene, hundreds of people line up outside the salt works. A man gives a simple speech. "They expect us to lose heart or to fight back; we will do neither." Then the first row of men walks slowly into the British lines, where they are clubbed and beaten. The women drag them away and apply first aid. The next row of men takes a deep breath and walks slowly into the clubs. The brutal, but inspiring, process continues.

Through it all, Walker is recording the event. He eventually goes to a phone and dictates the following story to the *New York Times*.

Without any hope of escape from injury or death, it went on and on and into the night. Women carried the wounded and broken bodies from the road until they dropped from exhaustion. But still it went on and on. Whatever moral ascendancy the West held was lost here today. India is free. She has taken all that steel and cruelty can give and she has neither cringed nor retreated.

In fact, it would take several more years before the British formally withdrew. But this amazing display of courage mattered as much as Walker suggests. It took place with Gandhi and all of India's formal leaders in jail. The system had become self-organizing.

Here again the critic might argue that Gandhi's goal was the unification of all India, yet once he died the system did not self-organize. The original India is still divided between Pakistan and India. This is correct. Gandhi ran out of time on unification. This does not negate the fact, however, that this man conquered the government of South Africa and later the entire British Empire. Gandhi changed the world. What is more important, he left a vision for the rest of us to ponder. In doing so he provided a service to all humankind for as long as history is written. Because of that service, the rest of us are more likely to achieve the transformational state of being.

Surrendering to the Process

Surrendering oneself to the process is a very difficult concept. It violates one of the primary rules of the normalized model: "Always appear to be in control." It therefore tends to be terrifying, and many people avoid trying. I have great faith in this concept and I am often willing to "walk naked into the land of uncertainty" (Quinn, 1996). And yet my experience falls into two categories: I sometimes do this with complete confidence and sometimes in complete terror. Let me share two examples. I will start with the confident version of surrender.

Once a group of doctoral students asked my colleague and me to talk to them about teaching. We agreed. The session began with a question. They asked, "How do you prepare for your classes?" My colleague told them that on a teaching day, he gets up at four A.M. and spends about six hours getting ready. Then he went into an analysis of the six-hour process. They took careful notes. After a while, they turned to me and asked how much time I spend preparing. I responded, "I do not prepare because there is never a time when I am not preparing." They stared at me as if I had come from another planet.

I explained that my courses are designed not to inform but to transform. I do not want my students to leave the course with only information. I want them to leave with an increased capacity to change the world. That means creating an environment where they are more likely to choose to empower themselves. Dispensing information is a very minor part of my classes. Instead, my classes are carefully designed to call forth divergent processes. I try to disturb the scripts of the class. I try simultaneously to challenge and support them. I do not prepare any lectures. Instead, I try to prepare myself to be fully present, to ask the right questions at the right time, and give them assignments that facilitate transformation.

Again, they looked at me as if I was from another planet. They asked me no more questions. Instead, they turned back to ask more questions of my colleague. No one there had any idea what I was talking about, and no one was very interested. I assumed that my time was wasted. Then, two days later, there was a knock on my door. It was my colleague. He wanted to explore my strange ideas.

The reaction of the students is very understandable. They have internalized the normal model of teaching: The expectation is to be an expert, gather information, and dispense it in an elegant way. I was suggesting two incomprehensible notions:

1. Be the message that you are trying to convey.
2. If you are clear on your purpose and in your design, then preparation is not about information, it is about being in the right state of being.

If you are there to transform the students, you will know what to say at the appropriate time. If you are always preparing in a transformational sense, there is no need to prepare in a normal sense.

This is not just a clever or cute philosophy. This is something I practice all the time. I thus walk into the classroom with the intention of surrendering to the conversational process. I do this with complete confidence. I have only a general sense of what will happen in the class, but I know that the class session will be very successful. Somewhere, my faith in this process turned to knowledge. I am certain about the outcome of the uncertain process.

Contrast this process to the same process in a different context. In Chapter Six, I recounted the story of a major intervention in a Fortune 500 company. Every other week for eight weeks we met with over a hundred of the top executives. The company was under great pressure and much was at stake. In Chapter Six, I described how the CEO came to hear the organizational voice and was able to articulate a vision. However, hidden within that story is another story that I did not reveal.

Each week, the hundred or so people arrived carrying a great deal of negative emotion. Our job as consultants was to take them through a cathartic process, facilitate the emergence of a common mindset, and commit them to a positive plan of action. We had a design, but it was very fluid. At every break, my colleagues and I would meet, assess where the group was, then make real-time decisions about what to do next. We would often decide that the person in charge of the next session should make an alteration of some sort. These decisions were almost always right, and the person taking the risk almost always succeeded. In the first two weeks, both groups turned around by the middle of the week and became very productive.

Everyone warned us that the third week would be the real challenge. In this company, there was a particular function, human resources, that played a Gestapo role. The wrong sentence uttered in the presence of someone from human resources could be a career stopper. People worked in terror of being in the same room with anyone from that function. On the third week, the head of human resources would attend. People argued that the group would be far less candid and there would be little or no progress during the third week. They were right. The program started, and we worked much harder and showed less progress. As each day dragged by, we felt more concerned that we were going to fail. Wednesday came and went.

On the Thursdays of the first two programs, I had made presentations pieced together from previous materials, and they had been smash hits. I spent Wednesday evening worrying about the morning session of the third Thursday. On Thursday, five minutes before I was to present, the faculty members I was working with held a huddle. One of them looked me in the eye and said: "We are in deep trouble. They have not had a catharsis. They are still in a whining mode. This is our last real shot at them. You have to pull this off. You cannot present your material. You cannot present anything you have ever presented before. You need to just walk up there and do what they need."

I stared at him in disbelief. I was due on stage in two minutes. My first reaction was anger. "It is easy for you to say! You're not the one in the hot seat!" I quickly moved beyond that; I knew he was right. As soon as I admitted this to myself, my anger turned to terror. I took a deep breath, realizing, beyond a doubt, that this was what I taught others to do, to trust the process. I needed to take a leap of faith—my faith. This was what I did in normal classroom situations. I had faith in this process, so why was I scared? Because there was so much at stake, and I did not even know what the first word out of my mouth was going to be when I got out on the stage. More honestly, I was afraid of failure and humiliation.

It was a long walk out to face my audience. Once there I took a breath and started talking. I described the situation the company was in. I described the two previous weeks. I contrasted that with the present week. I shared the analysis about why people thought it was not working. I just kept telling them things that no one would normally dare make public. I even described the conversation with my associate before I stepped out in front of them and the decision I had made to walk naked into the land of uncertainty, to come onto the stage with intent of doing what they needed. I shared the terror I felt.

My confession grabbed their attention and held them. They were paying close attention. I told them I was willing to take this risk because I was committed to the future of the company. I then told them that the future of the company rested on what happened this morning, and without their complete cooperation we would all fail. I began to ask questions. People started to give bold answers. The system started to churn and the dialogue between participants became honest for the first time.

On the spot, I invented an exercise and gave them an assignment. They left the room. When I returned to my colleagues in the back of the room, one of them said, "It worked, we are going to make it!" I collapsed into a chair.

Why would I take the risk I did that day? I could have ignored the advice to go up on the stage empty. I could have presented the material I had prepared. Was I motivated by money? No. It was simply because walking up there empty was what was needed. They were a human group in great need. Over the several weeks I had worked with them I had become committed to them, and out of this commitment came a vision of noble purpose. I was willing to serve that purpose. I did not like walking up there naked, but I did understand Dr. King's claim that, "whenever there is emergence of the new we confront the recalcitrance of the old." I knew the group needed a metaphor to engender their own metamorphosis. I was the metaphor.

As I stood up there, I was internally driven and other focused. The group could feel my state of being. It was palpable at that moment. I was in the middle of Gandhi's whirlpool, and I was working out my destiny in that whirlpool. In doing that, I was mindful of every cue. As I interacted with those cues, I created in real time. What I needed to say was given me, as Jesus suggested, in the "same hour."

The more vulnerable I became, the more the group reached out to help, to join in making a contribution. We were in a trusting relationship pursuing a shared purpose together. We were building a complex object with blindfolds on. Suddenly we had to bring the truth to the surface. No one was afraid of the truth anymore. The old fears were now inconsequential. We joined each other in a search for a new script. By the time the crowd left the room, a new larger system was in place, and it was beginning to self-organize. My colleagues in the back of the room could feel the new system forming. It was forming because we had surrendered to the emergent process.

CHAPTER NINE

ENTICE THROUGH MORAL POWER

The Eighth Seed Thought: Entice Through Moral Power

JESUS   *If ye continue in my word, then are ye my disciples indeed;*
And ye shall know the truth, and the truth shall make you free.
[John 8:31–32]

GANDHI   *We shall never be able to raise the standard of public life through*
laws. Only if the lives of leaders . . . are perfect will they be able to
produce any effect on the people. Mere preaching will have no effect.
[Iyer, 1990, p. 411]

KING   *If our words fail, we will try to persuade with our acts. We will*
always be willing to talk and seek fair compromise, but we are ready
to suffer and even risk our lives to become witnesses to the truth.
[King, (1968) 1986, p. 103]

Becoming Perfect

All three of the above statements express the importance of providing an example of moral power. Gandhi observes that in trying to raise the collective standard, the normal strategy of telling (preaching) and forcing (through laws) is not likely to be effective. If we want the relationship, family, group, unit, organization, or society to perform at a higher standard, the change agent must become a model. To do this, Gandhi says, we must be perfect.

As soon as we read the word *perfect*, we tend to disregard Gandhi as unrealistic and impractical. Yet few humans have ever been so realistic and so practical as was Gandhi. When he speaks of perfection I doubt that he means flawless. I do not think he sees perfection as a final, static state. I think he sees perfection as a dynamic state, a state of becoming.

I believe that perfection is a dynamic state that we enter whenever we sense we are closing one of our hypocrisy gaps, thus becoming more perfect. When we exercise the courage to close an important gap, we experience victory over the self and become connected to a deeper reality. We also gain increased moral power. People see and are attracted by our increased integrity. Our state of being state and our reality change.

Norma Rae illustrated this in the last chapter. She exercised the courage to commit herself totally to the change she valued. In doing so, she surrendered to the emergent process. When she stood on the table, she modeled perfect integrity in the pursuit of her purpose. She then attracted others to a higher level of performance.

In closing her integrity gap, she took on a different state of being and became conscious of a higher reality than the one that exists at the transactional level. She had contact with a new truth. She saw in herself a capacity that exceeded her imagination. She also could see that altering herself could alter the world. There is a higher reality. The world is not inherently transactional. Many of her fears were unnecessary. These truths made her free of the transactional reality in which most of us are embedded. Given her new reality, she became empowered and empowering to her community. That more empowered community then had the potential to become a productive community.

When we do as Norma Rae did, we become more inner directed and other focused. Since we are more aligned with some higher standard, we become a living symbol of that standard and are able to attract others toward it. In joining with these others, we become a productive community. Because we feel deeply for those we seek to influence, when we see their imperfections we are slow to condemn and more likely to find that the imperfections we would criticize in others are also in ourselves. A process of mirroring thus emerges. We learn more about ourselves as we reach out to help others.

This kind of perfection is a fragile. We may easily lose it. Further, this perfection may be focused on a single ideal or set of beliefs but not extend into every other area of our lives. Even as we experience this perfection in our special mission in life, we may still be guilty of many personal flaws. We are likely to still have many hypocrisy gaps. Yet becoming momentarily perfect on one higher standard increases the likelihood that we will develop the courage to recognize and work on other hypocrisy gaps.

Dr. King's example in history suggests that as powerful as he was with words, it was his acts and his courage to confront his adversaries peacefully that persuaded and ultimately changed both his friends and his enemies. Both his words and his actions, however, reflected a deep commitment that included a willingness to suffer and even die for his higher cause. When we have such commitment, both our words and our acts increase in persuasiveness. We acquire greater moral power.

Jesus states that as his followers strive to live his teachings and follow his example, they can become disciples in deed. In other words, as they struggle to live by a higher set of standards, their behavior must change, and this requires a change in scripts. He says, "And ye shall know the truth, and the truth shall make you free." I interpret this to mean that striving to live a higher standard reduces our hypocrisy gaps. As we transcend our scripts, we increase our awareness of emergent reality, and from this we gain a profound sense of liberation. We are temporarily free of the scripts and fears associated with the transactional realm. We discover our core values. We more clearly see the potential in self and others. In this state, we naturally attract others to transcend their scripts.

Moral Power and the Transcendence of Normal Scripts

Several years ago I agreed to coach a fifth grade, recreation league basketball team. I coached the team for four years, and then coached a second team. The boys on the original team were good athletes. They were very bright and all had great leadership capacities. This sounds like the makings of a fine team. There was, however, a problem. These boys were as unforgiving as they were intense. When anyone made a mistake, the team jumped all over that person. The criticism was poisonous to teamwork, risk taking, and learning and development. After a week, we developed a very small set of rules. The number one rule was that no one but the coach could criticize the performance of any player. I told them that negative feedback was a legitimate tool, but if they watched me carefully they would see that for every corrective statement made to a player, they would hear four or five positive statements directed to him as well. In the meantime, each of them could only give positive statements.

Each week, for four years, I would review this rule, and point out that when one of them criticizes a teammate, performance goes down, not up. In the years that followed with the second team, the same rule was necessary and I became a firm believer in it. Given my belief in this rule, it is useful to review a most striking exception. It involves Larry Bird, the basketball player. The exception is seen in an instructive incident that occurred at the end of the 1984 season.

Bird's career began in 1981. That year he led the struggling Celtics to the NBA championship and was rookie of the year. In the years that followed, Bird was a regular first team all-star. He was also recognized as the most valuable player in the league. As the 1984 season began, Bird was obsessed with winning the championship that had eluded his team in 1982 and 1983.

In recalling that year, his teammates describe the extent of Bird's dedication. He would arrive on the practice floor an hour and a half early and stay an hour afterwards. During this time he would discipline himself, running drills and practicing the basic aspects of his game. Although Bird never said a word about it, the rest of the players soon followed his example. As the season started, Bird continued to set the example of self-discipline and self-sacrifice. He continually extended himself, throwing himself into the crowd in pursuit of loose balls, taking painful charges on defense, and generally hustling on every play. Again, Bird said nothing, yet the other players were soon doing the same. The Celtics ended up with the best record in the league and had little difficulty getting to the championship series.

That series featured the first championship match-up of the league's two greatest stars. It was Magic Johnson and the Lakers against Larry Bird and the Celtics. The media coverage was intense. The Lakers won the first game in Boston and then destroyed the Celtics in game three in Los Angeles. The Celtics were down two games to one, and had lost their home court advantage. The situation was most discouraging. At the end of that third game, the quiet Bird disturbed the system. In the interviews after the game, he severely criticized his teammates. Among other things, he accused them of playing without heart. His comments were broadcast worldwide. Given my rule forbidding my players to criticize each other, it is interesting to analyze what happened.

M. L. Carr, one of Bird's teammates, indicates that as soon as he heard about those comments he knew what was going to happen. He said that the team would do anything for Bird, and when Bird said they had no heart, there was only one thing that could happen. The next game was one of the most memorable in NBA history. The Celtic players extended themselves to a level of intensity that was visible to everyone in the country. The entire game was played on the very edge of chaos. Several times it nearly erupted into violence. In the last moments the two teams were tied. With seconds left in overtime, Bird hit a most difficult shot to win. The Celtics then went on to win the next two games and the championship.

According to my logic, the Celtics should have disintegrated in the face Bird's criticism. Clearly, they did the opposite. Why? David Halberstam (1999) gives us some clues:

> The team was driven by the sheer force of his will. His greatness and toughness set him apart, and it was contagious. His teammates dared not disappoint him. He led more by example than by talking, although he was capable of stinging his teammates with words if he thought they were giving less than they should. His teammates knew that no one played or practiced in greater pain. He played in pain, indeed in great pain, and he expected them to do nothing less. Because Bird exuded mental toughness, a hatred of losing, and willingness to play at the highest possible level, his teammates gradually took on the same attitudes, as if absorbing his qualities by osmosis. "I saw that close up," Danny Ainge once noted. "None of us wanted to let him down. All of us wanted to be worthy of him. The great thing about Larry was his effect on his teammates. Everyone on that team rose with him not just to his expectations of them, which were high enough, but to his expectations of himself, which were even higher." [Halberstam, 1999]

When my kids criticized a teammate, they did so out of their own frustration and anger and in the process they dissociated themselves from one another. They were rejecting the person who erred, which was a little like a human body rejecting one of its limbs or organs, thus compromising the total organism—in this case, the team. When I criticized, it was clear that my corrective comments were made with the positive intent of helping the team improve. I spoke for a higher purpose, which the team as a whole presumably shared. Bird had all this and more. He had moral power. He was focused on the common good; he wanted the team to win; he had made enormous sacrifice for the common good; he knew that without productive community there could be no achievement of purpose. Without teamwork there would be no championship. He seldom made demands. He led by example. When it came to basketball, Bird was an inner-directed and other-focused leader. When he made his criticism, it was not offensive. It was an irresistible call to a noble cause. There is no questioning the motive of the moral leader. He or she is trying to build a productive community. The call for individual sacrifice is acceptable because the success of the collective is the success of the individual, and vice versa. Larry Bird called upon his people to meet the expectations of productive community and those players "wanted to be worthy of him."

The Paradox of Task and Person

Larry Bird had an intense drive to win, yet he also had incredibly positive relationships with his teammates. It might be fair to say that they loved him and were profoundly inspired by everything he stood for. In the transformational realm we almost always find moral power, and we almost always find paradoxical observations. In the normal, transactional realm, we have clear categories and clear cause-and-effect relationships. In the transformational realm we talk about oneness. Categorical differences melt and opposites interpenetrate. One of several such paradoxes is that transformational leaders tend to be high on both task and person. They place a very high value on getting the job done but they also value the person. At first glance one might conclude that it is impossible to do both, but as we shall see, this is not the case.

The major emphasis in this chapter is on the kind of moral power that people like Larry Bird exemplify, balancing the issues of person and task. For the moment, however, I would like to use the next few pages to return to the normal model and examine how we normally go about the change process. I will then return to the paradox of task and person.

Some Normal Perspectives on Changing People

The notion of encouraging people to transcend their scripts is rare in the normal model. In the normalized world we often work from the premise that people always resist change and will not be interested in transcending their scripts no matter what. I recall a discussion with a highly recognized consultant. He and I were working on different projects for the same organization. We met at lunch and learned that we would both be finished at mid-afternoon, so we agreed to go off for a round of golf when we were done. On the course we got into a discussion about human nature. My associate told me that people simply do not change. He said, "I tell managers to forget their dreams about changing people. Just replace the problem people and move on." He went on at great length defending his philosophy.

This man's cynical outlook is easy to understand. The truth is that it is indeed very difficult to change people, and researchers tend to verify this point. Professor Kim Cameron's (Cameron, 1997) research, for example, shows that as many as three quarters of all reengineering, quality management, strategic planning, and downsizing efforts have failed or created problems serious enough "to threaten the survival of the organization." Why? Because the change agents failed to address or alter successfully the key issues in the human system. It is difficult to change people. The important point I want to make here, however, is that people do in fact change.

We can all identify key moments in our own lives when we made significant changes. We decided to get married or divorced, to stop smoking, to go on a diet, to take school seriously, to intensify commitment to a job, to get further training, or to quit a job. We may have attended a workshop or read a book that gave us new insights that caused us to change the way we looked at our lives, at how we relate to others, or our work habits. Maybe we went through a rite of passage, a religious conversion, or a life crisis that caused us to see ourselves differently and change the way we were living. In each case, we were likely to come out of the process a different person. So if we, in fact, do change, as it seems that we surely do, why is changing other people so difficult?

One answer has to do with our inability to learn from our failed efforts to initiate change. When I fail in my attempt to change the behavior of another person, I do not exactly leap at the opportunity to question how or why my efforts did not work. It's all too easy simply to tell myself that the problem is not with me but with the person I tried to change. Even knowing better, I resist questioning my own values and behavior, the quality of my thought, or the effectiveness of my strategies. I wish for different results while continuing to do what I have always done. Given my lack of success and my definition of where the problem lies, how could I do anything but conclude that people do not easily change? Of course, with a little probing of my own position, I might very well discover that I am creating that world of no-change myself. Those people I am asking to change are simply mirroring my behavior and my beliefs.

To transform others effectively, we must transform ourselves. This proposition is not new. It is embedded in many of the world's great spiritual traditions. Yet it seems to defy normal understanding and application. Our defense mechanisms and our assumptions of authority seem to blind us to the notion that if we are to effect change in those around us, we need to change ourselves. When people assume roles of authority, they tend to plan and expect change in other people, but not in themselves. They see the core problem as the behavior of those they would change. This can be difficult to argue, of course, because the fact remains that there are problems outside us. If that's true, then why is it necessary for the change agent to change? We should consider three factors:

First, as a change agent, my first impulse, like the first impulses of the boys on my basketball team, is to assume an authority role. When I do so, I am likely to forget that other people find it difficult to change. Once I determine that they should change, I'm inclined to see the others as objects with obligations to do what I say. The mother-daughter case in the introductory chapter illustrates this. Despite her claims of love for Erin, the mother was, in fact, seeing Erin as a transactional object, and she was implicitly, but clearly, communicating that fact to her daughter. The normal executive sees the workforce as a collection of transactional objects obligated to do his or her will. The change agent ceases to see the change targets as human beings with feelings and the capacity for choice. Because I see them from the perspective of an expert or authority figure, I forget emotional reality. I forget to empathize. I forget that were I in their shoes I, too, would probably react just as they are reacting.

Second, in addition to the above, I also assume a problem focus. Like the boys on the basketball team, I assume that the person I am trying to change is the problem. When I do this I psychologically dissociate myself from that person. The person I am trying to change becomes an outsider, perhaps not even worthy of my attention. I see myself as the solution; the change target is the problem. The problem kid needs to learn to dribble; Erin needs to change her study habits; the employees need to more be responsive to their superiors' directives. We are two separate entities. But the fact is that we are not separate; we are one. Once I seek change in another person, we are in relationship. We are both parts of one system. The mother is part of the study problem and the members of the management team are part of the productivity problem.

Ironically, the change target usually sees the authority figure as part of the problem, but the change agent remains blind to this notion. Think about the last time a parent or a boss tried to solve a problem that required a change in your behavior. It is likely that you were highly aware that the problem was at least partially driven by the behavior of the authority figure, yet it is also likely that you were prevented from bringing this fact into the conversation. Once we have identified the problem with a particular change target, the die is cast. A particular perspective is set that will, in itself, determine the outcome. Again, the outcome will be exactly what we predicted.

Third, we fail to understand the dynamics of change. If I define the problem as being in the change target, there is no need for me even to look at the possibility that maybe I need to change, and so I do not. In maintaining my same behaviors I also maintain the existing "problem relationship." No matter what I say, my own behaviors cause the change target to react to me in exactly the ways they have in the past. I may tell the problem kid that I value his contributions to the team. I may tell Erin I love her. But if I don't change myself, my behaviors will be sending these people the same old messages—that I still see them as a problem and me as the solution.

I can say whatever I want, but if I do not change I will communicate who I really am, not who I claim to be in words. I may spend hours explaining the desired new culture in our organization, but as long as I behave as I have always behaved, the workers will just continue doing what they have always done. All the training programs and in-service workshops in the world become a waste of money.

But what happens if I do change my behavior? The short answer is that my change alters our relationships. Why? My new behavior distorts the balance or equilibrium. The changes in my behavior require the change target to pay attention, to seek a new way of operating, to make new choices. Erin is suddenly finding new messages in the behavior of her mother. Because Mom's motives, thought processes, and strategies have changed, Erin must alter her meaning system. The more unique and unexpected the change agent's behavior, the more the change target has to think and adjust. When a company brings in a new CEO, the change tends to create limited chaos, forcing people to be mindful and to make personal changes. An old CEO who makes a fundamental change, initiates the same stimulus. A parent who makes a fundamental change does the same.

Granted, it is difficult for us to change, regardless of which side of the desk we come from. New patterns of behavior usually only occur when I, the change agent, have a new viewpoint and a new purpose. But I have to care sincerely about these new viewpoints and purposes enough to motivate me to really be willing to be, think, and act differently. When, like Larry Bird criticizing his teammates, I do act outside the rules, others will naturally start to behave differently. Then, as I see others change, I am encouraged to change. The more often I change, the more often they change; my perception of the change potential in others is thus dependent on my own change potential. Again, the world I see is in fact mirroring the person I am. My behavior is playing a powerful role in creating what I perceive.

Finding New Perspective

The management team of a small manufacturing firm discovered that if they altered shift work from eight hours a day, six days a week, to twelve hours a day, four days a week, they could make considerable gains in efficiency. Furthermore, the employees, while working the same number of hours, could have three days off. It seemed a win-win. When the change was proposed, however, there was intense resistance. Many of the arguments made no sense. Finally, one senior person decided to interview each employee and really listen to what they had to say. He returned with a new perspective:

"What they had to say was a real eye opener. One guy, for example, has a farm. He leaves here at three and still has six hours of daylight to get his work done. The change would have destroyed his capacity to maintain that farm. That was just one example in a long list of reasons why the people did not want to make the change. From our view it was so straightforward, from theirs it was an enormous disruption."

Changing the hours employees work in an organization can seem like a no-brainer, simply a matter of people changing the days and the hours they put in at work. But unless we are willing to look through their eyes it is unlikely we will ever understand any resistance we might encounter. But looking through other people's eyes can mean that we have to change. We can't simply assume that telling people to change is going to get the results we want. Becoming an effective change agent means that we need to examine ourselves very carefully. We need to look at our own state of being, our own thought processes, or our own strategies for change. We might just discover, as the managers above did, that we can achieve the end results we desire simply by taking a closer look at the needs of the people we are asking to change.

Task-Person Paradox at the Organizational Level

When Jack Welch became the CEO of General Electric, he spent much of his time downsizing the company. He became known as "Neutron Jack," the reference being to the neutron bomb. People said that after Welch made one of his visits, the buildings were left standing but all the people were gone. Welch was defined as heartless.

As the downsizing came to an end, Jack Welch started to talk about the need to clarify and live the values of the company. He talked about the need to embrace positive organizational values that affected the way people related to each other. This caused an outcry. The devil himself was asking the people of GE to recite the Boy Scout oath. Journalists were quick to point out his blatant hypocrisy. Here was a man who had ruthlessly fired legions of loyal employees and now he was asking people to cooperate for the good of each other and for the company.

I had a different reaction. It seemed to me that Jack Welch was striving to be an effective leader. He had the courage to do the very painful task of downsizing, but he also had the wisdom to realize the necessity for cohesiveness. He was like Larry Bird. He desperately wanted to win and he knew it would require both discipline and teamwork. He was already applying very hard discipline and now he was trying to put an equal amount of emphasis on human cooperation.

I watched a similar evolution in David Whitwam, the CEO of Whirlpool. Dave is a brilliant man with a thirst for action and achievement. During his first five years as CEO, he not only globalized the company, he drove it to impressive levels of profit. Wall Street was delighted. As he entered his sixth year, things grew more difficult. He had stretched the system as far as it could stretch. As he wrestled with his challenges, he also began to talk about the need for values and the commitment to values. He wanted to develop a high-performance culture.

Many people reacted to this initiative as people had reacted to Welch at GE. How could such a hard-nosed and task-focused person talk about values and relationships? Whitwam was clear in his answer. Time after time he pointed out that he was not interested in being warm and fuzzy. He was interested in high performance. He had come to the conclusion that he could not have a high-performance company unless he tended to both task and people simultaneously. What brought him to such a conclusion? He made a profound, personal discovery that I think is central to the argument of this book. Whitwam said:

Sooner or later, every leader comes to understand how little power he or she really has. I will take you back to when this was just a North American business. A person could get things done continuously, consistently. As we became more complex and the environment more intense, it became impossible to get things done through the force of leadership. Everything in my mind has always been so clear and logical. I felt, if we just do what we know how to do every day, this thing will work. I had this grand scheme and grand design and grand vision and I thought I could articulate it and get people lined up. It did not happen. It absolutely did not happen. I think that I had to come to grips with the fact that it is not enough for me to be committed, to have a plan and understand where we are going. I realized I had to get everyone engaged and committed. [Quinn and Snyder, 1999, p. 191]

Earlier in this book, I reviewed the implicit theories of high performance. The most predominant theory is the journey of intense achievement. I think, and the data suggest, that most executives are trying to put this implicit theory into action. It basically assumes that an intense personality can make things happen. Such a person can drive others to high achievement, and the intense achiever can thus be recognized and rewarded. Whitwam is in essence saying that he was trying to enact such a journey. This is not surprising because it is the central theory of the transactional world.

Yet Whitwam, a brilliant thinker and shrewd student of management, discovered something astounding: "Sooner or later, every leader comes to understand how little power he or she really has." How could he say such a thing? He was the CEO. He was the king. Armies of people hung on his every word. He had all the authority one could ever hope to have. In making this statement, he is violating a core assumption of the normalized world—that a CEO can make things happen. He is violating a core assumption of the Machiavellian theory that drives the normal world.

Here is a radical statement: Formal leaders normally do not have the power necessary to transform a system.

In the beginning, Whitwam was internally driven. He had a clear vision and clear plans, and he was deeply committed to them. But he was not necessarily other focused. This was reflected in his statement: "I think that I had to come to grips with the fact that it is not enough for me to be committed, to have a plan, and understand where we are going." To accomplish the great purposes he had set out for his company, he needed to be more other focused, more aware of the people who worked for him. "I realized I had to get everyone engaged and committed," he finally said. Whitwam's discovery moved him from trying to enact the journey of intense achievement to trying to enact the journey of collective fulfillment. He could only build a great company by developing a culture of great relationships. He needed to build a productive community. So does every parent, teacher, coach, minister, or scout leader.

Transcending the Either-Or Perspective

In the normal world, our thinking is categorical, that is, we think in terms of dichotomies and polarities. Something is black or it is white; it is hot or it is cold; a person is effective or ineffective, and so on. In Chapter Two I discuss this kind of thinking in terms of hierarchies and adhocracies. I argue that productive community emerges when these two kinds of organizing processes interpenetrate. A similar analysis can be made in regard to our perceptions of change agents. In thinking about human influence, the most common differentiation is between task and person. We might say a manager is either task oriented or person oriented; is autocratic or democratic; is directive or participative; is a Theory X thinker or a Theory Y thinker; is left-brained or right-brained; initiates structure or provides consideration.

These can be useful differentiations in everyday communications, but they can also lead us to make value judgments that are less than accurate or decisions that are poor. The first polarity in each of the above pairs (task oriented; autocratic; directive; Theory X; left-brained; initiates structure) tends to be associated with notions such as orderliness, control, rationality, direction, and procedure. In contrast, the second element in each bipolarity (person oriented; democratic; participative; Theory Y; right-brained; provides consideration) tends to be associated with notions such as flexibility, spontaneity, trust, and development. When we observe other people, we tend inherently to value one orientation more than another. We may define one side of the polarity as positive and the other as negative, one good and the other bad. When this happens, it becomes virtually impossible for us to think that a healthy tension can exist that includes the presence of both orientations.

In the social sciences, we seek ways of creating clear categories: some managers are people oriented whereas others are task oriented, and never the twain shall meet. A review of the empirical studies using these measures, however, showed that in over 80 percent of the studies, the two measures were significantly correlated (Schriesheim, Hourse, and Kerr, 1976), that is, people who were high on people orientation were high on task orientation. Despite this fact, we tend to judge people by placing them in one category or the other.

By way of a popular example, consider the opening scene of the movie *Patton*. Patton gives a speech to his unseasoned troops as they are about to enter the war. He clearly states his expectations and objectives. If asked to explain why this speech is so effective, we might use words such as *expertise, authority, goal clarity, power, distance,* and *intimidation.* These words are traditionally associated with order and control. Judging from everything we can see at this moment, our assumptions would be correct. A deeper analysis, however, reveals that Patton embodies characteristics associated with the opposite side of the dichotomy.

Although Patton clearly uses symbols of power and expertise (an American flag, ivory-handled pistols, a swagger stick, medals, music, for instance) that differentiate him from his troops, he simultaneously uses language and metaphor (profanity, stories reflecting and resolving their inner-most fears) that convey closeness, identity, and understanding of their feelings. While maintaining distance and instrumental focus, he is sensitive and responsive to their most central fears. He helps them address their anxieties about dying and showing cowardliness. While directing and caring for his men, he lifts and empowers them. He does not dissociate himself from them; on the contrary, he creates a powerful bond.

This example illustrates that it is possible to integrate task orientation with person orientation. As I become more aware of this possibility, I can begin to transcend my own either-or thinking. I can begin to look for interrelationships between what I perceive as polarities. My new awareness makes it much more likely that I will be able to transmute my insights into real-world actions.

Why We Need Both Task and Person

In Chapter Seven, I used the example of jazz musicians and talked about Barrett's notion of provocative competence, that is, the ability to disrupt habit patterns. Barrett drew examples from artists such as John Coltrane and Miles Davis. Davis argued that the necessary disruptions must not be toxic, that they must be challenging but not overwhelming. Provocative disruption requires a deep understanding of the system and an appreciation for the people involved.

In the management literature we find reference to assigning stretch goals. But what Miles Davis is talking about is more than an authoritative request on the part of the leader. Davis helps group members by creating alternative paths for others to follow. We learn that he "imported new material that opened possibilities and suggested alternative routes for his players." I believe that transformational change agents recognize and meet the group's needs for learning whatever they need to learn to work in close relationship with one another. As I suggested earlier, the transformational change agent says, "Here is the standard, which I know looks impossible. But let's stand together and we will learn our way into a higher level of performance." I think that is what Larry Bird did in our earlier example.

Excellence Is About Learning on the Edge

Excellence is a dynamic process that involves real-time learning. It requires being connected to emergent reality. We are so used to describing performance in a linear and mechanistic way that we often cannot see the dynamic learning process that is actually occurring. An excellent description is provided by Pirsig:

> Sometime look at a novice workman or a bad workman and compare his expression with that of a craftsman whose work you know is excellent and you'll see the difference. The craftsman isn't ever following a single line of instruction. He's making decisions as he goes along. For that reason he'll be absorbed and attentive to what he is doing even though he doesn't deliberately contrive this. His motions and the machine are in a kind of harmony. He isn't following any set of written instructions because the nature of the

material at hand determines his thoughts and motions, which simultaneously change the nature of the material at hand. The material and his thoughts are changing together in a progression of changes until his mind is at rest at the same time the material is right. [Pirsig, 1974, p. 148]

The master sees things that the novice cannot. In the ideal situation, the master and the work become one. The point guard in basketball does not follow a set of rules; he or she flows with the situation, continually making choices. His or her behavior creates the situation and the situation creates the behavior. Great teachers and great leaders learn to do the same thing. This ability to be one with the process comes by discipline and growth. It is a learning process, yet it is not as mysterious as it may seem. It is something we all do.

Some researchers have suggested that the development of mastery is a five-stage process (Dreyfus, Dreyfus, and Athanasion, 1986). This process has been summarized as follows by Quinn, Faerman, Thompson, and McGrath (1996, p. 383).

1. In the novice stage, people learn facts and rules. The rules are learned as absolutes that are never to be violated. For example, in playing chess, we learn the names of the pieces, how they are moved, and their value; in parenting we take classes and read books; in management, we are exposed to the manuals and books of procedures.
2. In the advanced beginner stage, experience becomes critical. Performance improves as real situations are encountered. Understanding begins to exceed the stated facts and rules. Observation of certain basic patterns leads to the recognition of factors that were not set forth in the rules. A chess player, for example, begins to recognize certain basic board positions that should be pursued. The parent notices that the baby responds to a certain kind of soothing. The manager notices that people seem to regularly struggle with a certain problem.
3. The third stage is competence. Here we have begun to appreciate the complexity of the task and now we recognize a much larger set of cues. We develop the ability to select and concentrate on the most important cues. With this ability, our competence grows. Here our reliance on absolute rules fades. We take

calculated risks and engage in complex trade-offs. A chess player may, for example, weaken board position in order to attack the opposing king. This plan may or may not follow any rules that the person was ever taught. The parent begins to ignore certain kinds of cries. The manager begins to anticipate misunderstandings and prevents them.

4. The proficiency stage. In this stage, calculation and rational analysis seem to disappear, and unconscious, fluid, and effortless performance begins to emerge. Here we hold no single plan sacred. We unconsciously "read" the evolving situation. We notice and respond to cues which a casual observer wouldn't notice. Our attention shifts to new cues as our response to old ones becomes automatic. New plans are triggered in our minds as emerging patterns call forth plans that worked previously. Here there is a holistic and intuitive grasp of the situation. Here we are talking, for example, about the top 1 percent of all chess players, the people with the ability to intuitively recognize and respond to change in board positions. Here are the parents who maintain an extraordinary implicit communication. Here is the manager who regularly obtains extraordinary performance. Such people are rare, of course, and there is much to learn from them.

5. Experts. Those in this fifth stage do what comes naturally. They do not apply rules but use holistic recognition in a way that allows them to deeply understand the situation. They have maps of the territory programmed into their heads that the rest of us are not aware of. They see and know things intuitively that the rest of us do not know or see. They frame and reframe strategies as they read changing cues.

This is Pirsig's master craftsman at his machine. This is Bobby Fischer playing chess. This is Miles Davis disrupting his jazz group. This is Larry Bird making the impossible steal of the inbound pass with seconds on the clock. This is Patton speaking to his troops. This is Solomon telling the two women to cut the baby in half. This is mastery at the highest level.

But this is also you and me. We are all experts at something and we all, at times, experience the flowing process of Pirsig's craftsman. This notion of flowing performance deserves more attention.

Flow and the Autotelic Personality

Mihaly Csikszentmihalyi coined the term *flow*. It is a state that we all sometimes experience. Flow reflects complete absorption in a given activity. It is an experience of effortless action. In the flow state we feel no conflicts or contradictions. There is harmony among our feelings, desires, and thoughts. Athletes speak of it as "being in the zone"; mystics speak of "ecstasy"; and artists speak of "rapture."

Flow activities might include skiing, mountain climbing, singing, doing surgery, programming a computer, dancing, playing a card game, reading a novel, doing a task at work, or engaging in a conversation. Activities that lend themselves to the flow state often reflect a clear set of goals and a clear set of rules or expectations that require appropriate responses. Flow activities also provide immediate feedback. The actor knows how well he or she is performing. Flow usually reflects an appropriate match between level of challenge and level of skill. It occurs when our skills are fully employed in a challenge that we are just able to meet. This relationship is represented in Figure 9.1.

If an actor faces a challenging role for which he does not have the necessary skills, that person becomes frustrated, worried, and then anxious. If a person's skills exceed the challenge, the person gets relaxed and then bored. If both challenge and skills are low, the person tends to experience apathy. If challenge and skills are both high, then the person tends to feel both aroused and in control. It is then that they tend to experience flow. Notice that challenge and arousal are normally conceptually distant from skills and control. Yet it is when both of these are high that we enter flow. In this sense there is a creative tension.

In a normal day, most of us experience both anxiety and boredom, along with many other feelings. Flow experiences exist mostly during the high points. It is a time of full involvement. During flow there is a sense of timelessness. Physical and psychic energy are expended in a harmonious way. Our attention is highly ordered and we feel deeply invested in what we are doing, so that we are sharply and completely focused on the activity. We have no sense of distraction. Self-consciousness wanes or even vanishes altogether. We are at one with whatever we are doing. There is a sense of con-

Figure 9.1. Finding the Flow: The Psychology of Engagement with Everyday Life.

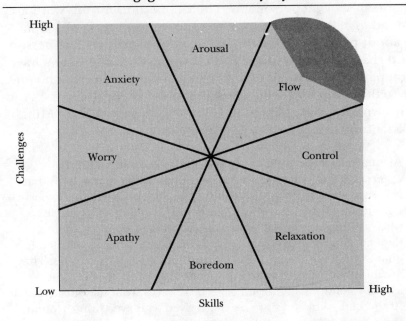

Source: From F. Massimini and M. Carli, 1988. "The Systematic Assessment of Flow in Daily Experience." In *Optimal Experience: Psychological Studies of Flow in Consciousness,* edited by M. Csikszentmihalyi and I. S. Csikszentmihalyi. New York: Cambridge University Press. Reprinted with permission of Cambridge University Press.

fidence and strength. We find flow activities inherently valuable; they are worth doing for their own sake.

Flow leads to growth, in part because it is a function of a creative tension between two conditions: arousal and control. In arousal, there is focus and involvement. Yet to move into the flow state, people usually need to be somewhat challenged by the task at hand, having to reach deep into themselves and garner resources that they may not have known they had. When that person's skill level is meeting the challenge, there is a sense of excitement or arousal, combined with a sense of control.

Flow—the simultaneous manifestation of arousal and control—tends to give rise to learning. States such as anxiety or boredom tend to undermine learning.

People who regularly enter the flow state are more likely to live lives of involvement and enthusiasm, and are more likely to develop an *autotelic* personality. The Greek roots for this word are *auto* and *telos*. *Auto* refers to self and *telos* refers to goal. We are talking about people who do things for their own sake. The person is internally driven and is fulfilled when they know they have accomplished something to their own standards. Although no one can be fully autotelic, some of us almost never engage in tasks for their own sake and some of us often do. In the words of Mihaly Csikszentmihalyi:

> An autotelic person needs few material possessions and little entertainment, comfort, power, or fame because so much of what he or she does is already rewarding. Because such persons experience flow in work, in family life, when interacting with people, when eating, even when alone with nothing to do, they are less dependent on the external rewards that keep others motivated to go on with a life composed of dull and meaningless routines. They are more autonomous and independent because they cannot be as easily manipulated with threats or rewards from the outside. At the same time, they are more involved with everything around them because they are fully immersed in the current of life. [Csikszentmihalyi, 1997, p. 117]

People who score high on autotelic evaluations tend also to spend a significantly high amount of time interacting with their families. They spend nearly four hours more per week than do people with lower autotelic scores. This perhaps suggests that internally driven people are not as likely to be coerced into working excessive hours. Perhaps, since they are less concerned about external rewards and punishments, they are more able to spend their time where they want to spend it. The results may also suggest that they invest in the relationships that matter most.

These people also demonstrate high levels of psychic energy. Normal people treat attention as a transactional good. We hoard attention carefully. We dole it out only for serious things, for things that matter; we only get interested in whatever will promote our welfare. The objects most worthy of our psychic energy are ourselves and the people and things that will give us some material or emotional advantage. The result is that we don't have much attention left over to participate in the world on its own terms, to be surprised, to learn new things, to empathize, to grow beyond the limits set by our self-centeredness. According to Csikszentmihalyi, "Autotelic persons are less concerned with themselves, and therefore have more free psychic energy to experience life with."

This research suggests to me that autotelic personalities are both inner directed (do things for their own sake) and other focused (practice empathy). They have less fear and more awareness of what is going on around them, making them much more likely to be connected to emergent reality. I suspect that since they are more likely to practice empathy and show concern, they are likely to be empowered and empowering.

It seems likely that our three sacred servants would have high autotelic scores, as would others we have discussed, such as Miles Davis and Larry Bird. At least hypothetically, I suspect these kinds of people are more likely to help others learn, experience flow, and become more autotelic themselves.

Becoming More Autotelic

As we read about the autotelic person, we are likely to dissociate ourselves from such profiles with the notion that these are not qualities that we presently have or could ever have. These are special people, we tell ourselves. These notions are not applicable to me. But let's not jump too quickly to that conclusion. The autotelic profile is much more prevalent than you might think.

From the research on flow we discover that it matters a lot how people focus their attention. Csikszentmihalyi differentiates between short-run intentions and long-term goals. Short-run intentions are how we plan to act in the moment; for example, we are going to finish reading this chapter and then go to dinner. Long-term goals are those desired ends that are clear to us and that guide our action over time; for instance, building a specific career or business. Together these determine how we will expend our psychic energy.

Because our actions over time help determine who we are, our sharp focus over an extended duration is important. Obviously, the person whose actions are predominantly determined by whatever outside stimuli happen by will not be the same kind of person as the one whose actions are determined by a clear inner goal to become a Nobel prize winner. Goals help establish the choices we make about how we will invest our psychic energy. These patterns bring order and predictability to our life experience, giving rise to a unique self, unique in the sense of being inner directed, driven by a very personal dream or goal.

Csikszentmihalyi suggests that the difference between Mother Theresa and Madonna is found by looking at the goals they hold. The reason for this is that their goals determine how they allocate their energy and attention.

The research on flow suggests that how we control our attention will determine the quality of our life experiences. This, in turn, suggests that we control what we become. We can better choose the kinds of lives we will live by developing personal disciplines that have to do with controlling our attention. These might include disciplines such as meditation, prayer, and athletic training. But such disciplines would also include any specialization or body of knowledge that we find enjoyable and that fosters self-improvement. The critical factor is attitude—engaging in tasks not for selfish gain but with a spirit of engaging in them for their own sake, for the joy of doing them.

We are accountable for what we become. The normal world-view suggests we are not. In the normalized mindset we complain about our context and our lack of freedom. There seems to be little room for choice in our lives. The normal person, for example, will argue that the notions of flow are very noble but if a person works in a routine job, in a hostile environment, such pursuits are spurious and ridiculous even to consider. Csikszentmihalyi dares to argue otherwise and provides some striking examples:

> A concrete example may illustrate best what I mean by leading a good life. Years ago my students and I studied a factory where railroad cars were assembled. The main workplace was a huge, dirty hangar where one could hardly hear a word because of the constant noise. Most of the welders who worked there hated their jobs, and were constantly watching the clock in anticipation of quitting time. As soon as they were out of the factory they hurried to the neighborhood saloons, or took a drive across the state line for more lively action.

Except for one of them. The exception was Joe, a barely liter-
ate man in his early sixties, who had trained himself to understand
and to fix every piece of equipment in the factory, from cranes to
computer monitors. He loved to take on machinery that didn't
work, figure out what was wrong with it, and set it right again.
At home, he and his wife built a large rock garden on two empty
lots next to their house, and in it he built misty fountains that
made rainbows—even at night. The hundred or so welders who
worked at the same plant respected Joe, even though they couldn't
quite make him out. They asked his help whenever there was any
problem. Many claimed that without Joe the factory might just as
well close. [Csikszentmihalyi, 1997, p. 2]

Most of the people in the above context did the normal thing.
They hated their bad environment and got out of there as soon as
possible. For most of them work was like a jail sentence. Yet even
in that kind of environment one man chose a unique response. He
stepped outside the norm and he created. In creating, he vastly
improved the quality of his job, the quality of his life, and the quality of his self. He became more autotelic than others around him.
He was doing things for their own sake and he was living in a
meaningful way. This very much reminds me of our earlier discussion of Victor Frankl and his accounts of the prisoners in the Nazi
concentration camps. Most people had a normal reaction to their
bad context. A small minority chose to not react. They chose to be
internally driven and other focused.

The exceptions that we find, in virtually every environment,
undermine the normal arguments of the normalized world.
Csikszentmihalyi claims that we can add value to the most routine
tasks by considering the larger context, focusing attention, and
seeking to add value. Like Joe in the above case, we can also seek
to exceed normal expectations. He gives another striking example:

One of the clearest examples I have ever seen was when I did
research in a factory where audiovisual equipment was being
assembled on a production line. Most of the workers on the line
were bored and looked down on their job as something beneath
them. Then I met Rico, who had a completely different take on
what he was doing. He actually thought his job was difficult, and
that it took great skill to do it. It turned out he was right. Although

he had to do the same sort of boring task as everyone else, he had trained himself to do it with the economy and the elegance of a virtuoso. About four hundred times each day a movie camera would stop at his station, and Rico had forty-three seconds to check out whether the sound system met specifications. Over a period of years, experimenting with tools and patterns of motion, he had been able to reduce the average time it took him to check each camera to twenty-eight seconds. He was as proud of this accomplishment as an Olympic athlete would be if, after the same number of years spent preparing, he could break the forty-four second mark in the 400 meter sprint. Rico did not get a medal for his record, and reducing the time to do his job did not improve production, because the line still kept moving at the old speed. But he loved the exhilaration of using his skills fully: "It's better than anything else—a whole lot better than watching TV." And because he sensed that he was getting close to his limit in the present job, he was taking evening courses for a diploma that would open up new options for him in electronics engineering. [Csikszentmihalyi, 1997, pp. 105–106]

Both of Csikszentmihaly's examples suggest that we can become more autotelic. We start by accepting a high level of accountability for our actions. We can also reinvent how we approach our tasks so that doing them becomes more desirable and more personally rewarding. We may hate to cut the lawn but we can redefine the task into a desirable challenge by setting the goal to do it in half the normal time or to use the time to be deeply attentive to the activity itself.

The idea is to increase the number times that we experience flow. This focuses our attention, orders our consciousness, and establishes inner harmony. The more things we want to do, the more times we can experience flow, the richer is our life. When what we have to do becomes what we want to do, we are no longer disempowered by external requirements but are more inner directed. We become enriched by what we once perceived as constraints, and this new perspective sets us free.

When we function in the world as autotelic personalities we make greater contributions to the world in which we live. Joe, in the above example, became the most important person in the plant that made railroad cars. The world around him was enriched by his presence and it enriched him in return. He thus co-created a better world and a better self. He become more able to seed the universe.

The Need to Support People in the Change Process

When challenged, most of us experience anxiety or even fear and may withdraw in the process. In order to learn, grow, and change, we need to feel capable of meeting the challenges before us, even though the challenges may require us to stretch our present capabilities. The long and short of it is that we need to feel in control of our destiny. Effective change agents understand and respect this human fact of life. Change agents see the need to both challenge and support people, recognizing that only when they feel supported and relatively safe will they take risks.

One of the best-selling books of all time is *The Road Less Traveled,* by Scott Peck, a psychotherapist. The job of the professional psychotherapist is to help people change, yet psychotherapists are not always effective in this. In the following passage, Scott Peck reflects on his own effectiveness, asking himself about the times that he really did make a difference with his patients:

It has been said that the successful psychotherapist must bring to the psychotherapeutic relationship the same courage and the same sense of commitment as the patient. The therapist must also risk change. Of all the good and useful rules of psychotherapy that I have been taught, there are very few that I have not chosen to break at one time or another, not out of laziness and lack of discipline but rather in fear and trembling, because of my patient's therapy seemed to require that, one way or another, I should step out of the safety of the prescribed analyst's role, be different and risk the unconventional. As I look back on every successful case I have had, I can see that at some point or points in each case I had to lay myself on the line. The willingness of the therapist to suffer at such moments is perhaps the essence of therapy, and when perceived by the patient, as it usually is, it is always therapeutic. It is also through this willingness to extend themselves and suffer with and over their patients that therapists grow and change. Again as I look back on my successful cases, there is not one that did not result in some very meaningful, often radical, change in my attitudes and perspectives. It has to be this way. It is impossible to truly understand another without making room for that person within yourself. This making room . . . requires an extension of and therefore a changing of the self. [Peck, 1978, pp. 148–149]

I would like to take great liberty in rewriting the above paragraph. I will change a few of his words for the sake of presenting eight key principles for creating productive community between change agents and change targets:

1. The change agent must bring to the relationship the same courage and the same sense of commitment that is being asked of the change target. The agent must therefore come to an intellectual and emotional understanding of what it means for the target to change.

2. In order to change, the target needs to step outside his or her ordinary life scripts. It is probable that the target has never made this particular change before. It is therefore terrifying and leads to paralysis. The change agent must understand this feeling.

3. To find the courage to change, the target needs the change agent to care enough to become a model of commitment and courage. The change agent needs to show the target how to step out of old life scripts. The agent must provide an example of integrity, courage, and love.

4. The change agent may be deeply experienced and may have been involved in many transformational processes. If this is the case, he or she has a complex script for how to facilitate a transformation. If the change agent has had few experiences, he or she has a simple script for how to facilitate a transformation. Yet every target is unique. What worked in the past is unlikely to work in the same way now. In each case, the change agent needs to behave in a new way. This means taking the risk to step outside the old script. It is a shift from the ordinary to the extraordinary. It means trusting intuition as the change agent tries new things. This is usually a cause for fear and trembling. It means modeling faith, commitment, courage, and love.

5. The willingness of the change agent to suffer through such personal change is the essence of the transformational process. It

leads to increased self-confidence and a more inner-directed and other-focused personality.

6. When the target sees the change agent suffering through the process and feels the increased concern of that person, the target feels inspired, that is, attracted or enticed by moral power.

7. It is also through this willingness to extend themselves and suffer with and over the target that change agents learn, grow, and change themselves. They are meeting a new challenge by developing new skills. They are in flow.

8. Each time the change agent goes through this process, it results in a radical shift in attitudes and perspectives. To facilitate change in the target, he or she has to make room for the target within her- or himself. This making room for the other requires an extension of self and therefore a changing of the self. When change agents go through this process, they become "empowered and empowering." The change agent is simultaneously focused on both task and person.

These eight statements present a demanding standard. If they seem too challenging, take heart. Peck was describing the essence of his successful transformations, not the normal relationships he had with most of his clients. Most of us have to make a great effort to perform at these high levels. But even though we may accept the values of ACT, we are all likely to be hypocrites most of the time. The transactional model is very powerful and it draws us all into normal patterns of externally driven and self-focused behavior. We have to struggle to discipline ourselves enough to be able to use moral power to entice others into transformation. The path to collective fulfillment is not an easy path to enter or stay on.

Appreciative Inquiry as a Method of Support

The practice of ACT is difficult because is requires clarity of purpose, courage, and concern. When we have these characteristics, we are much more likely to honor the volition of the change targets. We see them as whole people, not as objects. We are also more likely to see the potential in them. We understand that their ability to choose is the key to their potential, and we hold this power of choice sacred. In working with them, we are more likely to provide the noble purpose and the human concern necessary to attract the change target into transformation. The current philosophy of change that is most aligned with this orientation is called *appreciative inquiry*. Appreciative inquiry is currently revolutionizing the field of organizational development. The method was originated by David Cooperrider and his colleagues (Cooperrider and Srivastva, 1987; Cooperrider, 1986; Cooperrider and Whitney, 1999).

Appreciative inquiry is a process of search and discovery designed to value, prize, and honor. It assumes that organizations are networks of relatedness and that these networks are "alive." The objective of appreciative inquiry is to touch the "positive core" of organizational life. This core is called forth by asking questions. Humans have a tendency to evolve in the direction of questions that are asked regularly. Recall the story in the previous chapter of the consultant who asked simply, "What would it take for this project to end a week ahead of the deadline?" The simple intervention seemed to have miraculous impact. Appreciative inquiry would argue that asking this question drew out the human spirit. In a self-organizing way, the organization began to construct a more desirable future. This is the objective of appreciative inquiry. It is accomplished by bringing forth the positive change core of the organization, making it explicit and allowing it to be owned by all.

Appreciative Inquiry: A Four-Step Process

Step 1: Discovery. The assumption is that human systems are drawn in the direction of their deepest and most frequent explorations. The discovery phase is a systematic inquiry into the positive capacity of the system. Cooperrider and his colleagues designed this phase around an interview process. What is especially interesting is that the interviews are not conducted by outside consultants looking to define problems. They are carried out by members of the organization itself, often all the members of the organization, in what is thus a systemwide analysis of the positive core. The argument is that as people throughout the organization become increasingly aware of the positive core, appreciation escalates, hope grows, and community expands.

Step 2: Dream. Appreciation becomes a form of power that attracts people into a transformational state. As they come together, they are asked to share their findings. As they describe the actual, awareness of the potential invariably creeps into the dialogue. Positive feedback loops begin to emerge. A dream begins to form. It is usually stated in terms of three elements: (1) a vision of a better world; (2) a powerful purpose; and (3) a compelling statement of strategic intent. In my own words, the people are beginning to envision productive community.

Step 3: Design. Once the dream is in place, we turn our attention to how we would ideally redesign the organization to realize the dream fully. In normal change processes people tend greatly to resist any redesign. When they share a vivid dream of the potential of their organization, they are far more likely to cooperate in designing a system that might make that dream a reality. The authors assert that in their experience, every time an organization has been able to articulate a dream, they have been immediately driven to design for that dream.

Step 4: Destiny. In the initial work on appreciative inquiry, the fourth step was called "delivery," and it emphasized typical notions of planning and implementation. Over the years, Cooperrider and his colleagues discovered that the process is really about the transformation of existing paradigms. Scripts change. People discover that how they interpret the world makes a difference. They see that we actually do create the world in which we live! So instead of emphasizing planning and implementation, the authors now emphasize giving the process away. Give it to everyone, and then step back. This sounds like a recipe for chaos. It is instead a recipe for self-organization:

> Appreciative Inquiry accelerates the nonlinear interaction of organization breakthroughs, putting them together with historic, positive traditions and strengths to create a "convergence zone" facilitating the collective repatterning of human systems. At some point, apparently minor positive discoveries connect in accelerating manner and quantum change, a jump from one state to the next that cannot be achieved through incremental change alone, becomes possible. What is needed, as the Destiny Phase of AI (Appreciative Inquiry) suggests, are the network-like structures

that liberate not only the daily search into qualities and elements of an organization's positive core but the establishment of a convergence zone for people to empower one another—to connect, cooperate, and co-create. Changes never thought possible are suddenly and democratically mobilized when people constructively appropriate the power of the positive core and . . . let go of accounts of the negative. [Cooperrider and Whitney, 1999, p.23]

This statement brings us full circle. It takes us back to the very beginning of this book and our first seed thought: To obtain extraordinary results, one must start by envisioning a productive community. What Cooperrider and Whitney describe here is a vision of productive community in which every set of relationships has a living core. Suddenly we begin to see communities not as machines or as problems to solve but as living organisms with their own capacities of self-organization. In these communities, it is possible to have both hierarchical structure and adhocratic processes. It is possible to be simultaneously stable and flexible. It is possible to have hierarchy and equality at the same time. In such systems, people can connect, cooperate, and co-create a desired future. In such a community, people empower each other. Everyone becomes more autotelic in that they are more internally driven and other focused. Each person who takes part in a community like this is likely to grow; the system itself is likely to grow.

This is a very positive vision. However, I am aware that the cynic might exclaim, "Show me such a system!" In response, I'd suggest, Look at the one in which you presently live and I think you will quickly discover that every organization has a positive core that can be brought forth. When people find this core and allow themselves to be guided by it, they are less likely to depend on forcing change and more likely to entice and provide models for change in their own behavior. They are focused on the task that reflects the common good, and they have concern for the people with whom they are co-creating the future. Here again Csikszentmihalyi provides an inspiring insight:

Entropy or evil is the default state, the condition to which systems return unless work is done to prevent it. What prevents it is what we call "good"—actions that preserve order while preventing rigidity, that are informed by the needs of the most evolved systems. Acts that take into account the future, the common good, the emotional well-being of others. Good is the creative overcoming of inertia, the energy that leads to the evolution of human consciousness. To act in terms of new principles of organization is always more difficult, and requires more effort and energy. The ability to do so is what has been known as virtue. [Csikszentmihalyi, 1997, p. 146]

Carrying this definition of virtue in our minds, we can more fully understand the nature of moral power. When we become alert to this guidance, life becomes a choice between deep change and slow death. Deep change requires enormous effort. As we understand and embrace this notion, we become empowered and empowering. We seek to raise the standard of public life. As we close our own integrity gaps, our purpose clarifies and our commitment intensifies. We become more concerned, and we seek to persuade with our acts, enticing through moral power. We understand that through increased self-mastery, we experience a change in scripts and a change in awareness. We come to know the truth, and the truth makes us free.

Appendix A: A Summary of Advanced Change Theory

The purpose of this Appendix is to provide a summary of Advanced Change Theory (ACT). It does not contain the kinds of illustrations and stories that appear in previous chapters. It is a more abstract statement. For the person who has read Chapters One through Nine, this statement should prove easy going. The Appendix is organized into five parts. In the first part we consider the conceptual relationship of ACT to other realities and strategies. Next we explore the interpretation and use of ACT. Then we review the assumptions of ACT. Next we look at ACT as a fourth-level theory and discuss the dimensions of normal change theory from advanced change theory. Finally, I emphasize that ACT is a theory of action and not a theory of science.

The Location of the Transformational Strategy

Every theory of change mirrors a set of assumed values. ACT is no exception. In this book I have discussed four strategies for change, each one reflecting a different perspective or reality. In Figure A.1 we can see how these four realities and four strategies relate to each other. In this figure we also see the values associated with each reality and strategy.

Look at the lower right-hand corner of Figure A.1. You will find the words *technical reality*. Note that the strategy at work in this quadrant is the telling strategy. It is represented by the eight questions listed in the quadrant. Here the emphasis is on facts; the method tends to be rational persuasion. Three sets of values are reflected in this approach: structure and control *(bottom-center);*

Figure A.1. Four Perspectives on Change.

INTERPERSONAL REALITY   **TRANSFORMATIONAL REALITY**

Toward Win-Win   Toward Equality   Toward Vision
Negotiation and   and Change   Realization and
Long-Term Trust   Moral Courage

The Participating Strategy	**The Transforming Strategy**
Emphasis: relationship	Emphasis: emergent reality
Method: open dialogue	Method: transcend self
Questions:	Questions:
Is there a focus on human process?	Am I envisioning a productive community?
Is everyone included in an open dialogue?	Am I first looking within?
Do I model supportive communication?	Am I embracing the hypocritical self?
Is everyone's position being clarified?	Am I transcending the external sanctions?
Am I surfacing the conflicts?	Am I embodying a vision of the common good?
Are the decisions being made participatively?	Am I disturbing the system?
Is there commitment to a "win-win" strategy?	Am I surrendering to the emergent process?
Are the people cohesive?	Am I enticing through moral power?

Toward the Preservation   Toward the
of the System   Pursuit of Truth

The Forcing Strategy	**The Telling Strategy**
Emphasis: authority	Emphasis: facts
Method: leveraging behavior	Method: rational persuasion
Questions:	Questions:
Is my authority firmly established?	Am I within my expertise?
Is the legitimacy of my directive clear?	Have I gathered all the facts?
Do I understand their fears?	Have I done a good analysis?
Am I capable and willing to impose sanctions?	Will my conclusions withstand criticism?
Is there a clear performance-reward linkage?	Are my arguments logical?
Am I controlling the context and flow of information?	Are my arguments clear?
Am I using maximum leverage?	Do I have a forum for instruction?
Are the people complying?	Am I prepared to argue effectively?

Toward   Toward Structure   Toward Logical
Compliance and   and Control   Emplanation and
Personal Survival   Immediate Action

POLITICAL REALITY   **TECHNICAL REALITY**

logical explanation and immediate action *(lower right corner)*; pursuit of truth *(right-middle)*.

Now consider the upper left-hand quadrant. There you will find the *interpersonal reality*. It is represented by the eight questions listed there. The emphasis is on relationship. The method is open dialogue. There are three sets of values reflected in this approach: equality and change *(top-center)*; win-win negotiation and long-term trust *(upper-left corner)*; preservation of the system or relationship *(middle-left)*. Because these assumptions are in sharp contrast to the ones in the lower-right quadrant, the two realities and strategies are in sharp contrast.

Now move to the lower-left quadrant or the political reality. Note that the strategy at work here is the forcing strategy. The emphasis is on authority, and the method is leveraging the behavior of others. It is embedded in the values of structure and control; compliance and personal survival; preservation of the system. In contrast, the upper-right quadrant contains the transformational reality and the transforming strategy. The emphasis is on emergent reality, and the method is the transcendence of the self. The values are equality and change; vision realization and moral courage; pursuit of truth. Naturally these two realities and strategies are also in contrast with one another.

The two most normally practiced strategies—forcing and telling others to change—are found in the bottom two quadrants, sharing the core values identified as structure and control. In practice, as we assume the role of change agent, we tend first to tell people to change. If they fail to change, we then tend to look for ways to force them to change. This two-step dance is enacted everyday in virtually every aspect of our lives. It is normal. When we employ these two strategies we believe (often erroneously) that we are in control. The desire to be in control often blinds us to the fact that we may not be effective in this approach. For example, we may be able to get a person to perform a certain task in this way but we cannot totally control how well they perform it. Additionally, forcing often produces resentments that can build up into conflicts in the relationship that in turn can reduce productivity. Given the choice between being in control and being effective, it is normal for us to choose control. The problem is that this choice often blinds us to alternative change strategies that could be more effective and, in the long run, far more productive.

As we leave the assumptions of control, we move to the next most recognized change strategy, which is the *interpersonal perspective*. Here the emphasis is on mutual dependence, listening, open dialogue, clarifying values, surfacing and resolving conflict, and building commitment to win-win objectives. The desired outcomes are not imposed but are co-created with the change target. Rhetorically this is the most praised strategy, as it harmonizes with ideas of democracy and open dialogue. In practice, it sees limited use. For the few people with the discipline and strength to give up control willfully and pursue the honest negotiation of win-win outcomes, this strategy is most powerful. For most of us, however, it is not so easily understood or applied, and requires skills that many of us lack. In reality, the strategies represented here are too often misused, thus becoming a form of manipulation. Because it is misused, many people come to doubt the viability of this strategy, and so we return to telling and forcing, a strategy that at least seems to produce short-term results.

The *transformational* perspective, noted in the upper-right corner of the figure, is the least accessible of the perspectives. The transformational perspective and the strategy of self-change suggest that if we hope to produce long-term change, that process must begin and end with ourselves. This is the essence of ACT, with emphasis on engaging with emergent reality and co-creating the future.

The Interpretation and the Use of the Four Strategies

In the process of integrating these concepts, it is important to recognize that each strategy is a tool. The person who expands his or her awareness from, say, the technical reality to the political reality is likely to become a more effective change agent. That person does not give up the technical perspective but enriches it with a wider range of skills. The person who then goes on to master the interpersonal perspective keeps the tools of the technical and transactional perspectives but enlarges his or her awareness and skill set. That person is likely to be even more effective by having a richer perceptual map with which to see the context and with more skills to apply in trying to change it.

The person who embraces the transformational perspective becomes even more effective. But before making a choice between these four perspectives, or rating one above the other, note that Figure A.1 suggests that all four perspectives are related. In looking over the different perspectives, recognize that you can take an either-or interpretation, selecting one over another as inherently bad or good. Or you can take a more complex, both-and interpretation, drawing from each perspective as seems fitting or more appropriate. The latter clearly provides a much richer perspective that values positive opposites. It allows for creative tension and increased choice.

I think that each of the sacred servants saw life through the both-and lens. Jesus clearly taught the transformational perspective but he also employed the transactional perspective when he drove the money changers from the temple. Gandhi and King each absorbed great pain in pursuing the principles of the transformational perspective, but they made sure that the press was always present to expose the shame of the majority to the outside world. Raising that shame was a form of leverage that helped the minority change the majority.

Some people who are locked into the transactional perspective insist on seeing the three sacred servants through the transactional lens, and they interpret everything they did in terms of transaction. They sum up all their work as shaming the majority into change. Because they cannot look through the transformational lens, they miss some of the most important lessons to be learned from the sacred servants. The sacred servants were capable of using all four strategies. They used them effectively because they tended to begin by first looking within.

Some Assumptions of the Transformational Perspective

Throughout the book I have warned readers that the transformational perspective stands furthest from our normal assumptions. Here let me summarize some of the assumptions at the heart of ACT.

The World Is Change

From the transformational perspective of ACT, the social world occurs within the larger physical universe. Within that system, the basic building block is energy. Energy flows in ever-changing patterns that sometimes take on a state of equilibrium, sometimes not. As humans, we focus on the patterns that fit our time perspective, for example, from the perspective of our own life span. We see a table and to us it appears permanent. We think of our values, our body, the room and building we reside in, our families, organizations and our country, the planet and the universe. We see all of these as permanent. Yet the truth is that each of these is in the process of constant change. If our time perspective were to speed up, like a video on fast-forward, we would see many forms of energy come together to form the table or other object, and then we would see the table turn into other forms. The normal tendency is to take the permanence we perceive, that is, the moment of equilibrium when a table is a table, as our point of reference. ACT does not do that. It takes change as its point of reference, seeing the universe as being made up of constant movement, constant energy flows. The universe is continual change, only briefly punctuated by moments of equilibrium. We ourselves are change.

Systems Can Transform

We experience at least three kinds of systems: highly stable ones, driven primarily by negative feedback loops; unstable systems, driven primarily by positive feedback loops; systems in the state of "bounded instability," having both negative and positive feedback loops. These latter systems operate on the edge of chaos, and have the capacity to self-organize. They can transform to higher levels of complexity and integration. In ACT, the highest reality is experienced in the creative process in which a system transforms to a higher level.

Our greatest contribution is made by assisting in the growth and elaboration of the many systems of which we are a part. In doing so we experience a higher level of effectiveness and come to better understand the simplicity on the other side of complexity.

Organization Is Natural

Humans interact with one another and with their environment. Through our interactions, we send messages of how much we value each other. We develop notions of identity—our own and other people's. We sense that the existence of any organization is predicated on these patterns of interaction. We hunger for inclusion and for approval. We sense that the self exists in the eyes of others and that our value in the world is predicated on the value we add to the system of transactional exchange.

We humans form groups to pursue life purposes. In turn, the pursuit of our life purposes leads us to take risks. Over time, this leads to learning and growth for individuals and for the group. As we interact with each other, we naturally develop norms or patterned ways of being. We organize. We develop cultures or sets of shared beliefs that carry the explicit and the implicit rules of behavior. People take on roles and a hierarchy emerges. The hierarchy is a natural form that reflects the way we think.

Stable Hierarchy Tends Toward Frozen Bureaucracy

Human interaction can be seen as a system of transactions or exchanges. Under normal assumptions, we assume that actors are self-interested and that they seek to survive. With a self-focused worldview, we tend to conclude that survival is the first law of nature.

In a world of social exchange, the actors who have the most complex transactional skills tend to accumulate the most resources. These resources include physical objects or things and status. Since these have transactional value, it is considered normal to pursue wealth, recognition, and influence. Given these predilections, when the individual and collective good are seen as conflicting, it is normal for people to choose individual good. This, however, sends a signal throughout the system. If everyone is just out for themselves, cynicism grows and commitment ebbs. The system is only perceived as a means to an end. Any loyalty to it ends when the individual no longer sees it as serving them.

As self-interest becomes the core perception within an organization, conflicts increase in number. The resulting distrust escalates the costs of virtually every transaction. Within this climate, the system requires more and more formal controls because fewer people are willing spontaneously to work toward the common good of the system. Such systems become dominated by negative feedback loops. They become highly stable. Since the universe keeps changing, emergent reality is never the same. This external, emergent reality becomes a threat to the stabilized system. The most clever and powerful have the most to loose. They have the greatest need to deny the external realities that require internal adaptations. The most important issues thus become undiscussable. This process further erodes trust and further increases the cost of every transaction. The need for form controls these increases further, and the stable system moves toward stagnation and collapse. It becomes a frozen bureaucracy.

Stagnation Gives Rise to Adhocracy

Hierarchies are not inherently bad. Problems occur in them, however, when people pursue self-interest and no one has the courage to confront the inevitable conflicts that arise. When the common good is compromised, coalitions form. In a stagnant hierarchy, informal groups multiply. These informal groups, or adhocracies, come together to meet the collective purposes generated by the failure of human courage in the hierarchy. They are self-organizing groups.

Adhocracies, however, can be characterized by common concern and high trust. They make decisions quickly and are highly adaptive. They lend themselves to risk-taking, learning, innovation, and adaptation, and their initial success increases the attraction of further interest and resources. Like hierarchies, adhocracies are not bad. They can be a cancer that destroys the hierarchy or they can be the motor of adaptation. Some adhocracies are born outside any hierarchy. If they grow, however, they can be a challenge to coordinate, driving them in some cases into a hierarchical form. In a self-organizing universe, however, adhocracies unfold from hierarchies, and hierarchies unfold from adhocracies; each one contains the other. It is an endless process of yin and yang.

People Tend to Deny Emergent Reality

At an individual level most of us value control and predictability. Argyris (1991) tells us that there are gaps between what we say and what we do. He argues that there are some universal behavior patterns in which all professionals value control, winning, suppression of negative feelings, and the pursuit of rational objectives. Given these values we neutralize even the suggestion that we might be failing. We refuse to process such signals. If we did, the signals would give rise to learning anxiety, which is a negative emotion. So we suppress such emotions. We practice denial. We close down at the very time we most need to learn. We are all, without exception, hypocrites.

It is normal to have large gaps between our values and our behaviors. It is also normal to deny that these gaps exist. And it is normal to choose slow death over deep change. We keep exerting authority in order to preserve the old self. That self becomes increasingly disconnected and ineffective. We then consciously or unconsciously separate ourselves from others. The more disconnected we become, the more disempowered and worthless we feel. The divided self is the diminished self.

The hierarchy is an efficient mechanism for providing control and predictability. Individuals need routines, and such controlled organizations make it possible for complex organizations to function. However, people pay a price for routines, in large part because routines keep us from experiencing reality first hand. Increasingly, the people in a hierarchy get to the point of relying on their past perceptions and past behavioral patterns, expecting that what worked yesterday, last year, or five years ago will work just as well today. They start making unexamined responses to the stimuli they normally experience, and the chasm between emergent reality and their actions grows wider and wider each day.

People Become Transactional Objects

The normal world tends to reward exchange and compromise. Conformity is rewarded and nonconformity is punished. Systems of formal and informal sanctions give rise to fear. Even people in the most powerful positions are driven by fear. Among other things, people fear loss of control, loss of resources, loss of status, failure, rejection, and humiliation. We also fear our own potential and the possibility that we are compromising that potential for rewards of lesser value. Living in fear and compromising core beliefs lead to a divided self. Humans collude in the decision to diminish the self, and this gives rise to negative emotions that are often suppressed. Finally, the suppression of fears only magnifies the emotions we are trying to avoid!

As insecurity grows, innovation, risk taking, and learning decline, and we soon discover a simple truth—that stagnation is a function of fear. Under normal assumptions of transaction, people are not inherently valued. They are only valued according to what they contribute to the exchange. People become objects, machines. Ethics become situational, yielding to compromise. Loyalty is conditional, existing only as long as the organization meets the needs of the individual or the individual meets the needs of the organization.

Our Attempts to Change Others Stabilize Their Behaviors

In the normal model, the change agent seldom learns from failures because he or she denies that they even exist. When the effort fails, the agent feels it is because of a deficiency in the change target. We seldom question our own values, behavior, or integrity. We are thus doomed to repeat our ineffective patterns. We wish for different results while continuing to do what we have always done.

In normal attempts to make change, we tend to assume a position of authority and expect the change target to comply with our wishes. And if people have to make changes to accommodate us we underestimate the pain involved. We cannot understand or empathize. Once we determine that they should change, we think of them as objects with obligations to do what we say.

In assuming authority, we often have a narrow perspective: The change target is the problem. We thus dissociate from that person or persons. They are bad and we are good. The target becomes an object to be manipulated. In doing these things, we do not see the actual dynamics. We are always a part of the system, but since we define the problem as being elsewhere—certainly not with ourselves!—we see no need for self-change. We dig in and our behaviors remain stable. In maintaining a stable set of behaviors, that stabilization spreads through the existing system. Ironically, perhaps, since the system is stabilized and the change target is part of that system, he or she will continue to behave in the same manner no matter what we say or do.

ACT as a Fourth-Level Theory

In the previous chapters we have explored the concepts and principles of transformation and productive community. The process for achieving this kind of organization is seen primarily through the lens of Advanced Change Theory. I have compared ACT to three "normal" strategies for change: the telling strategy (persuading others); the forcing strategy (leveraging others); and the participating strategy (engaging others).

In Figure A.2 I have again listed the four strategies on the right side of the diagram. To the left I have listed twenty dimensions of differentiation. These dimensions have two anchor points. On the left side at the bottom is the normal model, and on the left side toward the top is the transformational model. To summarize what we have covered in this book, I will discuss the concepts associated with each dimension. I will present a brief description of each of the twenty dimensions, with subsequent comparisons between ACT and the normal models. Referring back to this figure may be helpful.

Core Vision

In ACT, the change agent has a core vision. It is a vision of high purpose and productive community. To have such a vision, the change agent must be inner directed and other focused. Bear in mind that when I say *productive community* I mean any relationship, ranging from two people to a large organization. The productive community is an envisioned set of relationships that are synergistic, in which the collective good and the individual good are one. As each pursues one's goals, the other is enriched.

In the productive community there is a continuous clarification of purpose. The roles and expectations may be hierarchical

Figure A.2. Four Strategies of Change.

DIMENSIONS OF DIFFERENTIATION		
NORMAL MODEL	**DIMENSION**	**ACT MODEL**
Personal survival	Core vision	Productive community
Fixed by position	Leadership	Spontaneous contribution
Equilibrium	Desired system state	Bounded instability
Prevent insurgency	Social movement	Enact insurgency
Responsive	Empowerment	Self-authorizing
Script driven	Consciousness	Mindful
Social expectation	Moral reasoning	Principle driven
Respond to sanctions	Sanctions	Transcend sanctions
Divided-guarded	Self	Authentic-open
Provokes closure	Stimulation	Provokes openness
Exotelic	Motivation	Autotelic
Uses symbols	Symbolic communication	Becomes a symbol
Controlled	Learning	Surrender-based
Imitation	Source of vision	Creation
Instruction	Vision transfer	Reframing
Problem solving	Mode of inquiry	Appreciative inquiry
Accountability	Cause and effect	Co-creation
Expertise	Stimulus for change	Improvisation
Negative force	Resistance and uncertainty	Positive force
Other	The target of change	Self

THE FOUR STRATEGIES

Level 4. The Transforming Strategy (ACT)
Method: transcend self; emphasis on emergent reality

Am I envisioning productive community?
Am I first looking within?
Am I embracing the hypocritical self?
Am I transcending the external sanctions?
Am I embodying a vision of the common good?
Am I disturbing the system?
Am I surrendering to the emergent process?
Am I enticing through moral power?

Level 3. The Participating Strategy
Method: open dialogue; emphasis on relationship

Is there a focus on human process?
Is everyone included in an open dialogue?
Do I model supportive communication?
Is everyone's position being clarified?
Am I surfacing the conflicts?
Are the decisions being made participatively?
Is there commitment to a "win-win" strategy?
Are the people cohesive?

Level 2. The Forcing Strategy
Method: leveraging behavior; emphasis on authority

Is my authority firmly established?
Is the legitimacy of my directive clear?
Do I understand their fears?
Am I capable and willing to impose sanctions?
Is there a clear performance-reward linkage?
Am I controlling the context and flow of information?
Am I using maximum leverage?
Are the people complying?

Level 1. The Telling Strategy
Method: rational persuasion; emphasis on facts

Am I within my expertise?
Have I gathered all the facts?
Have I done a good analysis?
Will my conclusions withstand criticism?
Are my arguments logical?
Are my arguments clear?
Do I have a forum for instruction?
Am I prepared to argue effectively?

but are being continually clarified. Different people serve different functions. Yet there is flexibility because there is high trust, and that trust allows for constructive confrontation. Issues are brought to the surface, not suppressed. People accept emergent reality and accept the need continually to change. Authority figures exist but they are servants to the system, not servants of the system. Everyone sacrifices for the common good. People are thus more able to accept the fact that their greatest service to the system may be to leave it. The pursuit of productive community begins to decay whenever anyone chooses personal good over collective good. It is a fragile journey of trial-and-error learning.

Productive community is not easily envisioned by people at a normal level of moral reasoning. Such people must be enticed to experience a higher purpose and a transformational mindset in order to pursue the envisioned productive community. Since nearly three quarters of all professionals hold a self-focused worldview, productive community is pursued in the professional world on an infrequent basis.

Leadership

Although there are authority figures in the productive community, leadership is not fixed by authority positions. It is spontaneously contributed by anyone whose skills or knowledge are needed at the moment. Everyone is expected to sacrifice for the common good. Change agents strive to avoid being too soft or too hard. The preferred style is high concern for task and high concern for people. People are expected to choose the collective good over personal good, and it is possible to challenge everyone—including the highest authority figures.

Because the leaders are internally directed and other focused, they encourage such challenges. They see themselves as servants to the higher purpose. Challenge is considered constructive. Risk and resistances are expected and accepted as part of the leadership process.

Desired System State

ACT envisions the productive community, and this is the kind of relationship that the change agent is trying to establish. Productive community is bounded by a clear structure, which includes well-defined purpose, roles, and procedures. These are constantly clarified. Yet within that structure is a great deal of flexibility. People work in a setting where there is a rich and open flow of information. Much time is devoted to productive dialogue. Openness, responsiveness, and flexibility ensure that emergent reality is recognized and constantly being tested. People here are accountable but free. They are empowered to make decisions. Negative feedback loops provide continuity while positive feedback loops allow for self-organization. The system can increase in complexity and integration. It can easily transform to higher levels of performance.

In ACT, the transformation to higher levels of performance emerges from conditions of bounded instability. Here positive opposites interact and the system moves to a higher level of order. This is difficult to conceptualize. Take a look at Figure A.3. It shows four examples of higher-order concepts associated with ACT. At the bottom is Csikszentmihalyi's concept of flow. He reasons that flow emerges when skills and challenge are both high. If challenge is high but skills are low, the result is a negative state, that is, anxiety. If skills are high and challenge is low, the result is also a negative state, but in this case boredom. Only when skills and challenge are both high does flow occur. In Figure A.3, by using the same logic, we can identify other higher-order concepts such as moral power, transformational influence, and productive community. In ACT these higher-order concepts are indicative of desired system states that operate at the edge of chaos. They cannot be conceptualized through the normalized, either-or lens. The capacity to think in both-and terms is central to transformation.

Social Movement

Productive community is not normal, yet instances of productive community emerge with regularity. In the negative state that I have previously described as a *frozen bureaucracy*, that is, a rigid and predictable structure, productive community can only occur through the initiation or spontaneous emergence of a social movement. A social movement is usually seen as a form of insurgency, however, and in the normal model the responsibility of authority figures is to prevent insurgency. Transformational people working within such organizations transcend this paradox.

Figure A.3. Dynamic Systems of Four Levels of Creative Tension.

Level 4. Organizational Form

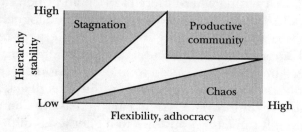

Level 3. Style of Influence

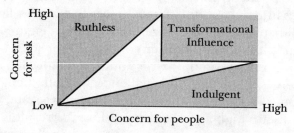

Level 2. Character

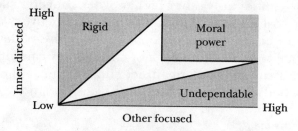

Level 1. Experience

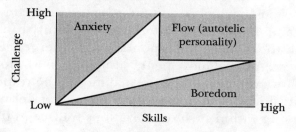

They maintain continuity while also transforming the system. They bring about social movements that allow the hierarchy to adapt. They become loyal social insurgents. They know how to challenge the old reality without threatening the authority system. They maintain the creative tension. Such a person is committed to the path of collective fulfillment.

Transformational change agents envision productive community and enact it. This generally requires them to follow some demanding patterns of self-mastery.

Empowerment

The understanding and practice of ACT requires self-mastery and the transcendence of self. To overcome the pressures of conformity, the change agent has to look within. Since all of us are self-deceptive and hypocritical, this involves considerable reflection and clarification of purpose. Clarification of purpose happens when one makes a fundamental choice (Fritz, 1989). A fundamental choice is a decision to live committed to some aspect of our own highest potential contribution.

When fundamental choices occur, our suppressed purposes and passions make their way into our consciousness. When we make such a choice, our outlook and our behaviors change. We develop constancy of purpose and tend not to bend with circumstance. When others would normally conform, we maintain the capacity for creative response. We initiate when others are reacting. We also increase our capacity for self-change. It is only when we make such fundamental choices that we find the capacity to transcend our fears of the sanction system and transcend our fears. We become free. We are empowered.

Consciousness

When we make a fundamental choice, we expand our vision beyond object reference and discover that the essence of reality is not transactional. Underneath the external props, such as identifying ourselves with a specific role or status within a hierarchy, we have an ongoing self. This self is of inherent value, which is best expressed when we are in pursuit of our unique purpose. With fundamental choice, we transcend our scripts, deviate from the norm, and begin to pursue our unique mission. When we let go of our old scripts, when we stop trying to serve ourselves and seek to serve others, a new self emerges. Our consciousness expands and we become aligned with emergent reality. We become more unified with our environment. The self becomes undivided. The self becomes mindful and creative. We begin to take initiative, and we begin to co-create our world.

Moral Reasoning

In the normalized model, change agents employ conventional levels of moral reasoning. In deciding what is right, they ask questions such as, "What is fair or just in the given situation?" In contrast, the transformational change agent operates at the highest level of moral reasoning and asks, "What is right?" The change agent then asks, "What result do I want to create?"

Whereas the normal change agent is driven by social expectation, the transformational change agent is driven by principle. Such commitment stimulates inner growth for the change agent. The willingness to pursue principle in a transactional world usually brings punishment and pain, but the willingness to persist is a form of purification that increases moral power and attracts others to the path of higher purpose. The transformational change agent does not pursue rewards or punishments but rather pursues a given contribution for its own sake. He or she creates for the sake of creation. The motivation is not self-interest but love. People with such a motive tend to attract and elevate others.

The Self

In the practice of ACT, the change agent looks within to face fears and self-deception and through this process is able to reduce integrity gaps. In this way the self becomes less divided. What is felt and what is said become congruent. The agent is more willing to make his or her personal issues public, and this is the first stimulus of cultural change. Because the change agent is more inner directed and other focused, the person is more empowered and empowering. Agents are more empowered because they have more awareness of how they are interpreting the world and are more attuned to the subtleties of the system. They see more deeply. They act more creatively. In doing so, the authentic self transcends its own culture.

Stimulation

As discussed above, flow is an experience we have when we engage in an activity that is challenging but achievable within our present skills and capacities (Csikszentmihalyi, 1997). When we're in the flow, we reach complete absorption. Whatever we are doing at this moment is worth doing for its own sake. Self-consciousness wanes. In this state there is harmony and a sense of timelessness. Physical and psychic energy expand. Attention is highly ordered and deeply focused. There is a positive tension between arousal and control. There is a sense of confidence and strength. Flow leads to growth. The simultaneous manifestation of arousal and control tend to give rise to learning. As a transformational change agent one understands this creative tension and invites people to it, provoking and disturbing but careful not to push the change target too far. They avoid the toxic intervention that results in anxiety and shut-down. This kind of person seeks mindfulness and openness to learning.

Motivation

People who enter flow regularly tend to live lives of involvement and enthusiasm. They tend to develop autotelic personalities. An autotelic personality is inclined to do things for their own sake and is internally and not externally driven. Such people are less focused on material possessions or external recognition. They are more autonomous and less likely to be driven by rewards and punishments, and they tend to be fully involved with everything around them.

The transformational change agent has the same characteristics as the autotelic personality. This kind of agent is internally driven and other focused, has high concern for task, and has high concern for people. A person who is a change agent understands the growth available on the edge of chaos and seeks to invite others to that same state of growth and empowerment.

Symbolic Communication

Acts are more persuasive than words. Principle-driven behavior is likely to be revolutionary because it distorts the normal system. It splinters people into supporters and resisters. The change agent becomes a living symbol, a "metaphor for metamorphosis" (Chatterjee, 1998). The transformational change agent embodies the common good, the new possibilities, and the vision. The change agent creates for the sake of the creation.

The kind of inner-directed behavior I describe here is rare, however. For it to work, people around the change agent must be able to grasp what that change agent is doing. If we want to become change agents within the framework of the ACT model, we must become mindful. In doing so, we become open to influence. The living symbol radiates signals that repel some people while attracting others. Change agents usually attract others because they symbolize the potential within each person or within an organization. As attracted people come together they engage in a new dialogue and this gives rise to productive community.

Learning

To be fully alive we need to be engaged with what is really happening around us. Engaging emergent reality requires confidence and courage. It means leaving our zone of control, familiarity, and comfort to go to the edge of chaos. It means going forward without answers and learning as we go. Professional knowledge gives us confidence that we can perform as long as the context does not change, but learning at the edge of chaos means learning in the present moment. Our capacity to do this increases as our integrity increases. With increased integrity, authenticity, and an undivided self, we can successfully process more information; we are conscious of more cues. With increased integrity, we are better able to surrender control and trust the processes of co-creation, self-organization, and transformation. As we surrender control, we are filled with intelligence. As we stand in our truth, the path opens. We learn our way to transformational power and accomplishment.

Source of Vision

Such learning gives rise to a vision of what can be. Conscious leaders see potential. They are familiar with the power of a self-organizing universe. Transformational change agents have reverence for the potential in the universe. Their purpose is to call forth such potential. Their vision is always unique.

Transformation comes about not as a result of imitation but through creation. The vision must be unique to the moment. It is not a result of rational analysis but of living on the edge of chaos and hearing the voices within the system. Listening is a form of co-creation, and vision emerges from such listening. Nor is vision the result of political compromise. The human spirit will simply not resonate with such incentives. Only an authentic voice can call forth the necessary human commitment.

Vision Transfer

Having a vision is one thing; helping others share that vision is another thing. This seldom happens by didactic telling. Mindfulness must be created through disturbance of the routines. The transformational change agent thus seeks to reframe meaning systems. In the transformational state, the change agent is able to see deeply and to have a more complex theory of the context. Complex understanding is often the foundation for reframing. A common tool for reframing is the bold-stroke image. It may be conveyed by a profound question, a revealing story, or a metaphor. The communicated image distorts the normal assumptions of the actors and sets them on a new behavioral course. The CEO of Coke asks, "What is our share of the stomach?" and the entire company changes.

Mode of Inquiry

As they invite others to growth and empowerment, the transformational change agent strives to transcend the "problem-solving" mode of inquiry that is at the core of the normal model. For the normal change agent, the language of problem solving is a language of deficit, of focusing on finding out what's wrong rather than building on what's right.

When we shift from the language of problem solving to the language of appreciative inquiry (Cooperrider and Whitney, 1999), we begin building a human system with a great capacity to construct the future. Until then, this capacity is constrained by normal assumptions and behaviors, so the object of appreciative inquiry is to bring forth the "positive core" of the system, to tap the untapped potential, to call forth the best in every person, group, and organization. This is done by posing questions that ask us to reframe our perspectives and understandings, drawing out the hopes and commitments of the people and awakening the human spirit. Such questions distort the existing frames and force us to look at how we are relating to our worlds.

As a shared vision begins to emerge, with more and more people participating in that vision, the organization begins to self-organize. At this point the system itself actualizes its own positive essence, becoming its own agent of change. Just as people can be autotelic, so it may be possible that larger systems become autotelic, too. Such systems learn to enact productive community, create tasks that are worth doing for their own sake, and give rise to continuous learning and adaptation.

Cause and Effect

Transformation cannot be explained or produced in terms that we ordinarily associate with the cause-and-effect paradigm. We begin to understand it only when we grasp the concept of co-creation. The transformational change agent engages in purposive, principle-driven behaviors, and these disrupt the system. We humans are driven to make sense of new behavior, so the change agent must stimulate this sense-making process. When that dynamic switches into action, an interdependent system begins to emerge. There are an increased number of positive feedback loops, and the system moves to the edge of chaos. Here small acts can bring transformation, yet the change agent is not the sole cause. The change agent, the individuals within the organization, and the context are co-creating the new system. The agent is necessary but alone is insufficient to produce this kind of change. Indeed, as it begins to occur, this process has sacred overtones, drawing upon the mysteries of the universe itself.

Stimulus for Change

All efforts at transformation involve improvisation, thus challenging us to commit ourselves to an objective for which there is no known path. The way must be learned. The transformational state must be created. If we are functioning within a normalized system, this is going to be particularly difficult to understand or enact. You'll remember that within the normalized system, authority is equated with expertise. We are slow to question the expert or authority figure.

Transformational change agents stimulate improvisation by continually disturbing the system, bringing forth positive feedback loops, and attracting the organization into a state of high performance. On the edge of chaos, the cause-and-effect relationships are not clear. The change agent often does not know what to do. There are periods when they cannot predict from moment to moment what will happen next. They can only stand in their place and trust the process. They eventually reach high performance because they self-organize to a level of increased complexity and integrity. This occurs to them and not to others because others do not have the commitment or the courage to risk acting on the edge of chaos. Transformational change agents lead. Leadership means to go forth to die.

Resistance and Uncertainty

In normal theories of change, resistance is a negative force that must be overcome. In ACT, resistance is a necessary ingredient for the transformational process. In fact, transformation begins with resistance. It is a necessary part of gestation. It calls for an adaptation on the part of the change agent (Palmer, 1998, p. 165). It requires mindfulness. In the midst of an encounter with resistance, the change agent must imagine other alternatives. The change agent and the change target then become more tightly joined in a larger process of self-organization. Out of the tension caused by the resistance, a new system is born.

Creating a turbulent system means living in a turbulent system. The transformational change agent does not prescribe change. He or she must endure the pain of resistance and the pain of uncertainty. The change agent must trust the process, which is an act of courage and faith. Afterward we may say that the transformation was driven by the change agent. But this is only a half-truth at best. The change agent was necessary but not sufficient. The outcome was predictable in a general but not a specific sense.

The Target of Change

For better or worse, we all embody our own vision, even when we do not have one. People live in accord with how they see the world. From the influence of our visions we model our behaviors, which then influence whatever environment we are in. The environment (this includes people) adapts and then expects these behaviors from us. It calls forth what we have been and tends to hold us within the pattern of behavior that we originated. The world we operate in thus becomes normalized and we have a grooved path that encourages us to continue the same behaviors. So who and what we are matters. But what we embody is a choice we can make. We can make a fundamental choice, and new behaviors will follow. The context in which we live and work will then call forth new behaviors.

We can control who we are. The transformational state is not a fixed and final state. We can become inner directed and other focused for a time. We can be on the journey of collective fulfillment and then fall back to an outer-directed and self-focused stance. We can, for example, move to the path of intense achievement or to some other path. Yet the more often we make fundamental choices and experience transformational power, the more our basic character changes and the more likely we are to stay on the path of authentic living.

When we change ourselves we change the world.

ACT Is a Theory of Action

As we come to a close in our journey, I want to make a point about the name I have given this work. I must confess that *Advanced Change Theory* is a bit of a misnomer.

Whereas *theory* is a term we associate with normal science, where we deal with rigorous statements of testable and reproducible propositions, ACT focuses on the realm of the actual, where things are not quite as tidy. The normalized world is captivated by normal science largely because it is characterized by linear logic, clear categories, and statements of cause and effect. It seems to be neat and clean, promising us that life, after all, can be predicted, easily understood, and controlled.

But ACT is not a theory in the above sense. Rather, the transformational realm that it delves into is an alternative form of reality. It is not about the actual but the potential. It is about enacting and co-creating the future and delivering it into the present. It does not deal with the normal and predictable but with the unique and unpredictable.

When people start sharing stories about their transformational experiences, we frequently find the conversations turning to the subject of paradox and contradiction. We get descriptions of a world in which categories seem to collapse and opposites inter-penetrate. In this strange realm, cause and effect blur and fall out of focus. Deductive predictability gives way to inductive creation and discovery. It is very messy—yet effective and, at times, victorious.

But ACT will never become a linear theory of normal science. It will always remain a rough set of instructions for how a person might pursue transformation. ACT can never be precise, complete in scope, or final in statement. It is not intended to be subjected to scientific scrutiny. Its goals are modest but, I would like to think, noble—to support and encourage human commitment and explo-ration. As a philosophy of changing, it serves as a statement for understanding and guiding action, a map through a wilderness that all travelers, each in their own way, will have to navigate for themselves. I would like to believe that the words of this book might help make these journeys more fulfilling and successful.

Appendix B:
Some Criticisms of ACT

This book is intended to stimulate thinking about how to effect change in human systems. By articulating ACT and publishing this book, I hope not only to extend the traditional theories of change but also to expand the array of approaches that will be available to people who want to bring change to human systems. However, in the process, I would be remiss were I not to address some of the criticisms I anticipate.

Criticism 1: ACT Is Not a Unique Approach

One point of criticism is that ACT is not conceptually different from existing change strategies, such as rational persuasion, coercion, and participation. Not a mutually exclusive category, ACT overlaps and includes other influence strategies. In Appendix A, I show how these are related and how they are differentiated. ACT is different in that it puts a much greater emphasis on self-change than do other strategies of change. In ACT, change agents must first change themselves; their individual changes, in turn, bring change into the organization in which they are immersed. This feature—the change of the change agent—seldom appears in standard organizational literature.

As a change agent following the principles of ACT, one asks questions that are very different from those found in most books on change. And the answers that ACT offers reflect a more complex view of change than one might expect to find in the more traditional discussions of strategies.

Criticism 2: ACT Is Not Relevant to Modern Organizational Life

Another possible criticism of ACT is that it has nothing to do with the more utilitarian nature of most contemporary organizations. Jesus, Gandhi, and King, some critics point out, were spearheading social revolutions, transforming whole cultures where there were vast social injustice. One might wonder whether ACT is less relevant for the person trying to make a change in some straightforward process—for example, an employee trying to change some aspect of quality.

To respond to this criticism, I return to the issue of why so many change efforts fail. Many changes that on the surface appear simple are not. Rather, they have a widespread impact on the culture, and their success depends on extensive work to help people adapt. Since doing this adaptive work is difficult and complex, it is often met with denial. The change agents involved may deceive themselves into believing that incremental or technical changes will be enough. Make the changes and everything will fall into place. Too often, as we all know, such efforts fail. I believe that any change that requires altering well-established behavior patterns can only succeed if we recognize and work with the complex social processes that will be set into motion.

In any organization, change in the culture requires the authority figure to become a social insurgent, the leader of a social movement. This is a radical thought! It is radical because the notion of change driven by authority, as well as the notion of change being driven by social insurgency, are assumed to be mutually exclusive, if not at war with one another. Authority exists to resist insurgency, and vice versa. The notion that a CEO, or even the humblest employee, needs to model moral power and become the leader of a social movement is both intellectually and behaviorally difficult to fathom.

Criticism 3: ACT Is a Formula for Failure

This criticism suggests that ACT isn't applicable because under the veneer of civility that we find in most organizations is a treacherous, Machiavellian world in which the weak always lose. It also suggests that notions of principle are fine for rhetorical posturing, but leverage is the only thing that matters. In other words, in the end, social life is a Darwinian game, an adversarial environment where only the fit survive and thrive.

Those who take this position also imply that ACT is even dangerous because it can lead normal people to get hurt. It would only make people weak. The reality, however, is that practitioners of ACT are anything but weak. It took tremendous strength and courage for Gandhi and King to willingly submit themselves to the club of an enraged, racist policeman. Similarly, it takes tremendous courage for a CEO to invite external analysts into the company to make a brutal assessment of the strategy upon which he has built his own reputation and the future of the company.

Such people are neither weak nor naive. They have discovered an advanced theory of change, one that includes but exceeds the logic of transaction. They are less naive than the seemingly politically astute advocates of the Machiavellian position. They have a larger perspective on power and have more choices available to them. Yet their choices do highlight the fact that change is dangerous. Making a deep change always involves risk or walking on the edge of chaos. The transactional perspective wishes this reality away, whereas ACT recognizes the danger and embraces the associated pain. This is possible for the agent of ACT because his or her purpose is now more important than self. It is not possible for the transactional agent because the survival of the current self is more important than purpose.

Criticism 4: Gandhi, Jesus, and King Were Flawed

Another potential criticism is that all three of our sacred servants had personal imperfections, and the long-term consequences of their efforts were not always so laudable. Gandhi, for example, might be criticized for his child-rearing practices and for the fact that when he died the machinery was not in place that would allow ordinary leaders to continue his legacy. Jesus might be criticized because of the terrible crimes committed in his name. King might be criticized for the lack of personal discipline in some aspects of his life, and though his cause was righteous many innocent people suffered or died in the wake of his efforts. I respond by emphasizing the fact that ACT does not require human perfection; instead, it requires the change agent to have the courage to continually acknowledge and be willing to take responsibility for his or her own lack of perfection.

It requires the change agent to search continually for patterns of self-deception and hypocrisy. The requirement is to be in the process of reflection aimed at closing integrity gaps. This results in a transformational state of being. It is a state of temporary perfection, not a state of perfection in a final or total sense. The fact that one or more of our three models were imperfect humans doesn't disqualify ACT. On the contrary, this engagement with our imperfections is a key part of its strength and effectiveness.

Bear in mind that the change patterns that flow from the personal change process I describe in ACT are not controlled or predictable. Since every creative act suggests that something is being destroyed, all social change will be objectionable from the point of view of one or more of the involved parties. The key here is not the specific change agents nor the specific outcomes but the principles that can be learned from their general patterns of behavior.

Criticism 5: Gandhi, Jesus, and King Were Heroes

This is basically the opposite of the above criticism. The courage and wisdom of our three sages are going to be seen by most as being bigger than life. Hence, another potential criticism is that although ACT is powerful, it may not be suitable for application by the average person. How could we ask an ordinary human being to live up to the standards of such obviously extraordinary leaders? The risks are enormous. The required personal accountability is beyond the capabilities or fortitude of normal people. My response is that every one of us is continually facing the dilemma of making deep change or accepting slow death (Quinn, 1996). Either choice necessitates great risks.

In any cross section of people, the majority will choose slow death. They will choose to live disempowered lives of "quiet desperation." However, as I tried to show in many case illustrations, ordinary people, from mothers to professors to CEOs, may occasionally employ and experience ACT. Hence, ACT behaviors may be rare in any given social context, but are much more common than we think if we view the total spectrum of our individual life experiences. We can escape accountability by separating the three sacred servants from ourselves, by making them bigger than life, but the alternative is to lock ourselves into patterns of stagnation. The deep change or slow death dilemma is ever with us.

Criticism 6: ACT Can Only Work Under the Most Positive Conditions

The potential criticism here is that although there may be some validity to ACT, it has only very limited usefulness. The argument in this case is that for this change strategy to work, change targets must be open and ready for change and have a strong identification with both the organization and the change agent. They also must be "attracted" to a vision of working for the collective good. It is further argued that it is easier to bring this sort of radical change to an organization that has a culture of respect and honor for its employees. For example, it would be difficult to implement ACT in an organization that has been slashed by frequent downsizing while maintaining extreme levels of executive pay, or in an organization where employees have been conditioned to be fearful and passive.

In fact, ACT works in the most impossible of situations. Witness the work of Jaime Escalante at Garfield High School in East Los Angeles. His true story is recounted in the film *Stand and Deliver.* The school where he taught had degenerated to a level of despicable conditions, yet Escalante built an astounding community of success and pride. He did this despite the fact that there was no honor or respect in the culture. The change targets were close-minded, with no identification with the organization, and there was no respect for the change agent. Escalante had to establish a vision, build respect, and attract the highly resistant actors into the transformational process. Furthermore, he was not the senior authority figure in the school; he was merely a teacher. In that supposedly disempowered role, he transformed an impossible situation. He did it by behaving in ways consistent with ACT, proving that the principles inherent in ACT are applicable even in the most oppressive of settings.

Summary

In summary, all these criticisms share the logic of transaction. This logic reflects the reality that most of us experience most of the time. That is, we believe the transactional paradigm, we enact it, and in doing so we co-create a world that is transactional. In doing this, all of our assumptions are confirmed. The agent of ACT, however, alters his or her state of being and enters the transformational reality. There, another logic emerges and the change agent becomes empowered and empowering.

References

Argyris, C. "Crafting a Theory of Practice: The Case of Organizational Paradoxes." In R. E. Quinn and K. S. Cameron (eds.), *Paradox and Transformation*. Cambridge, Mass.: Ballinger, 1988.

Argyris, C. "Teaching Smart People How to Learn." *Harvard Business Review,* May-June, 1991, pp. 99–109.

Argyris, C. "Empowerment: The Emperor's New Clothes." *Harvard Business Review,* May-June, 1998, pp. 98–105.

Barrett, F. J. "Creativity and Improvisation in Jazz and Organizations: Implications for Organizational Learning." *Organization Science,* 1998, *9*(5), 605–622.

Bass, B. *Handbook of Leadership: Theory, Research, and Managerial Applications* (3rd ed.). New York: MacMillan, 1990.

Block, P. "Foreword." In Roger Harrison (ed.), *A Consultant's Journey: A Dance of Work and Spirit*. San Francisco: Jossey-Bass, 1995.

Bridges, W. *Transitions: Making Sense of Life's Changes*. Reading, Mass.: Addison-Wesley, 1980.

Cameron, K. S., and Quinn, R. E. *Diagnosing and Changing Organizational Culture*. San Francisco: Jossey-Bass, 1997.

Campbell, J. *The Hero with a Thousand Faces*. New York: Bollingen Foundation, 1949.

Charan, R., and Tichy, N. *Every Business Is a Growth Business: How Your Company Can Prosper Year After Year*. New York: Random House, 1998.

Chatterjee, Debashis. *Leading Consciously*. Boston: Butterworth-Heinemann, 1998.

Chin, R., and Benne, K. D. "General Strategies for Effecting Changes in Human Systems." In W. G. Bennis, K. D. Benne, and R. Chin (eds.), *The Planning of Change: Readings in Applied Behavioral Sciences*. New York: Holt, 1969.

Cooperrider, D. L. "Appreciative Inquiry: Toward a Methodology for Understanding and Enhancing Organizational Innovation." Unpublished Doctoral Dissertation, Case Western University, Cleveland, Ohio, 1986.

Cooperrider, D. L., and Srivastva, S. "Appreciative Inquiry in Organizational Life." In W. Pasmore and R. Woodman (eds.), *Research in Organization Change and Development*, vol. 1, pp. 129–169. Greenwich, Conn.: JAI Press, 1987.

Cooperrider, D. L., and D. Whitney. "A Positive Revolution in Change: Appreciative Inquiry." In P. Holman, *Change Handbook*. San Francisco: Berrett-Koehler, 1999.

Csikszentmihalyi, M. *Finding Flow, The Psychology of Engagement with Everyday Life*. New York: Basic Books, 1997.

Dreyfus, H. L., Dreyfus, S. E., and Athanasion, T. *Mind Over Machine: The Power of Human Intuition and Expertise in the Era of the Computer*. New York: Free Press, 1986.

Frankl, V. E. *Man's Search for Meaning, An Introduction to Logotherapy*. New York: Washington Square Press, 1963.

Fritz, R. *The Path of Least Resistance: Learning to Become the Creative Force in Your Own Life*. New York: Fawcett Columbine, 1989.

Goss, T. *The Last Word on Power: Re-invention for Leaders and Anyone Who Must Make the Impossible Happen*. New York: Currency Doubleday, 1996.

Graham, G. *Change Is an Inside Job*. Seattle: Gordon Graham & Company, 1998.

Gross, S. J. "The Process of Change: Variations on a Theme by Virginia Satir." *Journal of Humanistic Psychology*, 1994, *34*(3), 87–110.

Halberstam, D. *The Reckoning*. New York: Avon, 1986.

Halberstam, D. *Playing for Keeps: Michael Jordan and the World He Made*. New York: Random House, 1999.

Heifetz, R. A. *Leadership Without Easy Answers*. Cambridge, Mass.: Belknap Press of Harvard University Press, 1994.

Iyer, R. *The Essential Writings of Mahatma Gandhi*. England: Oxford University Press, 1990.

Jaworski, J. *Synchronicity: The Inner Path of Leadership*. San Francisco: Berrett-Koehler, 1996.

Katzenbach, J. R., and The RCL Team. *Real Change Leaders: How You Can Create Growth and High Performance at Your Company*. New York: New York Times Business, Random House, 1995.

King, M. L., Jr. *A Testament of Hope: The Essential Writings and Speeches of Martin Luther King, Jr.* (J. M. Washington, ed.). New York: Harper & Row, 1986. (Copyright 1968, 1996.)

Kohlberg. L."Stage and Sequence: The Cognitive-Developments Approach to Socialization". In D. A. Goslin (ed.), *Handbook of Socialization Theory and Research*. Chicago: Rand McNally, 1969.

Nair, K. *A Higher Standard of Leadership*. San Francisco: Berrett-Koehler, 1994.

Palmer, P. *The Courage to Teach: Exploring the Inner Landscape of a Teachers Life.* San Francisco: Jossey-Bass, 1998.

Payne, R. *The Life and Death of Mahatma Gandhi.* New York: Dutton, 1969.

Peck, S. *The Road Less Traveled: A New Psychology of Love, Traditional Values, and Spiritual Growth.* New York: Simon & Schuster, 1978.

Pirsig, R. M. *Zen and the Art of Motorcycle Maintenance.* New York: Morrow, 1974.

Quinn, R. E. *Deep Change.* San Francisco: Jossey-Bass, 1996, p. 201.

Quinn, R. E., Faerman, S. R., Thompson, M. P., and McGrath, M. R. *Becoming a Master Manager: A Competency-Based Framework.* (2nd ed.) New York: Wiley, 1996.

Quinn, R. E., Brown, M., and Spreitzer, G. M. "The Empowering Self Modification Strategy: A Fourth General Strategy for Effecting Changes in Human Systems." Working Paper Available from the Authors, 1998.

Quinn, R. E., and Snyder, N. T. "Advanced Change Theory: Culture Change at Whirlpool Corporation." In J. A. Conger, G. M. Spreitzer, and E. E. Lawler III (eds.), *Leader's Change Handbook: An Essential Guide to Setting Direction and Taking Action.* San Francisco: Jossey-Bass, 1999.

Redfield, J., and Adrienne, C. *The Celestine Prophecy: An Experiential Guide.* New York: Warner Books, 1995.

Rogers, Carl R. *On Becoming a Person.* Boston: Houghton Mifflin, 1961.

Schlesinger, L. A., Eccles, R. G., Gabarro, J. J. *Management Behavior in Organizations: Texts, Cases, and Readings.* New York: McGraw Hill, 1983.

Schriesheim, C. A., Hourse, R. J., and Kerr, S. "Leader Initiating Structure: A Reconciliation of Discrepant Research Results and Some Empirical Tests." *Organizational Behavior and Human Performance,* 1976, *15*(2), 297–321.

Shechtman, M. R. *Working Without a Net: How to Survive and Thrive in Today's High Rise Business World.* New York: Pocket Books, 1994.

Smith, C. *The Merlin Factor: Keys to the Corporate Kingdom.* McLean, Va.: Kairos Productions, 1995.

Spreitzer, G., Quinn, R. E., and Fletcher, J. "Excavating the Paths of Meaning, Renewal, and Empowerment: A Typology of Managerial High-Performance Myths." *Journal of Management Inquiry,* 1995, *4*(1).

Thoreau, H. D. "Civil Disobedience." Booten, N.J.: Liberty Library, 1946. (Originally published 1849.)

Torbert, W. R. *Managing the Corporate Dream: Restructuring for Long-Term Success.* Homewood, Ill.: Dow Jones-Irwin, 1987.

Van de Ven, A., Polley, D., Garud, R., and Venkataraman, S. *The Innovation Journey.* New York: Oxford University Press, 1999.

Waldrop, M. M. *Complexity: The Emerging Science at the Edge of Order and Chaos.* New York: Touchstone, 1992.

Warner, C. T. *Bonds of Anquish, Bonds of Love.* Provo, Utah: Brigham Young University Moral Studies Group, 1992.

Weick, K. *Sensemaking in Organizations.* Thousand Oaks, Calif.: Sage, 1995.

Wheatley, M. J., and Kellner-Rogers, M. *A Simpler Way.* San Francisco: Berrett-Koehler, 1996.

Whyte, D. *The Heart Aroused.* New York: Currency Doubleday, 1994.

Williamson, M. *A Return to Love.* New York: HarperCollins, 1994.

Wright, K. *Breaking the Rules: Removing the Obstacles to Effortless High Performance.* Boise, Idaho: CPM Publishing, 1998.

Youngblood, M. D. *Life at the Edge of Chaos: Creating the Quantum Organization,* J. Renesch (ed.). Flower Mound, TX: Perceval Publishing, 1997.

Index

Credits

Table 1.2

From Mark Youngblood in *Life at the Edge of Chaos: Creating the Quantum Organization*, edited by John Renesch, 1997, Perceval Publishing. Used by permission of Perceval Publishing, a division of Quay Alliance.

Martin Luther King epigraphs, Chapters 2–9

From *A Testament of Hope: The Essential Writings of Martin Luther King, Jr.*, edited by James M. Washington, Harper & Row, 1986. Reprinted by arrangement with The Heirs to the Estate of Martin Luther King, Jr., c/o Writers House, Inc. as agent for the proprietor. Copyright © 1968 by Martin Luther King, Jr. by The Heirs to the Estate of Martin Luther King, Jr.

Text excerpt, Chapter 2

From Mihaly Csikszentmihalyi, *Finding Flow, The Psychology of Engagement with Everyday Life*. Copyright © 1997 by Mihaly Csikszentmihalyi. Reprinted by permission of Basic Books, a member of Perseus Books, L.L.C. and by permission of The Orion Publishing Group Ltd.

Text excerpts, Chapter 5

From Mark Youngblood in *Life at the Edge of Chaos: Creating the Quantum Organization*, edited by John Renesch, 1997, Perceval Publishing. Used by permission of Perceval Publishing, a division of Quay Alliance.

From J. Jaworski, *Synchronicity: The Inner Path to Leadership*, 1996, Berrett-Koehler Publishers, Inc., San Francisco, CA. Reprinted by permission of the publisher. All rights reserved. 1-800-929-2929.

Text excerpts, Chapter 6

From Ron Charan and Noel Tichy, *Every Business Is a Growth Business*. Copyright © 1998 by Ron Charan and Noel Tichy. Reprinted by permission of Times Books, a division of Random House.